THE

MAGNOLIA BAKERY

HANDBOOK

THE
MAGNOLIA
BAKERY
— HANDBOOK —

A Complete Guide for the Home Baker

Baking Made Easy with
150 Foolproof Recipes & Techniques

BOBBIE LLOYD
Chief Baking Officer

HARPER
DESIGN

An Imprint of HarperCollinsPublishers

290 ADDITIONAL RE

This book is for my great-grandmother, both grandmothers, and my mother, for inspiring a love of baking, and for keeping family recipes and traditions alive from generation to generation.

CONTENTS

INTRODUCTION

I have always loved the way baking brings people together. Some of my earliest and fondest memories are of making family recipes alongside my great-grandmother, grandmother, and mother: the delicate and buttery cut-out cookies during the holidays, my mom's home-made rhubarb pies—with rhubarb picked from our backyard—cooling on the kitchen counter in summer, or her insanely rich chocolate cake with fudge icing all year long.

When I was eight years old, my mother went to work full-time. We had a family meeting to discuss how each of us would pitch in around the house, and I volunteered to help get dinner ready. I signed up for my first cooking class at the local YWCA, a twelve-week course called "International Cooking." The first week we made cinnamon toast and hot chocolate. Twelve weeks later, we wrapped up with paella. Since that moment, cooking and baking have been my true passion.

During college, I decided to become a professional chef. After packing up my grand-mother's collection of cookbooks from the 1940s and 1950s, and her beautiful, handmade vintage aprons, I left my hometown of Chicago to study at the Modern Gourmet Cooking School in Boston under the renowned French chef Madeleine Kamman. Upon graduating, a partner and I opened American Accent, a restaurant and café in nearby Brookline with a small retail bakery where we made everything from scratch daily.

Since then, I've been a personal chef, service manager at Union Square Café, a controller, and co-owner of several New York eateries. I was lucky enough to work with some of the best in my industry, learning about each facet of running a food business. All these formative experiences ultimately led me to Magnolia Bakery and my love of baking.

When my business partner, Steve Abrams, and I took over the reins of Magnolia Bakery in 2007, it was a cozy shop with a welcoming, vintage vibe on the quiet, tree-lined corner of West Eleventh and Bleecker Streets in New York City's Greenwich Village. At the time, cupcakes were all the rage, due in no small part to Magnolia Bakery's cameo appearance in a 2001 episode of *Sex and the City*. Carrie Bradshaw (Sarah Jessica Parker) and Miranda Hobbes (Cynthia Nixon) perched outside the shop discussing Carrie's love life as they ate vanilla buttercream cupcakes and licked pink icing from their fingers. Aired around the world, that episode made Magnolia Bakery—and those pink cupcakes—a global phenomenon. Six years later, the bakery was still drawing in *Sex and the City* fans, as well as anyone passionate about classic American baked goods.

I've managed to stay true to the bakery's original spirit while upgrading the ingredients and expanding its offerings. I listened to our loyal customers and our devoted staff (the ones who we say "bleed pastel") and responded accordingly. There are now a greater variety of cakes, cupcakes, and banana pudding flavors, plus scones and insanely good pies. And we've taken the Magnolia Bakery experience to other locations—first in New York, then to other cities across the country, and now we have an international presence. Wherever we go, there we are: a little corner shop with that welcoming feeling of entering an old-fashioned kitchen, where everything is made by hand, carefully, and with love.

That welcoming feeling will come to you as you bake your way through this book. In these pages, you'll find Magnolia Bakery's most beloved recipes for American homestyle baked goods made from scratch, updated for today's tastes; some of my family recipes that have been handed down through the generations; and some favorites of mine that I've perfected over the years. I guide you through all the tools and techniques I've found most useful and provide helpful tips so you can up your baking game. If you're at all like me, you'll agree that few things are more satisfying than baking. It demands precision, but there's always an element of surprise that comes from having to relinquish control while your goodies spend time in the oven. You follow the process as best you can, and at the end there's a big, rewarding transformation. There's nothing sweeter.

Invaluable Tips and Techniques for the Home Baker

My home kitchen is my happy place. It's where I retreat when I'm stressed. All the careful measuring, chopping, and mixing calms and refocuses me. My husband lovingly teases me when he sees me dicing ingredients into tiny pieces— he knows it's a sign I've had a rough day, and before you know it, I'll be refreshed and happy.

Many professional pastry chefs say that baking is a science, but I say it's a study in preparation and patience. It's essential to read a recipe through from beginning to end. Then do it again. On this second go-around, check the ingredients and be sure you have everything required. There's nothing worse than getting halfway through a recipe, only to find out you don't have any eggs. Confirm you have all the tools and the right pan sizes and that your ingredients are at the correct temperature. If a recipe calls for ingredients at room temperature, remove them from the refrigerator a half hour before you begin. Premeasure as many of the ingredients as possible.

If you have the counter space, portion them all into little bowls, so they are ready when you need them. If using a scale—and I highly recommend you do—weigh out all your dry ingredients first (you can even do this ahead of time and keep them covered on the counter). Finally, take your time! Being in a hurry makes you more likely to forget the vanilla or salt (speaking from experience).

ESSENTIAL TIPS FOR BAKING

Ingredients at the Right Temperature

It's important for ingredients to be at the proper temperature to ensure the recipe is successful. Some types of baked goods, such as cakes and cupcakes, call for butter, eggs, and dairy ingredients at room temperature; others, such as pie doughs and scones, require cold butter. Room temperature is around 68° to 70°F. Allot at least 30 minutes to attain that. If you aren't sure, use an instant-read thermometer to confirm. I have a very warm kitchen (no AC and too much heat), and carefully check my ingredients with a thermometer before baking. Butter beats up creamier at room temperature; eggs will foam more, which is an important requirement to create an emulsion that traps air and makes a lighter batter. On the other hand, it's easier to separate cold eggs and cut in cold butter; heavy cream won't whip if it's not cold.

Preheat Your Oven and Verify the Temperature

Before placing anything in an oven, be sure that it hits the correct temperature. Ovens vary greatly and some have "hot spots" where the temperature spikes. Buy an oven thermometer and check all areas of your oven: top, bottom, front, and rear. For even baking, cakes, cupcakes, and cookies should be baked on the center rack.

Prepare Your Pans

If the recipe calls for lining your pan with parchment paper or greasing and flouring the pan, do this step before you undertake other recipe steps. Grease the pan all over with butter or shortening, being sure to get into the corners. Place a little flour (or cocoa, if making chocolate cakes) in the pan and shake until the bottom and sides are covered. Invert the pan and give it a firm tap to remove any excess flour.

Line the pan neatly with parchment paper. You can purchase precut parchment paper rounds online or place your cake pan on a piece of parchment paper, trace the pan size, cut out the round, and place it on the buttered and floured surface of the pan.

Don't skip this important step or you may not be able to get your cake out of the pan. A dear friend called me late one night when this happened with her daughter's birthday cake, and I rushed over to help her. Turns out, she hadn't greased and floured her pan before lining with parchment.

UNSTICKING CAKES

If your cake sticks to the pan, here's a trick to save the situation. Place the cake back in a 325°F oven on the bottom shelf for about 10 minutes, just to warm the pan. Then, carefully turn the pan upside down onto a flat baking sheet and firmly rap on the bottom of the pan a few times. If the cake doesn't fall out easily, turn the pan right side up again and run an offset spatula around the cake, gently nudging it away from the sides of the pan. Try flipping the cake again.

Use a Scale

Professional bakers use a scale for a key reason: It's precise. All ingredients in this book are in cups (for those without a scale), and in grams and ounces. Baking is so much neater and more reliable when you use a scale. For example, when measuring dry ingredients, place a bowl large enough to hold all the ingredients on the scale, tare or zero it out, add the flour, zero it out again, then add the remaining ingredients one at a time, zeroing out between additions. This saves on cleanup, as you are only using one bowl.

Measuring Dry Ingredients

I really want to emphasize how important it is to weigh flour in grams and ounces rather than trusting a measuring cup. I have done a few experiments with our bakers at Magnolia Bakery in which five people all scooped a cup of flour from the bag and, when we weighed the scoops, they ranged from 126 grams to 140 grams per cup. This adds up to a big difference when a recipe calls for 2 or 3 cups of flour. You could end up with ¼ to ⅓ cup more flour than needed, leaving you with either flat cookies or dry cake. If you must use a measuring cup, I recommend that you scoop your flour. Whisk the flour in the bag first to lighten it up, then gently scoop and swipe with the flat edge of a knife. If you have a scale and want to have a little fun, check your scoop in weight. One cup of all-purpose flour should weigh 4.8 ounces/135 grams.

Measuring Liquid Ingredients

Place a liquid measuring cup large enough to hold all the wet ingredients on the counter and confirm at eye level that you hit the measuring marks on the cup. However, it's much easier to measure liquid ingredients by weight. It's also faster, and you won't have to clean another cup.

Measuring Sticky Ingredients

When measuring sticky foods, such as honey, peanut butter, or syrup, coat the inside of your cup with a nonstick spray. The sticky stuff will slide right out.

When to Sift

If a recipe calls for "3 cups sifted flour," it means you must sift the flour *before* measuring it out. If the recipe calls for "2 cups flour, sifted," it means you sift *after* you measure. If there is no mention of sifting, you don't need to do it at all. I recommend you always sift ingredients that easily clump, such as cocoa, cornstarch, and powdered sugar.

Most of the recipes call for whisking the dry ingredients together. Whisk for a solid minute to be sure that the dry ingredients are fully incorporated.

Cracking Eggs

If the recipe calls for separated eggs, it's much easier to separate them when they are cold. The whites, however, will whip to a greater volume when they are at room temperature. Crack eggs into a separate bowl, one at a time, before adding them to a recipe. It's much easier to remove a piece of shell from a small bowl than from your batter. And egg whites will not whip if there is any trace of egg yolk. I always separate my whites one at a time into a small bowl, then combine the total into another bowl.

Adding Eggs to Dry Ingredients

I like to put all my eggs in a liquid measuring cup with the vanilla extract. It's much easier to pour one egg at a time into a batter this way. Carefully tilt the measuring cup over the mixer; the weight of the yolk will drop one egg at a time. Mix until incorporated before adding the next egg. If the recipe calls for eggs mixed with milk or another liquid, lightly whisk them together in a liquid measuring cup or a bowl with a spout.

Whipping Egg Whites

Be sure your mixing bowl and beaters are completely clean and grease-free or the whites will not whip. Your bowl needs to be big enough for the egg whites to expand to as much as eight times their original volume. I use a tiny amount of cream of tartar or lemon juice to stabilize the egg whites so they reach their full volume without collapsing. If making meringue, gradually add the sugar once your egg whites have just about doubled in size and are foamy. Take your time. Don't add additional sugar until the previous addition has dissolved. To confirm if the sugar is completely dissolved, rub some of the egg whites between your thumb and finger; if it's smooth, you can add more sugar.

Scraping the Mixer Bowl

Scraping is essential to successful baking because it ensures that all ingredients are well mixed. If butter is stuck to the side or bottom of the bowl, your cake won't rise properly. If flour isn't fully incorporated, it can leave streaks in your batter. Stop the mixer and use a large-headed rubber spatula to scrape the sides and bottom of the bowl, as well as the paddle. Scrape after every step of a recipe. You really can't scrape too much.

Folding in Ingredients

Folding is that part of mixing where you blend two mixtures together. In most of the recipes that require folding, you are blending something lighter, such as whipped egg whites, into a heavier batter. Start by placing about one-third of the whipped egg whites on top of the batter. Place a rubber spatula in your dominant hand and gently insert it under the batter in the bowl at the twelve o'clock position. Scoop underneath the batter and fold the batter over from the six o'clock position. Using your other hand, give the bowl a quarter-turn and repeat this process, adding the rest of the egg whites until all the egg whites are no longer visible and you have a cohesive batter.

Scooping Cupcake and Cookie Doughs

I use a scoop to evenly portion cupcake batter and cookie doughs. (See Tools of the Trade, page 19.) Unless otherwise instructed, for cupcakes use a #20 scoop, which is about a ¼ cup, and scoop directly from the mixer bowl, pressing the scoop against the top edge of the bowl to smooth the batter out flat. For cookies, if the recipe specifies a rounded ball, use the scoop to evenly portion the dough, then form a ball in the palm of your hands.

Checking for Doneness

Why is bake time given in a range? Because ovens tend to vary and there are other factors, like how often you open the oven door. You'll know your pie is done when the crust is golden brown and the fruit is tender. Cheesecake and custard pies are ready when they're just set; the batter should jiggle slightly and evenly over the whole surface when you give the pan a tiny shake. Brownies and bars are ready when they're just set, or when a cake tester inserted in the center comes out with moist crumbs. For muffins, coffee cakes, cakes, and cupcakes, I use a few different tests: First, the room will start to smell like cake. Second, touch the center of the cake with your finger. If it springs back and holds a slight indentation, it's done. If you're not sure, try the skewer test: Using a wooden skewer or cake tester, pierce the center of the cake. If the skewer comes out clean, the cake is done. (The cake will continue to cook out of the oven.) If the batter is wet, it needs another 3 to 5 minutes in the oven. Final doneness indicator? When the cake starts to pull away from the pan ever so slightly and begins to turn a light golden brown.

Melting Chocolate

There are two methods for melting chocolate: microwave or hot water bath. I usually use my microwave, because it's faster and easier. Place chopped chocolate or chocolate chips in a glass bowl and heat in the microwave in 30-second increments. Depending on how much chocolate you are melting, you may need to do this several times. After 30 seconds, check the chocolate. If it's shiny and starting to melt, remove it from the microwave and stir with a rubber spatula. If you still see a few large pieces of chocolate, return to the microwave and heat for another 20 to 30 seconds. Stir again until the chocolate is smooth and pourable. Do not overheat! You don't want hot chocolate, just melted chocolate.

To create a hot water bath, pour an inch of water into a medium saucepan and bring to a simmer over low heat. Place the chocolate in a heatproof glass or stainless steel bowl. Place the bowl over the simmering water, being careful that the bowl does not touch the water. You want the steam to melt the chocolate, not the water, since the steam is considerably hotter. Also, water and chocolate are not friends. If you get even a droplet of water in your chocolate, the chocolate will seize up.

As the chocolate softens, stir it from time to time with a spatula. Before the chocolate is completely melted, remove the bowl from the pot and continue to stir until completely smooth. Let cool to room temperature before using.

The Ingredients Used in My Kitchen and at Magnolia Bakery

The most delicious baked goods rely on the freshest and finest ingredients. High-quality butter is paramount, and be sure to buy the best flour, sugar, eggs, and chocolate that you can.

BUTTER AND OTHER FATS

BUTTER: The be-all, end-all. So much of baking relies on butter. Butter provides flavor, and the necessary fat, moisture, and texture. For all the recipes in this book, I use a good-quality 81 to 82 percent butterfat, unsalted butter. The reason for using unsalted is that the amount of salt in salted butter varies. With unsalted butter you can control how much salt you add. Always make sure your butter is fresh. It can pick up smells from the refrigerator and quickly go rancid. Don't keep butter in your fridge for more than a month. If you buy too much and need to store it longer, place wrapped sticks in a resealable freezer bag and be sure to write the date on the bag. Butter may be kept frozen for up to 3 months.

Why is butter temperature so important? Butter and flour are the building blocks for cakes, cookies, scones, and most of the muffins in this book, as well as for the all-butter pie crust. Cake and cupcake recipes call for softened butter at room temperature. Butter needs to be soft enough to cream so that the fat molecules can hold the moisture from the sugar, which makes for a tender, lifted cake. Pies, scones, and biscuits need chilled butter to be tender and flaky.

Typically, room temperature is 68–70°F. I teach our bakers to pull out their instant-read thermometers to check the temperature before using the butter. Butter will not cream correctly if too cold, cakes won't rise, and cookies won't be tender. Take your butter out of the refrigerator at least 30 minutes before you need to use it. If you have a warm kitchen, take the butter straight from the refrigerator, unwrap each 4-ounce stick, and place in the microwave for 10 seconds on the defrost cycle. Rotate and press the butter gently; if it dents slightly, it is at room temperature. If you leave the butter out on the counter, do the same test. Gently press the butter with your finger and it should dent just a little. If the butter is shiny and oily looking or smooshes easily when you press it with your finger, it is *too* soft.

Chilled butter is essential for flaky, tender pies and scones. I can't recall where I first saw this excellent method for cutting and shredding cold butter, but in the last few years it's been all over the Internet. Open a 1-pound package of butter and place all four unwrapped 4-ounce sticks in the freezer for 10 to 15 minutes until

frozen. Line a baking sheet with foil or parchment paper. Remove one stick at a time from the freezer and unwrap. Roll the butter in flour just to coat. Using the large holes of a box grater, quickly grate the butter onto the lined baking sheet. As soon as the grater is full, spread the butter over the pan; continue until you have grated all four sticks. Transfer the baking sheet back to the freezer until the butter pieces are fully frozen. Place the shredded butter pieces into a freezer bag and store up to 3 months for future use. I usually grate 2 or 3 pounds at a time so that it's ready when I need it. When making pies or scones that call for chilled cut butter, take out what you need, weigh it, and gently toss with your flour mixture. This really saves a lot of time!

MELTED BUTTER: If a recipe calls for melted and cooled butter, you can melt it in the microwave or on the stove, but be careful not to cook the butter. You just want to heat it to where it's melted and pourable, not hot. If you heat it too much, allow it to cool to body temperature before using. Hot butter will melt the sugar, which is not good. Place the butter in a microwave-safe bowl and microwave in 30-second increments. When about half the butter is melted, with a few large pieces remaining, stir until it's all melted. You want it to melt slowly but not cook.

BROWNED BUTTER: Browned butter adds a depth of flavor that can change the overall taste of a recipe. Blondies made with browned butter, for instance, have a deeper butterscotch flavor. To brown butter, heat it on low heat until the butterfat solids sink to the bottom of the pan and gives off a toasty, nutty aroma. Remove the pan from the heat immediately to stop the butter from cooking. Be sure to cool browned butter to room temperature before using.

VEGETABLE OIL: Vegetable oil or canola oil is used in some of our cake and muffin recipes. Vegetable oil is 100 percent fat and doesn't have the water content of butter, so does not contribute to rise or lift. Vegetable oil can come from soybeans, corn, or rapeseeds (canola), with little difference in taste or color, which makes the different types interchangeable for baking.

FLOUR

I use two types of flour: all-purpose and cake.

ALL-PURPOSE FLOUR: The versatility of all-purpose flour means it's used the most frequently. It has a protein content between 10 and 11.7 percent, which provides structure yet is light enough for cakes and cookies. I prefer unbleached flour and recommend any of these brands of all-purpose flour: Hecker's, Gold Medal, and King Arthur.

CAKE FLOUR: Almost all the cake and cupcake recipes in this book call for cake flour, which is finely milled, soft winter wheat. It has a lower protein content than all-purpose flour and less gluten, producing a fine crumb and a lighter, softer texture. You will be amazed at the difference the first time you make a cake with cake flour instead of all-purpose flour. I recommend Softasilk or Purasnow.

SUGARS AND SWEETENERS

Sugar is necessary for adding sweetness and texture to baked goods. White sugar should be scooped and leveled. Using a scale is the easiest and most consistent way to measure out sugar.

SUGAR: If a recipe calls for "sugar," it means granulated white sugar. I prefer Domino extra-fine granulated cane sugar. Extra-fine sugar dissolves perfectly when creaming with butter for cakes and cookies. If you cannot find extra-fine sugar, you can make your own by processing regular granulated sugar in the food processor for about 30 seconds.

BROWN SUGAR: Unless otherwise stated in a recipe, I use light brown sugar that is packed and leveled into the measuring cup. I love what brown sugar does to a recipe and have changed up many a cookie or bar recipe over the years by using half white and half brown. More white sugar results in a crispy cookie; more brown sugar in a chewier one. You can play with your favorite recipes to see which you prefer. Always store brown sugar in a tightly sealed bag. If it becomes dry and clumpy, it will not mix properly. You can refresh brown sugar that is dried out by placing it overnight in a tightly sealed plastic bag along with a slice of grocery store white bread.

POWDERED SUGAR: I prefer to use Domino 10X powdered sugar. Because powdered sugar is prone to clumping, measure (or weigh) the quantity of powdered sugar you need, then sift it.

MAPLE SYRUP: I use Grade A "dark" maple syrup for its richer, deeper flavor. Always purchase the real thing. No artificial syrups allowed!

CORN SYRUP: I rarely use corn syrup as a sweetener, but occasionally it is a necessity. For instance, you can't make pecan pies without it. I use dark corn syrup in both the Pecan Pie (page 172) and Black Bottom Pecan Pie (page 174), but if you prefer a lighter taste, you can opt for light corn syrup.

SWEETENED CONDENSED MILK is made from cow's milk that has been heated to remove the water and concentrate the liquid and then sweetened. Sweetened condensed milk is an essential ingredient in all the banana pudding recipes. I recommend either Eagle Brand or Magnolia by Borden.

EGGS

I only use Grade A Large eggs for baking. A large egg weighs about 50 grams. Eggs have many responsibilities in baking. The yolk is high in fat and adds richness, tenderness, and color to baked goods. The white is high in protein and provides structure and moisture. Beaten eggs also act as a leavening agent, as air is pushed into the tiny cells that expand during baking. If you make sure your eggs are at room temperature before baking, you will get greater volume. It's also easier to separate eggs when they are cold.

DAIRY

MILK: All my recipes that call for milk use whole milk unless otherwise specified.

CREAM: I only use 36 percent fat heavy cream, never light cream or whipping cream. You'll never get that cream whipped to fluffy perfection unless everything is cold. Place your bowl and beaters or whisks in the freezer for 5 to 10 minutes before you begin whipping. If whipping by hand, use two whisks at the same time and the cream will whip up faster and fluffier.

CREAM CHEESE: Philadelphia brand cream cheese is my pick because it guarantees a consistent outcome. Bring cream cheese to room temperature before mixing. Most recipes call for cutting it into 1-inch pieces. I usually just pull chunks with my fingers as I add it to the mixer.

BUTTERMILK is made by culturing low-fat milk with a lactic acid bacteria. The result is a thicker, tangier milk. It is used in baked goods for added flavor, as well as to whiten and tenderize cakes. If you find that you are in the middle of a recipe and don't have any buttermilk, you can make your own. Add 1 tablespoon lemon juice or distilled white vinegar to 8 ounces low-fat milk. Let sit for 10 minutes. If you have a farmers' market near you that sells fresh buttermilk, give it a try. It's amazing what a difference it can make.

SOUR CREAM is made by culturing light cream with a lactic acid bacteria. Use only full-fat sour cream in these recipes.

CHOCOLATE

The most important thing to know about chocolate is that quality really counts. I was lucky to be able to travel to Ecuador to visit an organic cacao farm, where I learned so much about the importance of how we source ingredients. Ultimately, provenance and quality really affect the outcome of your baked goods.

Most of my recipes call for semisweet chocolate. Most grocery stores carry Ghirardelli, Guittard, and Valrhona. If you want to splurge, I recommend Scharffen Berger 62% Cacao Baking Chunks. Some gourmet retailers carry these, and you can always find them on the Internet. Always store your chocolate at room temperature.

COCOA POWDER is the liquor from chocolate rendered in a powder form. There are two types available on the market, Dutch process and natural. I prefer a Dutch process cocoa with a cocoa fat content of 22 to 24%. It provides a richer, darker flavor, which makes brownies and cookies much fudgier. My favorite brand is República del Cacao from Valrhona. Other more readily available brands are Droste and Guittard.

WHITE CHOCOLATE is made from cocoa butter, sugar, and milk solids, so it doesn't contain any of the dark cocoa solids. "White baking chips" contain partially hydrogenated oil instead of cocoa butter. When buying white chocolate in any form, make sure it has at least 20% cocoa butter.

LEAVENING AGENTS

Ever notice how some recipes call for both baking powder and baking soda? They are both leavening agents but they behave differently and have somewhat different roles. Think of baking soda as the ingredient that helps spread your batter and baking powder as the one that gives you "poof," or lift.

BAKING SODA is much stronger than baking powder. In order for it to become active, it requires that an acid be present, such as buttermilk, sour cream, lemon juice, or vinegar (as in the Red Velvet Cake, page 52). The soda reacts to the acid and releases carbon dioxide, which creates lift. To test for freshness, place 3 tablespoons distilled white vinegar in a small bowl, add ½ teaspoon baking soda, and watch for it to bubble up.

BAKING POWDER contains some baking soda. I only use double-acting baking powder, which reacts twice: once when added to liquid and again when exposed to heat. Make sure your baking powder is fresh. A good habit to get into is to date the containers when you purchase them. To test for freshness, place ½ teaspoon baking powder in a small bowl and mix in 3 tablespoons water. If the powder is fresh, it will fizz a little like soda.

MISCELLANEOUS

COCONUT MILK isn't a true dairy product, as it is made from a blend of coconut and water. However, it has the same consistency as cow's milk. Be sure you purchase canned coconut milk and not coconut cream or coconut milk beverage. Shake the can well before using and store any leftovers in the refrigerator.

SWEETENED SHREDDED COCONUT is my go-to in all the recipes calling for coconut. You can use unsweetened flaked coconut as a garnish if you prefer, in which case I recommend toasting it.

PEANUT BUTTER: Skippy peanut butter is the brand I recommend for the recipes. Be sure to purchase creamy peanut butter, not chunky. Don't purchase natural peanut butters; they will separate as they don't contain stabilizing ingredients.

PUMPKIN PUREE: Libby's 100% Pure Pumpkin is an excellent canned puree. Don't mistakenly buy pumpkin pie filling, which already has the spices added to it.

JAM OR JELLY: For the recipes that call for jam or jelly, choose a high-quality brand such as Bonne Maman. However, the grape jelly I use for my PB&J Cupcakes (page 96) is Welch's. My childhood PB&J was made with Wonder bread, Skippy peanut butter, and Welch's Grape Jelly. I still crave one every now and then.

EXTRACTS: Vanilla extract should always be the real thing; substitutes just don't cut it. I prefer vanilla from Madagascar. For other extracts, including peppermint and almond, always buy the best quality since the recipes call for very small quantities.

SPICES: With spices, freshness really counts. Their aroma and flavor dissipate over time, so purchase smaller quantities that you will use up faster. When we opened our first Magnolia Bakery location in the Middle East, I bought nutmeg and cinnamon from the local grocery store. The spices were so fresh and potent, I had to cut the amount in the recipe by half!

FOOD COLORING: I much prefer thick, highly concentrated gel paste over liquid food coloring for dying buttercream. AmeriColor and Wilton both offer student kits with a large selection of colors. It takes very little, sometimes just a touch, to get the color you want. The technique I use is to dip a toothpick into the gel paste and touch the buttercream in my bowl to get a lovely pastel color. If you overdo it, there is no going back. The only time I use liquid food coloring is for red velvet cake. At Magnolia Bakery we use a pastel color palette for decorating our famous swirled cupcakes. We use gel powders to hand-dye white sprinkles in yellow, pink, green, blue, and lavender. For 4 quarts of white sprinkles it takes just a smidge of gel powder. You can purchase special measuring spoons with a smidge, a pinch, and a dash.

CUPCAKE DECORATIONS: There are many online sites that offer a wide variety of fun cupcake decorations. I love the custom sprinkle blends from Layer Cake Shop. Michaels craft stores carry a huge section of Wilton cake decorating supplies.

HOW TO FILL A PIPING BAG

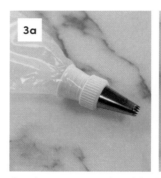

Put one hand into the bag, folding the top over so that the rim extends toward your fingertips. You can also use a wide-mouth jar, folding the top of the bag over the sides.

If you're only using one tip or a large tip like the Wilton #1M, drop it to the bottom of the bag and push it down to the point. Cut the bag so that about half of the tip is exposed.

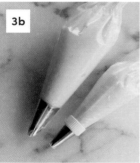

If you're using a coupler, slide the large part into the bag, with the narrow end pointing toward the bag's tip. Cut the bag just past the end of the coupler (3a). From the outside of the bag, place the decorating tip onto the coupler. Twist the small part of the coupler over the tip and onto the larger part of the coupler to secure it (3b).

Using a spatula or icing wand, add buttercream, being careful to fill the bag no more than ⅔ or ¾ the way up. Scrape any excess off of the wand or spatula before withdrawing it.

Unfold the bag and push all the buttercream down toward the tip. Do this a few times to remove any air bubbles, as air in the bag can cause uneven pressure, causing icing to spurt out of bag and/or create an uneven design. To make sure the icing is flowing evenly, give the bag a squeeze over a small bowl.

Tightly twist the top of the bag closed and set aside until you're ready to use it.

Tools of the Trade

The best piece of advice I can give to the home baker is to purchase the right assortment of good-quality tools. It's an investment in your future baking success that will definitely pay off.

STAND MIXER: Your first and most essential purchase should be a stand mixer. My favorite is the KitchenAid 5-quart mixer. If you bake a lot, consider purchasing an extra bowl, as there are a few recipes that require you to whip cream or eggs whites and add them to a batter. Having both a glass and metal mixer bowl really comes in handy. Get the spouted clear glass one, if you don't have it; it's fun to watch your batter mix.

HAND MIXER: For whipping up small amounts of whipped cream, I like to have a hand mixer available. Hamilton Beach made one just for Magnolia Bakery.

FOOD PROCESSOR: I use a Cuisinart DLC 10 Pro Classic 7-cup, a workhorse I've had for years. It's the ideal size for a small kitchen, yet big enough to make a batch of two-crust pie dough.

DIGITAL SCALE: A more modest investment, this adds an important element of consistency to your measurements. I like the OXO 6-pound scale, which is available almost everywhere.

BAKING PANS

CUPCAKE AND MUFFIN PANS: You'll need several of these. I prefer the WinCo AMF 12-cup aluminum pan. It has a low, wide cup that gives your cupcake or muffin a larger top surface. I also have a couple of mini-muffin pans, which come 24 to a pan, and an extra-large muffin pan with 6 to a pan.

13 × 9 × 2-INCH BAKING PAN: Purchase a couple of different styles. This is the pan size used for most of the brownie and bar recipes in this book. Metal is good for basic baking, and glass or ceramic work well if you are presenting your dish in its cooking vessel, such as the Blueberry Jamboree (page 233).

12 × 17 × ½-INCH BAKING SHEETS: Amazingly versatile tools. These are the perfect size for baking cookies and scones. Be sure to purchase some without a rim, because they work best for the cut-out cookies, as you can slide the parchment paper directly off the sheet and onto the cooling rack.

PIE PANS: I use a 9-inch glass Pyrex deep-dish pie pan for my apple pies. It's helpful to be able to see the crust browning. For pies with a single crust, I prefer to use 9-inch metal pie pans. Metal conducts heat much better and ensures that the bottom crust will be fully baked and not soggy. Stoneware is pretty, but I don't like baking pies in it. The pans are never consistent in size, and crusts don't bake up as crisp and flaky. Use a metal pan for baking and place it in a stoneware one for serving.

9 × 2-INCH ROUND CAKE PANS: You should have at least three of these. I prefer Fat Daddio's anodized aluminum pans. They reflect heat rather than absorb it, and heat evenly, which is very important to the outcome of your cakes. These are available on Amazon and at some specialty stores and websites.

9-INCH SPRINGFORM PAN: Most specialty stores carry springform pans. Be sure to get. Get a good-quality, heavy-duty nonstick pan, such as Calphalon. Cheap ones leak and break quickly.

BUNDT PAN: For the full-size pan, get the 12-cup-capacity pan from Nordic Ware: It's the best one out there. For the mini-Bundt cakes, Wilton and Sur La Table offer nonstick pans that make 12 or 20 mini-bundt cakes.

9 × 2-INCH FLUTED NONSTICK TART PAN WITH REMOVABLE BOTTOM: This is the one I use for the Sour Cream Coffee Cake (page 198).

SAUCEPANS: Stainless steel saucepans with lids in 4-quart and 2-quart sizes are the most useful and also work with induction burners.

SMALL WARES

In the professional kitchen, these make up the arsenal of supplies we need for all our baking functions. Listed in alphabetical order, each is equally important for a well-stocked baking kitchen.

BENCH SCRAPER: I prefer all-stainless or stainless with a wooden handle.

COOKIE CUTTERS: A package of assorted round cookie cutters in stainless steel is a good start. My Cut-Out Sugar Cookies (page 136) are perfect for any cut-out shapes you can find.

COOKIE PRESS: A necessary and fun tool to make the Holiday Spritz Cookies (page 133).

COOLING RACKS: It's good to have two or three.

GRATERS: A Microplane grater is excellent for grating lemon, lime, and orange zests. A box grater with large

holes works well for grating butter and carrots. Get a good-quality stainless steel one with a solid handle and a nonslip rubber base.

KITCHEN SHEARS: These are helpful for cutting pie dough.

KNIVES: You should have at least three knife sizes in your arsenal, including a good 10-inch chef's knife, a 10-inch serrated knife for cutting cakes in half, and a good-quality paring knife.

Measuring Cups and Spoons

DRY MEASURING CUPS: Purchase good-quality stainless steel, accurate measuring cups. Don't purchase cheap ones, which sometimes are not precise. Get a set that includes 1 cup, ¾ cup, ½ cup, ⅔ cup, ⅓ cup, and ¼ cup measures. KitchenMade is a reliable brand.

LIQUID MEASURING CUPS: Purchase a 1-cup and a 2-cup. I like having options. If you bake a lot, get a 4-cup as well. OXO makes quality plastic cups, and Pyrex is reliable for glass versions.

MEASURING SPOONS FOR DRY INGREDIENTS: Get a stainless steel set that has all the sizes, from 1 tablespoon to $1/16$ teaspoon and everything in between. Don't use decorative spoons; they are not accurate.

PARCHMENT PAPER: Totally essential. Get the half-sheet size and cake rounds. You can usually get these at specialty stores or online. I also have a few silicone baking mats that I love to use for cookies.

PASTRY BRUSH: I like the all-natural, 2-inch white boar bristle brushes by Ateco.

PEELER: I like the OXO Y-Peeler. It has a good grip.

PIE SHIELDS: Pie is done when the crust is browned, but sometimes the edge will start to burn. This simple little invention sits on the edge of the crust to protect it. You can also make your own with a piece of foil rolled into a cylinder and then formed into a circle the size of your pan.

PIE WEIGHTS are used to keep your pie crusts from bubbling and shrinking. I prefer Mrs. Anderson's ceramic pie weights.

ROLLING PIN: I prefer a big, moist-resistant hardwood rolling pin with handles, such as Farberware classic wood rolling pins. I like to let the rolling pin do the work for me.

RUBBER SPATULAS OR BOWL SCRAPERS: These are mostly used for scraping down the sides, bottom, and paddles of the mixing bowl. Get a variety of sizes from a reliable brand like Rubbermaid or Ateco. I also like to have a spatula that is heat-resistant for stirring lemon curd and melted chocolate.

RULER: You would be surprised by how many times you'll need one—for measuring pie dough to evenly cutting bars and brownies.

SCOOPS: It's so much easier to portion batter and dough uniformly if you use a scoop. I use two sizes: a #20 and a #40. The higher the number, the more scoops you will get out of your batter. For cupcakes and muffins, I use a #20 scoop (¼ cup); for cookies, I mostly use a #40 (1-ounce) scoop. Norpro and OXO both make good-quality stainless steel scoops with food-release blades.

SIEVES: Cuisinart carries a set in three handy sizes, 3⅛ inch, 5½ inch, and 7⅞ inch. I use the large size to sift flour, cocoa, and powdered sugar, and the smaller ones when I need to dust powdered sugar over cakes or cookies.

THERMOMETERS: Purchase an oven thermometer, an instant-read thermometer, and a candy thermometer. My favorite candy thermometer is from Taylor Precision. It clips to the side of your pan and is easy to view.

TIMERS: You'll need two. I frequently use my phone alarm as a timer, but sometimes you have two things working at the same time, so a good old-fashioned timer is always helpful.

WHISKS: I have six whisks in my kitchen and I use them all, from a 12-inch French whip to a 6-inch whisk.

WOODEN SKEWERS AND TOOTHPICKS: These are used for testing cakes, cupcakes, and muffins.

WOODEN SPOONS: In all shapes and sizes, for stirring those hot sauces.

CAKE-DECORATING SUPPLIES

ATECO ICING SPATULAS: At Magnolia Bakery we have always referred to these as "icing wands." Invest in a 6-inch straight spatula as well as a 4½-inch offset and a 9¾-inch offset spatula.

CAKE BOARDS: These are indispensable for moving cake layers around, decorating cakes, and serving cakes.

CAKE TURNER OR CAKE STAND: I love the Ateco cast-iron nonslip 12-inch cake stand that revolves. It will last a lifetime. If you don't want to spend this much, Wilton makes an inexpensive cake turntable for less than twenty dollars that is available almost everywhere.

PIPING OR DECORATING BAGS: Wilton and Ateco make disposable bags.

PIPING TIPS AND COUPLERS: Wilton offers several variety packs of tips and couplers, which include just about every tip you would ever need to have on hand for basic cake decorating.

RECIPES

CHAPTER ONE

CAKES

I grew up during a time when you would never think of going to someone's house for dinner without bringing a cake. My mother had a repertoire of her favorites that she could whip up in no time. Every week, she would bake us a chocolate sheet cake with fudge icing that we would slowly whittle away at, a sliver a day. It's one of the quintessential tastes of my childhood. If by chance there was a slice left that got a little dry, my dad would just put it in a bowl and pour milk over it. We wouldn't dream of wasting a crumb.

Cake is such an important part of our culture. We slice into delicious and beautifully decorated cakes to commemorate birthdays, weddings, baby showers, and whatever else we're celebrating. At Magnolia Bakery, we bake thousands of cakes each year to help make these occasions special. In this chapter, I've included some of our best-selling ones, as well as some of my personal favorites for you to enjoy.

Almost all the cakes in this book are two-layer 9-inch cakes. I tend to prefer thicker layers, but you can also use the same amount of batter to make three thinner 9-inch layers. You'll just need to reduce the baking time by 15 to 20 minutes. Either way, these cakes will serve up to sixteen people, depending on how big you cut the slices.

CAKE (AND CUPCAKE) BAKING TIPS

Cake and cupcake batters are easy to make and easy to mess up. Most failures are caused by undermixing or overmixing. Follow these simple tips carefully and you will be baking cakes and cupcakes like a pro in no time.

Make sure that all the ingredients are properly mixed: Scraping the bowl and paddles after each step of the recipe is very important for proper mixing. Stop the mixer and scrape down the bowl, being sure to get all the ingredients from the bottom and sides as well as from the paddle.

Be careful not to undermix the batter: When a recipe calls for creaming butter until light and fluffy, it will be 3 to 5 minutes, or until the butter is very light in color and the ingredients are about double in size. I suggest setting a timer so that you can get used to what 5 minutes feels like. Stop the mixer (and timer) halfway and scrape down the bottom and sides of the bowl and the paddle. If your ingredients are not properly mixed, you won't get that lift that your cakes need. When adding dry ingredients, be sure they are thoroughly blended, leaving no streaks of flour.

At the same time, you want to be careful not to overmix: When a recipe calls for mixing just until combined, stop the mixer before the ingredients are fully mixed. Remove the bowl from the mixer and fold in any remaining ingredients with a rubber spatula.

HOW TO GREASE AND FLOUR A CAKE PAN

Grease the pan all over with butter or shortening, being sure to get into the corners. Place a little flour (or cocoa, if making chocolate cake) in the pan and shake to cover the bottom and sides. Invert the pan over a piece of paper towel and give it a firm tap to remove any excess. Line the pan with a parchment paper round.

HOW TO FILL THE BAKING PANS: For smooth, even cake layers, fill the pan a little more than halfway with batter, unless the recipe states otherwise. Smooth the batter with an offset spatula then gently tap the pan on the counter a couple of times to remove any air bubbles.

COOLING THE CAKE IN THE PAN: Don't be tempted to remove the cake from the pan right away! Allow your cakes to cool in the pan on a cooling rack for 30 minutes. Loosen the cake from the sides of the pan with a small knife. Invert the pan over the cooling rack or a sheet pan, firmly tap the bottom, and the cake should fall right out. If you used a parchment liner, be sure to remove it at this stage. Using another rack or pan, turn the cake right side up and place on the cooling rack to finish cooling. Once completely cool, you can continue to assemble and decorate your cake or wrap the cake layers in plastic wrap and store at room temperature for up to 2 days.

STORING CAKE LAYERS: If you are not going to use your cakes immediately, wrap the cake layers in plastic wrap or foil (I do both when freezing) and store for up to 2 days at room temperature. You can freeze the layers for up to 2 months. Thaw at room temperature when ready to decorate.

SETTING UP THE CAKE FOR ICING: These are the basic instructions for setting up all your cakes. If you are using a cake board, tape the board to the cake turner, or wet a small piece of paper towel and place the board on top of it. Both these techniques keep the board from slipping. If you are placing your cake on a decorative serving plate, arrange four overlapping strips of parchment paper around the plate, which helps to keep the plate clean while you are icing the cake. When you are done icing your cake, pull the strips away to leave a clean serving plate.

LEVELING THE CAKE LAYERS: If your cakes have rounded during baking, you may need to level them off. Using a large serrated knife, slice off the rounded top part only.

Leveling a cake layer.

ASSEMBLING THE CAKE LAYERS: These basic instructions apply to all cakes, as shown in the photos below. Place the first layer top side up on a cake turner or serving platter. Add 1 to 1½ cups buttercream or icing in the center. Using an icing wand, spread and smooth the buttercream to the edges. Top with the second cake layer, top side up. Use about 3 cups icing to finish the top and sides of the cake You may need more buttercream for specific designs, which are discussed in each recipe.

Assembling the cake layers.

CUTTING LAYERS IN HALF FOR A 4-LAYER CAKE: To cut each cake into 2 layers, it's easier to slice if your cake layers are chilled first. This will firm them up with less chance of a breakage while slicing. Place one layer at a time on a flat surface. With a long, sharp serrated knife, working your way around the cake, score the outside edge as a marker before you fully cut through the cake.

Carefully and slowly cut through the cake with a sawing motion while holding your other hand on the top of the cake. Once you have completely cut through the cake, carefully lift the layer with two knives crisscrossed over each other and move it to a flat surface. Place the bottom cake slice on a cake turner. Start assembling your cake layers before cutting into the second layer. You want to use the layers immediately, so they don't dry out.

CRUMB-COATING A CAKE: If you had to cut away the domed top or the sides of your cake layers, you may have loose crumbs and will need to "crumb coat" your cake. Assemble the layers with whatever filling you are using. With a pastry brush, swipe any loose crumbs on the top and sides. Use an icing wand to spread a thin layer of buttercream all over your cake, covering it so that you don't see any cake. Crumbs are okay at this point. Transfer the cake to the refrigerator until the buttercream is firm, about 30 minutes. Finish icing the cake, this time making it pretty and smooth.

USING A PIPING BAG: If you haven't used a piping bag before, practice on a piece of parchment paper until you are comfortable applying the right amount of pressure. Write some words and draw some lines on the paper to use as a guide. Purchase tips and couplers so that you can easily switch to new designs using the same color. There are plenty of videos online to help you perfect your piping game; also see How to Fill a Piping Bag (page 18). Both Ateco and Wilton make decorating tips, although the numbering systems are not directly transferable from one brand

TIPS FOR DECORATING YOUR CAKE

I've included some basic decorating instructions with each cake recipe and named the technique for each design as follows. In this chapter, I recommend specific buttercreams to complement the cake flavor, but you can use any combination you enjoy. I love our chocolate cake with just about any of our buttercreams and icings. Experiment and see what you like—from classic American buttercream to a cream cheese icing, the possibilities are endless!

NAKED CAKE
- Ultimate Carrot Cake with Cream Cheese Icing
- Hummingbird Cake
- Lemon Cake with Lemon Meringue Buttercream
- Razzy Cake

SPACKLE CAKE
- Chocolate Cake with Peanut Butter Buttercream
- Banana Chocolate Chip Cake

SMOOTH SIDES
- Everyone's Favorite Vanilla Cake
- Chocolate Cake with Caramel Meringue Buttercream
- Chocolate Cake with Peppermint Buttercream
- Confetti Cake

HORIZONTAL SWIPES
- Super-Rich Chocolate Cake
- Pumpkin Spice Cake with Caramel Cream Cheese Frosting
- Strawberry Cake with Strawberry Meringue Buttercream
- Caramel Cake with Caramel Meringue Buttercream

STARS & ROSETTES
- Red Velvet
- Everyone's Favorite Vanilla Cake

to the other. I used all Wilton tips in this book: #1M (large open-star tip), #2A (round tip), #12 (round tip), #22 (open-star tip), #30 (closed-star tip), #32 (open-star tip), #104 (petal tip), #199 (open-star tip).

STORING CAKES: Most cakes do not need to be refrigerated. The cold dry air is not good for cakes, especially if any cake is exposed, as with the naked cake designs.

Rubbermaid Servin Saver Cake Keeper is the ideal way to store cakes. Its airtight seal keeps cakes from drying out and the buttercream from crusting. If your cake is iced with a cream cheese icing, I recommend keeping it in the refrigerator. Place it in the refrigerator first to firm up, then either cover loosely with plastic wrap or place in a cake keeper. Bring your cake to room temperature before serving.

EVERYONE'S FAVORITE VANILLA CAKE

Vanilla cake is the heart and soul of Magnolia Bakery. It's the basis for this cake and for our best-selling cupcakes, the perfect foil for our Classic Vanilla and Classic Chocolate Buttercreams. In 2007, when we took over the bakery, we noticed that while people liked the buttery vanilla flavor of our cake, they no longer cared for its dense, pound cake–like texture. As you can imagine, we make a lot of vanilla cake every day at all our bakeries, so we needed a foolproof recipe that would produce consistently delicious results.

I went back to the drawing board and developed a new recipe with an updated texture and enhanced flavor. Now, we use cake flour and all egg whites to produce a very tender crumb. I also added a little sour cream for extra richness. The result is a moist cake that is irresistibly buttery and perfectly light.

The Confetti Cake shown on the next page is a simple variation on Everyone's Favorite Vanilla Cake. A festive cake, with pastel confetti throughout as well as sprinkled around the sides, it makes a memorable and celebratory addition to any special occasion.

MAKES two 9-inch layers;
serves 8 to 16

INGREDIENTS

4⅓ cups (498g/17.3oz) cake flour

1¼ teaspoons baking powder

½ teaspoon baking soda

½ teaspoon salt

1¾ cups (420g/10.6) whole milk

⅔ cup (150g/5.3oz) sour cream

1¼ cups/2½ sticks (282g/10oz) unsalted butter, at room temperature

2½ cups (500g/17.7oz) sugar

1 tablespoon pure vanilla extract

6 egg whites

Magnolia Bakery Vanilla Buttercream (page 265) or Chocolate Buttercream (page 266)

FOR THE CONFETTI CAKE

1½ cups (195g/6.9oz) confetti sprinkles

1. Preheat the oven to 325°F. Grease and flour two 9-inch cake pans. Line the bottoms with rounds of parchment paper.

2. In a medium bowl, whisk together the flour, baking powder, baking soda, and salt; set aside.

3. In a liquid measuring cup, whisk together the milk and the sour cream until no lumps remain; set aside.

4. In a stand mixer with a paddle, cream the butter, sugar, and vanilla on medium speed until light and fluffy, about 3 to 5 minutes. Scrape the sides and bottom of the bowl and the paddle.

5. With the mixer on medium speed, slowly add the egg whites, a little at a time, beating until incorporated before adding more. Once the egg whites have been incorporated, stop the mixer and scrape the sides and bottom of the bowl and the paddle.

6. With the mixer on low speed, add the flour mixture in three additions alternating with the milk and sour cream mixture, beginning and ending with the dry ingredients. Mix for about 15 seconds, just until incorporated. Scrape down the bottom and sides of the bowl.

7. If making the confetti cake add 1¼ cups (162.5g/5.75oz) of confetti. Mix again for 15 seconds. Scrape down the bottom and sides of the bowl and the paddle.

(continued)

8. Evenly divide the batter between the prepared pans. Bake 45 to 47 minutes, or until the tops spring back when touched and a cake tester inserted in the center comes out clean.

9. Let the cakes cool in the pan for 30 minutes. Remove from the pan and cool completely on a wire rack.

10. To decorate the cake as in the image with smooth sides, place one cake layer top side up on a cake turner. Use an icing wand to evenly spread 1½ cups of vanilla buttercream over the surface. Add the second cake layer top side up. Using an icing wand, spread about 1 cup buttercream on the top of the cake and about 2 cups on the sides, spreading as you go around the top and sides of the cake until the cake is smooth.

11. For the scallop border, place ½ cup buttercream in a pastry bag with a #32 tip. With even pressure, squeeze the bag and pipe around the top and bottom of the cake. Sprinkle with confetti sprinkles.

VARIATION

GENDER REVEAL CAKE: Cakes that reveal a child's gender— through the color of the icing sandwiched between the top and bottom layers—have become a popular dessert at baby showers. To create one, follow the instructions for the Confetti Cake above. To fill and ice the cake, you will need one recipe of Magnolia Bakery Vanilla Buttercream (page 265). Tint about 1½ cups pink or blue for the filling and tint 2½ cups a neutral tone (like yellow, white, or pale green) for the top and sides of the cake. For tips on creating icings in different colors, see Food Coloring on page 17 and Tinting Buttercream on page 264.

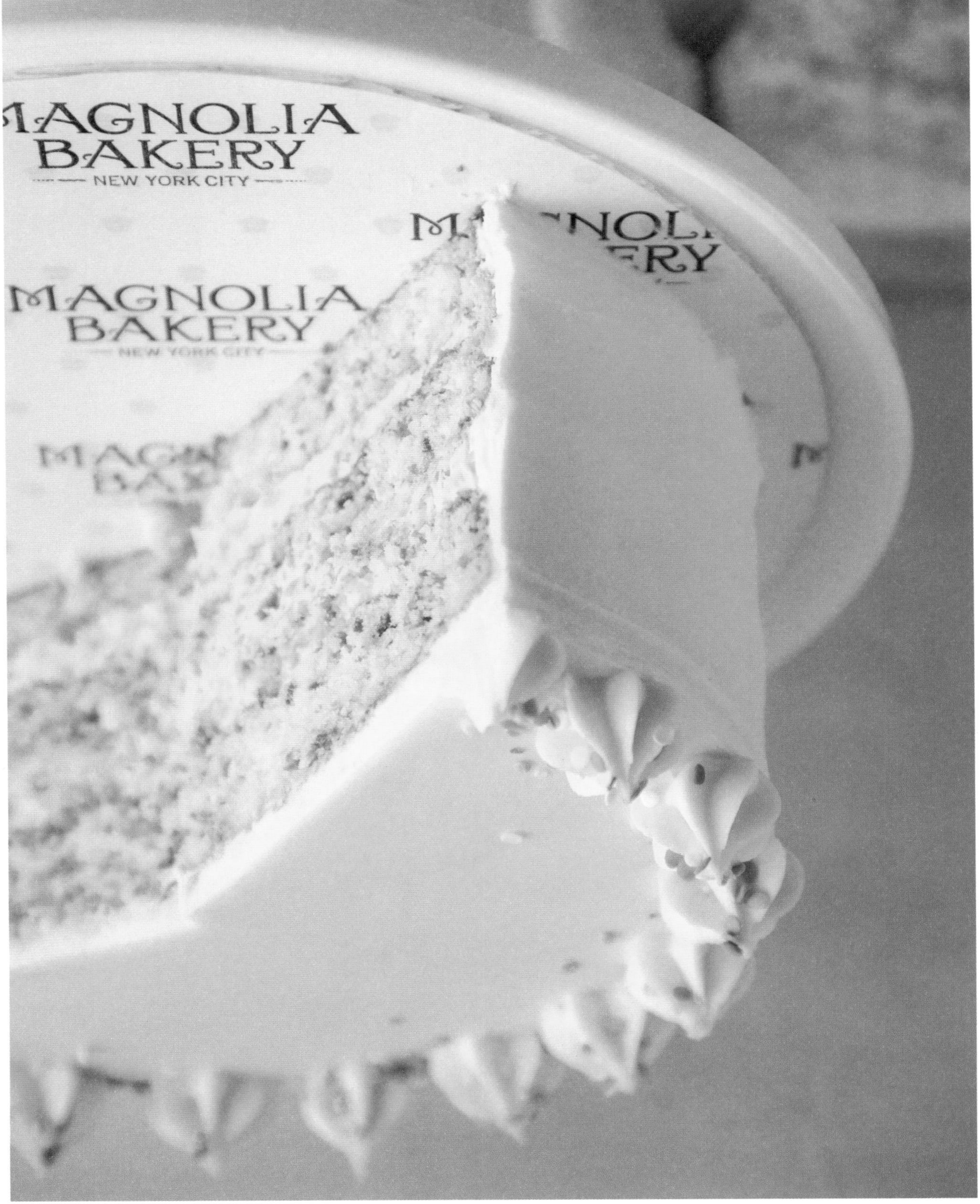
MAGNOLIA
BAKERY
NEW YORK CITY
MAGNOLIA
BAKERY
NEW YORK CITY

STRAWBERRY CAKE WITH STRAWBERRY MERINGUE BUTTERCREAM

This showstopping cake is a pink-tinged variation on Everyone's Favorite Vanilla Cake (page 31) that substitutes strawberry puree for the milk. It's an ode to the berry and the essence of summer, though the year-round availability of frozen strawberry puree means you can make it any time. I swear you taste sunshine in every bite.

MAKES two 9-inch cake layers; serves 8 to 16

INGREDIENTS

Everyone's Favorite Vanilla Cake (page 31)

1¾ cups (395g/14oz) fresh strawberry puree (see Tip), or frozen, if fresh is not available.

Strawberry Meringue Buttercream (page 272)

1 cup (175g/6.1oz) halved fresh strawberries, plus whole strawberries for garnish (optional)

NOTE

If you want to use fresh halved strawberries as shown in the photograph, it's important to fill and ice the cake no more than a few hours before serving so the berries are firm and look fresh. Otherwise, they may become soggy and their color may bleed into the cake.

1. Make Everyone's Favorite Vanilla Cake as directed, substituting the strawberry puree for the milk in step 3.

2. To assemble the cake, place one layer top side up on a cake turner. Use an icing wand to evenly spread 1 cup buttercream over the surface. If using the 1 cup (175g/6.1oz) fresh strawberries, place them halved side down around the perimeter of the cake.

3. Place the second cake layer top side up on the first layer. Using an icing wand, cover the cake with the rest of the buttercream, smoothing the top and sides.

4. To create the horizontal swipes effect shown in the photo, follow these steps. Starting at the bottom of the cake, gently press the tip of a small icing wand against the side of the cake while you spin the cake turner. Repeat round by round as you work your way up to the top of the cake. To decorate the top, repeat this method, working from the outside in.

5. Garnish the top with the whole strawberries.

TIP

Strawberry puree is simple to make. One 16-ounce container from the grocery store will yield about 1¾ cups (395g/14oz) of puree.

Wash and dry 16 ounces of strawberries. Remove the hulls and cut them into 1/4-inch pieces. Place them in a food processor and puree until smooth. This puree can be made ahead and refrigerated for up to 3 days or frozen up to 2 months.

STARS & ROSETTES CAKE

Creating the stunning cake design that appears on the cover of this book is not for the faint of heart. There's no question that it is time-consuming and requires a lot of buttercream. You need four times the Vanilla Buttercream recipe to fully cover this cake. Once you've gotten comfortable with some basic cake designs, how to use a piping bag and the different designs each tip can create, you'll be ready to make a cake that will impress even the most discerning of your friends. Have everything set up beforehand because, once you start, you really can't stop.

MAKES two 9-inch layers;
serves 8 to 16

INGREDIENTS

Everyone's Favorite Vanilla Cake
(page 31), through step 10

Magnolia Bakery Vanilla Buttercream
(page 265), quadruple the recipe

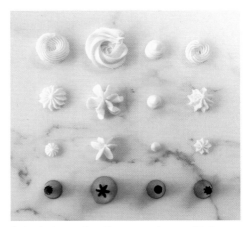

A single decorating tip can produce multiple effects. Here are the four Wilton tips you'll need to make this cake. From left to right: #22, #1M, #12, and #32.

1. Make Everyone's Favorite Vanilla Cake, as directed on page 31, through step 10.

2. Make the buttercream. Keep one batch white to ice the cake as directed in step 10. This can be done ahead of time and covered while you make the rest of the buttercream. Divide the remaining 3 batches into 6 bowls. Keep one white and dye the rest yellow, pink, blue, green and purple, as desired.

3. Gather your supplies. You will need eight 12-inch piping bags, four couplers and the following Wilton tips: four #1M tips, two #32 tips, two #12 tips, and two #22 tips.

4. Set up 4 of the bags with the #1M tip (see How to Fill a Piping Bag, page 18) with 4 different colors of buttercream of your choice.

5. Set up the remaining bags with couplers and the buttercream colors of your choice.

6. Beginning with the #1M-tipped bags, randomly place large rosettes around the cake. Position the tip where you want the center of the rosette and, with even pressure, squeeze the bag while moving clockwise in a circle, ending at 3 o'clock. Make large and small rosettes.

7. Be as creative as you want to be at this point. These four tips can create a variety of designs. Switch out colors and tips. Changing the pressure you apply when piping will create a star or rosette in different sizes. You can use the same tip to create a rosette by moving in a circle or a star by just pulling your bag straight up.

8. Stop and look at the cake periodically and fill in the empty spaces with any color or tip you choose. Have fun! This is your cake.

SUPER-RICH CHOCOLATE CAKE

As with our vanilla cake, the chocolate cake we were serving at Magnolia Bakery in 2007 needed an update. Early on, I developed this super-rich version that customers now obsess over. It's incredibly easy to make and doesn't even require a mixer. The resulting cake is moist with a beautiful dark chocolate aroma and flavor. The addition of a little espresso powder—boiling water helps it dissolve evenly through the cake—enhances the chocolate's intensity. This recipe is the base for all the chocolate-inspired cakes in this chapter.

Chocolate cake with chocolate buttercream is pure heaven, but this dark beauty is so versatile that it can pair with almost any buttercream. Over the next several pages are variations on this cake that offer delicious flavor options.

MAKES two 9-inch layers; serves 8 to 16

INGREDIENTS

2 cups plus 2 tablespoons (428g/15oz) granulated sugar

1¾ cups (237g/8.3oz) all-purpose flour

¾ cup plus 2 tablespoons (87g/3oz) unsweetened dark cocoa powder (22 to 24%), sifted

1½ teaspoons baking powder

1½ teaspoons baking soda

1½ teaspoons salt

2 eggs

1 cup (240g/8.5oz) whole milk

½ cup (104g/3.6oz) vegetable oil

1 tablespoon pure vanilla extract

2 tablespoons instant espresso powder

¾ cup (180g/6.3oz) boiling water

Chocolate Buttercream or Chocolate Mocha Buttercream (page 266)

1. Preheat the oven to 325°F. Grease and flour two 9-inch cake pans. Line the bottoms with rounds of parchment paper.

2. In a large bowl, whisk the together the sugar, flour, cocoa, baking powder, baking soda, and salt. Set aside.

3. In a medium bowl, whisk together the eggs, milk, oil, and vanilla.

4. Whisk the egg-milk mixture into the flour mixture just until incorporated. Scrape the bowl with a rubber spatula.

5. Place the espresso powder in a liquid measuring cup, add the boiling water, and whisk until dissolved. Carefully whisk into the cake batter until fully mixed. Scrape the bowl again.

6. Divide the batter evenly (it will be thin) between the prepared pans. Bake for 30 to 35 minutes, or until a cake tester inserted in the center comes out clean.

7. Let the cakes cool in the pans for 30 minutes. Transfer the cakes to a cooling rack to cool completely.

8. To assemble and decorate the cake with horizontal swipes, place one layer top side up on a cake turner. Use an icing wand to evenly spread 1½ cups buttercream over the surface. Add the second layer top side up. Using an icing wand, spread 1 cup buttercream on the top and the remaining buttercream on the sides. Smooth the icing around the cake, leaving a somewhat thick but smooth coating on the sides. Gently press the tip of an icing wand against the side of the cake, starting on the bottom, while spinning the cake turner, evenly move the wand to the top of the cake to create the horizontal swipes effect.

CHOCOLATE CAKE WITH CARAMEL MERINGUE BUTTERCREAM

~~~~~~

Caramel meringue buttercream is rich and smooth with buttery toffee notes that perfectly complement a rich chocolate cake. This divine duo is sure to delight lovers of both caramel and chocolate. The impressive crosshatch drip design is remarkably simple, with no special tools required.

MAKES two 9-inch layers; serves 8 to 16

INGREDIENTS

Super-Rich Chocolate Cake (page 39), prepared as directed through step 7

Caramel Meringue Buttercream (page 272)

½ recipe Caramel Sauce (page 287), at room temperature

1. To assemble and decorate the cake with the crosshatch pattern, place one cake layer top side up on a cake turner. Use an icing wand to evenly spread 1 cup buttercream over the surface. Add the second layer top side up. Using an icing wand, spread about 1 cup buttercream on the top and about 1 cup buttercream on the top and about 1½ cups on the sides, smoothing as you go until the cake is fully iced and smooth.

2. Place the room temperature caramel sauce in a squeeze bottle or a resealable plastic bag with a small hole cut in one corner. Drizzle the sauce in thin lines in one direction over the top of the cake, then switch directions and continue drizzling to create a crosshatch pattern all over the top of the cake. Allow the excess caramel to drip down the sides.

CHOCOLATE CAKE WITH PEPPERMINT BUTTERCREAM

Inspired by the York Peppermint Patty's classic combination of mint and chocolate, this cake is a year-round favorite. A touch of refreshing peppermint extract gives the meringue buttercream a hit of flavor that is a bright counterpoint to the sultry chocolate. To make the cake even more festive, you can add a drop or two of red food coloring to the peppermint meringue buttercream and decorate with crushed peppermint candies.

MAKES two 9-inch layers; serves 8 to 16

INGREDIENTS

15 peppermint candies

Super-Rich Chocolate Cake (page 39), prepared as directed through step 7

Peppermint Meringue Buttercream (page 272)

1. To assemble and decorate the cake with smooth sides and small rosettes, place one cake layer top side up on a cake turner. Use an icing wand to evenly spread 1 cup buttercream over the surface. Add the second cake layer top side up. Using an icing wand, spread about 1 cup buttercream on the top and about 1½ cups on the sides, smoothing as you go until the cake is fully iced and smooth.

2. For the rosette border, place ½ cup buttercream in a piping bag with a #30 closed star tip and pipe rosettes at even intervals around the top of the cake. Lightly sprinkle crushed peppermint candies over the surface of the cake.

> **TIP**
>
> To crush the candies, place the unwrapped peppermint candies in a heavy-duty plastic bag. Using a heavy rolling pin or a hammer, smash each one directly in the center and crush them into small, even-sized pieces.

CHOCOLATE CAKE WITH PEANUT BUTTER BUTTERCREAM

I am haunted by the luxuriously rich combination of chocolate and peanut butter. This isn't the last time you'll hear me rave about this match made in heaven. A prime example of how well the flavors go together, this cake is nothing short of a modern classic.

MAKES two 9-inch layers; serves 8 to 16

INGREDIENTS

Super-Rich Chocolate Cake (page 39), prepared as directed through step 7

Peanut Butter Buttercream (page 267)

½ cup (70g/2.4oz) chopped peanuts

½ cup (80g/2.8oz) mini chocolate chips

To assemble and decorate the cake, place one cake layer top side up on a cake turner. Use an icing wand to evenly spread 1 cup buttercream over the surface. Add the second layer top side up. Using an icing wand, spread about 1 cup buttercream on the top and about 1½ cups on the sides. Once the buttercream is evenly applied and smooth, use the icing wand to create a rustic look by swirling the wand unevenly around the cake, with a spackling motion. Sprinkle with chopped peanuts and mini chocolate chips.

CHOCOLATE WHITE-OUT CAKE

Smothered with a fluffy marshmallow meringue icing, this chocolate cake's impressive look belies the easy technique. The icing, light as air, offers the perfect textural and visual contrast to the cake's rich, dark chocolate magnificence.

MAKES two 9-inch layers; serves 8 to 16

INGREDIENTS

Super-Rich Chocolate Cake (page 39), prepared as directed through step 7

Marshmallow Meringue Icing (page 271)

½ cup (80g/2.8oz) mini chocolate chips

To assemble and decorate the cake, place one cake layer top side up on a cake turner. Use an icing wand to evenly spread a heaping cup of icing over the surface. Add the second cake layer top side up. Using an icing wand, spread about 1 cup buttercream on the top and about 1½ cups on the sides, smoothing around the top and sides of the cake as you go. To get the meringue to look fluffy, touch the end of the icing wand to the icing and pull away quickly to create peaks of icing. Sprinkle with the mini chocolate chips.

RAZZY CAKE

This pretty chocolate cake is filled with raspberry jam and an ethereal white chocolate raspberry meringue buttercream. This naked cake design—with the sides left exposed—is easy to assemble but still looks quite impressive thanks to the fresh raspberries and a drizzle of ganache.

MAKES two 9-inch layers; serves 8 to 16

INGREDIENTS

Super-Rich Chocolate Cake (page 39), prepared as directed through step 7

½ cup (170g/6oz) raspberry jam

½ recipe White Chocolate Raspberry Meringue Buttercream (page 272)

½ recipe Chocolate Ganache (page 268)

½ pint raspberries

1. To assemble and decorate this naked cake, place one layer top side up on a cake turner. Using an icing wand, evenly spread the raspberry jam over the cake layer. Place 1½ cups of the buttercream in a piping bag and cut a 1-inch hole in the tip. Evenly pressing the bag, start on the outer edge of the cake layer while pressing the piping bag and spiral in to the center until you have used all the buttercream to cover the jam.

2. Add the second layer bottom side up. Using an icing wand, spread 1 cup buttercream on the top surface while spinning the cake turner. Smooth the excess buttercream to the sides of the cake with a firm hand, then spread the buttercream around the cake in a very thin layer to create an almost naked cake.

3. Place the chocolate ganache in a heatproof glass bowl. Heat in the microwave in 30-second increments, stirring after each, until the ganache is pourable but not hot. Pour the ganache into a plastic squeeze bottle or a plastic bag with a small hole cut in the corner. To create the drizzle effect, hold the squeeze bottle on the edge of the cake. Squeeze the bottle while spinning the cake turner with the other hand, letting the ganache drip down the sides as you go around the cake.

4. For the rosette border, place ½ cup buttercream in a piping bag with a Wilton #1M tip. Pipe large rosettes at even intervals around the top of the cake. Place 1 raspberry in the center of each rosette just before serving.

COCONUT CAKE WITH COCONUT FILLING AND MARSHMALLOW MERINGUE ICING

The ultimate triple threat, this towering confection is three layers of coconut cake filled with a sweet and chewy coconut filling, smothered with marshmallow meringue icing, and topped with shredded coconut.

MAKES three 9-inch layers; serves 10 to 20

INGREDIENTS

4 cups (460g/16oz) cake flour

2 teaspoons baking powder

½ teaspoon salt

1½ cups/3 sticks (340g/12oz) unsalted butter, at room temperature

2¼ cups (450g/16oz) granulated sugar

1½ teaspoons pure vanilla extract

1½ teaspoons grated lemon zest

3 eggs

3 egg yolks

1½ cups (357g/12oz) full-fat coconut milk

2½ cups (250g/8.8oz) sweetened shredded coconut

Coconut Filling (page 286)

Marshmallow Meringue Icing (page 271)

1. Preheat the oven to 350°F. Grease and flour three 9-inch cake pans. Line the bottoms with rounds of parchment paper.

2. In a medium bowl, whisk together the flour, baking powder, and salt. Set aside.

3. In a stand mixer with the paddle, cream the butter and sugar on medium speed until light and fluffy, 4 to 5 minutes. Stop the mixer and scrape down the bottom and sides of the bowl and the paddle.

4. With the mixer on medium speed, beat in the vanilla and lemon zest until combined. Beat in the whole eggs and yolks, one at a time, mixing after each addition until fully incorporated. Scrape down the bottom and sides of the bowl. Reduce the mixer speed to low. Add the flour mixture in three additions, alternating with the coconut milk, beginning and ending with the dry ingredients.

5. Scrape down the bottom and sides of the bowl and beat for 30 seconds, until you no longer see streaks of flour.

6. Remove the bowl from the mixer. With a rubber spatula, fold in 1¼ cups (125g/4.4oz) of the coconut just until incorporated.

7. Divide the batter between the prepared pans. Bake for 28 to 30 minutes, or until a cake tester inserted in the center of the cake comes out clean.

8. Let the cakes cool in the pans for at least 30 minutes. Transfer the cakes to a cooling rack to cool completely.

9. To assemble and decorate the cake, place the first cake layer top side up on a cake turner. Use an icing wand to evenly spread 1 cup coconut filling over the layer. Add the second cake layer top side down and spread 1 cup coconut filling over it. Place the third layer over the filling top side up. With an icing wand, spread the meringue over the top and sides, making sure to use all the icing for a really lavish cake. To get the meringue to look fluffy, touch the end of the icing wand to the icing and pull away quickly to create peaks. Garnish with the reserved 1¼ cup (125g/4.4oz) shredded coconut.

MAGNOLIA BAKERY'S RED VELVET CAKE
WITH WHIPPED VANILLA ICING

Much has been debated about the origins of red velvet cake, widely considered a Southern tradition dating back to the late 1800s, although the Waldorf-Astoria Hotel in New York City is thought be among the first to introduce a very red cake to its menu in the late 1950s. Wherever it began, red velvet cake has been a staple at Magnolia Bakery since its opening in the mid-1990s and remains a beloved classic.

My contribution has been to increase both the cake's richness and chocolate flavor by adding a darker cocoa, which has more fat, and buttermilk, to create a softer texture with more body. We serve our red velvet cake with an old-fashioned whipped vanilla icing (also known as ermine icing), which is made with a milk and flour roux, sugar, and butter. It's similar in texture to whipped cream but richer and lusher. If you prefer cream cheese icing, choose from our classic Cream Cheese Icing (page 268) or Sweet Cream Cheese Icing (page 269), which has a slightly sweeter flavor.

MAKES two 9-inch layers;
serves 8 to 16

INGREDIENTS

3⅓ cups (383g/13.5oz) cake flour

1½ teaspoons salt

¾ cup/1½ sticks (170g/6oz) unsalted butter, at room temperature

2¼ cups (450g/16oz) granulated sugar

3 eggs

6 tablespoons liquid red food coloring

3 tablespoons (22.5g/0.75oz) unsweetened dark cocoa powder (22 to 24%), sifted

1½ teaspoons pure vanilla extract

1½ cups (240g/8.5oz) buttermilk

1½ teaspoons cider vinegar

1½ teaspoons baking soda

Whipped Vanilla Icing (page 270)

1. Preheat the oven to 325°F. Grease and flour two 9-inch cake pans. Line the bottoms with rounds of parchment paper.

2. In a medium bowl, whisk together the flour and salt. Set aside.

3. In a stand mixer with the paddle, cream the butter on medium speed until smooth. Gradually add the sugar and beat until very light and fluffy, 4 to 5 minutes.

4. With the mixer on medium speed, add the eggs, one at a time, beating well after each addition. Scrape down the bottom and sides of the bowl and the paddle.

5. In a small bowl, whisk together the red food coloring and cocoa powder. With the mixer on low speed, carefully pour the mixture into the batter, mixing until combined. Scrape down the bottom and sides of the bowl.

> **TIP**
> Liquid red food coloring can stain your hands and your kitchen counters. When working with any liquid food coloring, place the bottle on a baking sheet lined with paper towels. If any droplets escape your watchful eye, they land on the paper towels and not on your counter.

(continued)

Starting at the bottom of the cake and moving counterclockwise, work rosettes in rows.

Position the first rosette in each new row in the center of two lower-row rosettes.

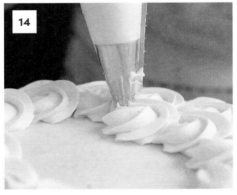

On top of the cake, work the rosettes from the outside in.

6. In a liquid measuring cup, whisk together the vanilla and buttermilk. Beginning and ending with the dry ingredients, add the dry ingredients to the mixer bowl in three additions, alternating with the buttermilk. With each addition, being careful not to overmix, beat until the ingredients are just incorporated. Scrape down the bottom and sides of the bowl.

7. In a small bowl, stir together the cider vinegar and baking soda. With the mixer on low speed, carefully add the cider vinegar and baking soda mixture to the batter and combine well. Scrape down the bottom and sides of the bowl.

8. Evenly divide the batter between the prepared pans. Bake for 40 to 45 minutes, or until the tops spring back when touched and a cake tester inserted in the center of the cakes comes out clean.

9. Let the cakes cool in the pans for 30 minutes. Transfer the cakes to a cooling rack to cool completely.

10. To assemble and decorate the cake, place one cake layer top side up on a cake turner. Use an icing wand to evenly spread 1½ cups whipped vanilla icing over the surface.

11. Add the second cake layer top side up. Using an icing wand, spread about 1½ cups icing over the tops and sides in a thin layer.

12. To decorate the cake with the rosette pattern shown in the photos at left, place the remaining icing in a piping bag with a #1M Wilton tip. Starting at the bottom layer of the cake, place the tip where you want the center of the first rosette to be. With even pressure, squeeze the bag while moving counterclockwise in a circle, ending at 3 o'clock. Start the second rosette where the last one ended.

13. Work your way around the cake, then start a second row above the first, positioning the first rosette in the center of the two lower-row rosettes. Continue until the entire cake is covered.

14. When placing rosettes on the top of the cake, work in the round, from the outside in, starting new rounds with the first rosette positioned between two on the previous row.

S'MORES CAKE

There's something wonderfully homey and yet still special about the familiar flavors of s'mores. And there's no denying that they definitely make you want some more! This gorgeous cake uses ground graham crackers, cinnamon, and honey to really nail that taste, plus a layer of chocolate ganache and fluffy marshmallow meringue icing to evoke the classic campfire treat.

MAKES two 9-inch layers;
serves 10 to 20

INGREDIENTS

3⅓ cups (450g/16oz) all-purpose flour

1 cup (110g/3.9oz) finely processed
   graham cracker crumbs

1 tablespoon baking powder

1½ teaspoons salt

1½ teaspoons ground cinnamon

1⅔ cups/3⅓ sticks (376g/13.2oz)
   unsalted butter, at room
   temperature

1 cup plus 2 tablespoons (225g/8oz)
   granulated sugar

1 cup (200g/7.1oz) light brown sugar

½ cup (150g/5.3oz) honey

6 eggs

1 tablespoon pure vanilla extract

¾ cup (180g/6.3oz) whole milk

Chocolate Ganache (page 268),
   cool but not stiff

Marshmallow Meringue Icing
(page 271)

1. Preheat the oven to 325°F. Grease and flour two 9-inch cake pans. Line the bottoms with rounds of parchment paper.

2. In a medium bowl, whisk together the flour, graham cracker crumbs, baking powder, salt, and cinnamon. Set aside.

3. In a stand mixer with the paddle, cream the butter, both sugars, and honey on medium speed until very light and fluffy, 4 to 5 minutes. Scrape down the sides and bottom of the bowl and the paddle.

4. Reduce the mixer speed to low and add the eggs, one at a time, mixing well after each addition. Add the vanilla and mix for 30 seconds. Scrape down the sides and bottom of the bowl.

5. With the mixer speed on low, slowly add the flour/graham cracker mixture in three additions, alternating with the milk, beginning and ending with the dry ingredients, until just barely incorporated. Remove the bowl from the mixer. Finish mixing with a rubber spatula by folding and scraping the bowl until you no longer see streaks of flour. Scrape down the sides and bottom of the bowl.

6. Evenly divide the batter between the prepared pans. Bake for 35 to 40 minutes, or until the tops spring back when touched in the center and a cake tester inserted in the center comes out clean.

7. Let the cakes cool in the pans for 30 minutes. Transfer the cakes to a cooling rack to cool completely.

8. Place 1½ cups of the ganache in a mixer bowl and beat on medium speed for 3 to 5 minutes, forming slight peaks with a mousse-like texture. Set the whipped ganache aside.

9. Place ½ cup of the chocolate ganache in a heatproof glass bowl. Heat in the microwave in 30-second increments, stirring until the ganache is pourable but not hot. Pour the ganache into a plastic squeeze bottle or a plastic bag with a small hole cut in the corner. Set aside while icing the cake.

(continued)

Drizzling ganache over the top of the cake.

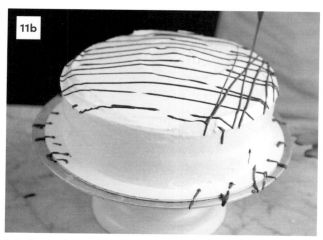

Drizzling more ganache after giving the cake a quarter turn.

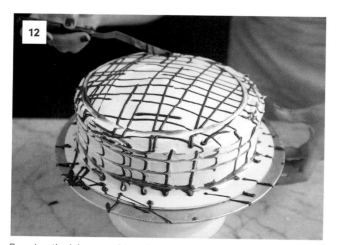

Pressing the icing wand into the meringue.

Reaching the center and lifting the wand.

10. To assemble and decorate the cake, place one cake layer top side up on a cake turner. Use an icing wand to evenly spread the whipped ganache to the edges. Add the second cake layer top side up. Using an icing wand, spread the meringue icing over the top and sides of the cake, smoothing it as you go.

11. To finish, drizzle the pourable ganache in a crosshatch pattern all over the top of the cake, letting the excess drip down the sides.

12. To create the beautiful horizontal swipe pattern in the photo, spin the cake turner and, starting at the bottom of the cake, gently press a small cake icing wand into the meringue icing.

13. Twirl the cake stand with one hand while moving the wand up to the top of the cake. While spinning the cake turner again, move the wand to the center of the cake, lifting the wand when you hit the center.

ULTIMATE CARROT CAKE WITH CREAM CHEESE ICING

I have been making this cake for so many years, in part because it's requested so much. I've been told by many people that this is the best carrot cake they've ever had. No doubt it's because of the generous amount of carrots, raisins, walnuts, pineapple, and coconut. I coarsely shred the carrots so they add a great texture and retain lots of flavor. And then there's the cream cheese icing—so delectably tangy and rich. Add just enough so the cake really shines through. There are a lot of ingredients in this recipe. Take the time to get everything set up and measured before you begin.

MAKES two 9-inch layers; serves 8 to 16

INGREDIENTS

3 cups (405g/14.3oz) all-purpose flour, plus 1 tablespoon for the raisins

1 tablespoon baking powder

1½ teaspoons baking soda

1 tablespoon ground cinnamon

¼ teaspoon grated nutmeg

1 teaspoon salt

1 cup (150g/5.2oz) raisins

3 cups (318g/11.2oz) lightly packed shredded carrots (about 3 large)

1½ cups (368g/13oz) canned juice-packed crushed pineapple, drained

1 cup (120g/4.2oz) coarsely chopped toasted walnuts

1 cup (100g/3.5oz) sweetened shredded coconut

6 eggs

3 cups (600g/21.2oz) granulated sugar

2 teaspoons pure vanilla extract

2 cups (416g/15oz) vegetable oil

Cream Cheese Icing (page 268)

1 cup (120g/4.2oz) coarsely chopped toasted walnuts (see Tip, page 288) for garnish (optional)

1. Preheat the oven to 325°F. Grease and flour two 9-inch cake pans. Line the bottoms with rounds of parchment paper.

2. In a medium bowl, whisk together the flour, baking powder, baking soda, cinnamon, nutmeg, and salt. Set aside. Toss the raisins with the remaining 1 tablespoon flour. Set aside.

3. In a medium bowl, toss together the shredded carrots, pineapple, toasted walnuts, coconut, and raisins.

4. In a stand mixer with the paddle, beat together the eggs and sugar on medium speed for 2 minutes, or until light and thick. Add the vanilla and oil and beat well. Scrape down the bottom and sides of the bowl.

5. On low speed, gradually add the flour mixture, mixing until just barely incorporated. Remove the bowl and scrape down the bottom and sides. Use a spatula to fold and mix the batter until no streaks of flour remain.

6. Fold in the carrot mixture. Note: This is a lot of fruit and nuts, so it's easier to mix the batter if you transfer it to a large wide bowl.

7. Evenly divide the batter between the prepared pans. Bake for 50 to 60 minutes, or until a cake tester inserted in the center comes out clean.

8. Let the cakes cool in the pans for 1 hour. Transfer the cakes to a cooling rack to cool completely.

9. To assemble and decorate this naked cake as in the photo, place one cake layer top side up on a cake turner. Use an icing wand to evenly spread 1½ cups cream cheese icing over the surface. Add the second cake layer top side up. Using an icing wand, spread the remaining icing over the top of the cake. Use the back of a soup spoon to swirl simple designs into the cream cheese. Garnish with toasted walnuts, if desired.

HUMMINGBIRD CAKE WITH SWEET CREAM CHEESE ICING

Created on the island of Jamaica, where it is also known as the Doctor Bird cake, the Hummingbird cake was adopted as a Southern tradition after the recipe was first published in *Southern Living* magazine in the 1970s. It's a bestseller at Magnolia Bakery, popular for its unique combination of banana, pineapple, and pecans.

MAKES two 9-inch layers; serves 8 to 16

INGREDIENTS

6 very ripe bananas (700g/24oz)

3 cups (405g/14.3oz) all-purpose flour

1½ teaspoons baking soda

1½ teaspoons ground cinnamon

¾ teaspoon salt

3 eggs

2¼ cups (450g/16oz) granulated sugar

1 cup plus 2 tablespoons (225g/8oz) vegetable oil

1½ teaspoons pure vanilla extract

1½ cups (342g/12oz) canned juice-packed crushed pineapple, drained

¾ cup (86g/3oz) coarsely chopped pecans, lightly toasted (see Tip, page 288), plus ½ cup (58g/2oz) for garnish (optional)

Sweet Cream Cheese Icing (page 269)

1. Preheat the oven to 325°F. Grease and flour two 9-inch cake pans. Line the bottoms with rounds of parchment paper.

2. Break the bananas into large pieces and place them in the stand mixer bowl with the paddle. Beat on medium speed until pureed. Transfer them to a bowl, scraping the mixer bowl clean, and set aside.

3. In a medium bowl, whisk together the flour, baking soda, cinnamon, and salt. Set aside.

4. In a stand mixer with the whisk, combine the eggs and sugar. Whisk on medium speed for 5 minutes, until pale and creamy. Pour in the oil and vanilla and whisk for another 2 minutes, until everything is well combined. Scrape down the bottom and sides of the bowl.

5. Switch to the paddle and with the mixer on low speed, mix in the mashed bananas and the pineapple just until incorporated.

6. Remove the bowl from the mixer. With a spatula, scrape down the bottom and sides of the bowl, then fold in the flour mixture in three additions, mixing until just combined and there are no longer any streaks of flour. Fold in the ¾ cup chopped pecans.

7. Evenly divide the batter between the prepared pans. Bake for 40 to 45 minutes, or until a cake tester inserted in the center comes out clean.

8. Let the cakes cool in the pans for 1 hour. Transfer the cakes to a cooling rack to cool completely.

9. To assemble and ice the cake, place one cake layer top side up on a cake turner. Use an icing wand to evenly spread 1½ cups cream cheese icing over the surface. Add the second layer top side up.

10. Using an icing wand, spread the remaining icing over the top and sides of the cake, leaving some of the cake slightly exposed for the naked cake effect. Sprinkle the remaining chopped toasted pecans around the top edge of the cake, if desired.

LEMON CAKE <small>WITH</small> LEMON MERINGUE BUTTERCREAM

This divine citrus-infused cake is for all the lemon-heads out there. It's filled with lemon cream and iced with lemon meringue buttercream. Because the filling is so addictive, I wanted to get more of it in every bite, so I sliced each of the two layers in half to create a four-layer cake. It manages to be delicate and luscious, creamy and tangy, all at once.

MAKES two 9-inch layers; serves 8 to 16

INGREDIENTS

5¼ cups (613g/21.3oz) cake flour

1½ tablespoons baking powder

1¼ teaspoons salt

3 cups (600g/21.2oz) granulated sugar

2 tablespoons grated lemon zest

1½ cups/3 sticks (340g/12oz) unsalted butter, cut into 1-inch pieces, at room temperature

5 egg whites

2¼ cups (540g/19oz) buttermilk

2 tablespoons fresh lemon juice

Lemon Meringue Buttercream (page 272)

Lemon Cream Filling (page 286)

1. Preheat the oven to 325°F. Grease and flour two 9-inch cake pans. Line the bottoms with rounds of parchment paper.

2. In a medium bowl, whisk together the cake flour, baking powder, and salt.

3. In a stand mixer with the paddle, combine the sugar and lemon zest. Mix for 1 minute, until fragrant. Add the flour mixture. Mix on low speed for 1 minute.

4. Add the butter to the mixer bowl all at once. With the mixer on low speed, mix until the mixture looks like wet sand, 2 to 3 minutes.

5. In a large liquid measuring cup, whisk together the egg whites, buttermilk, and lemon juice.

6. With the mixer on low speed, slowly pour in the egg white mixture. Mix for 1 minute. Scrape down the bottom and sides of the bowl. Mix again for 1 minute, until the batter is smooth and creamy. Scrape down the bottom and sides one more time.

7. Evenly divide the batter between the prepared pans. Bake for 45 to 50 minutes, or until the tops spring back when touched and a cake tester inserted in the center comes out clean.

8. Let the cakes cool in the pans for 1 hour. Transfer the cakes to a cooling rack to cool completely.

9. To make it easier to cut each cake into 2 layers, chill the layers first. This will firm them up with less chance of breakage while slicing. Place one layer at a time on a flat surface. With a large sharp serrated knife, score the outside edge as a marker before you fully cut through the cake. Carefully and slowly work your way around the cake, cutting through the cake with a sawing motion while holding your other hand on the top of the cake. Once you have completely cut through the cake, carefully lift the layer with the knife or two knives across each other, and move it to a flat surface.

10. Place the bottom cake slice on a cake turner, cut side up. Start assembling your cake layers before cutting into the second layer. You want to use the layers immediately so they don't dry out.

11. To assemble and decorate the cake as in the photo, place 1 cup of the lemon meringue buttercream in a piping bag, no tip necessary. Pipe a dam around the perimeter of the first layer. You may not need to use all the buttercream, it's there just to hold the lemon filling in place. Fill the center with about ½ cup of the lemon cream. Repeat with the next two layers, placing the final layer bottom side up. Using an icing wand, spread the remaining buttercream over the top and sides, smoothing with the icing wand to create the naked cake effect. There is enough buttercream to fully cover the cake with smooth sides and a rosette border on top (see the Everyone's Favorite Vanilla Cake on page 31).

CARAMEL CAKE WITH CARAMEL MERINGUE BUTTERCREAM

This caramel cake's pronounced butterscotch flavor is not overly sweet; brown sugar and butter build rich layers echoed by caramel meringue buttercream. While optional, the caramel sauce—either drizzled or applied in a cross-hatch pattern (see the Chocolate Cake with Caramel Meringue Buttercream on page 40)—adds an extra dimension for the palate and the eye.

MAKES two 9-inch layers; serves 8 to 16

INGREDIENTS

4½ cups (517.5g/18oz) cake flour

1 tablespoon plus 1½ teaspoons baking powder

1½ teaspoons salt

2½ cups (300g/10.6oz) light brown sugar

1 cup (200g/7.1oz) granulated sugar

1½ cups/3 sticks (340g/12oz) unsalted butter, cut into 1-inch pieces, at room temperature

7 eggs

1 tablespoon plus 1½ teaspoons pure vanilla extract

1½ cups (360g/12.7oz) whole milk

Caramel Meringue Buttercream (page 272)

½ recipe Caramel Sauce (optional; page 287), for drizzling

1. Preheat the oven to 325°F. Grease and flour two 9-inch cake pans. Line the bottoms with rounds of parchment paper.

2. In a stand mixer with the paddle, combine the flour, baking powder, salt, and both sugars. Mix on low speed for 1 minute.

3. Add the butter to the mixer bowl all at once. With the mixer on low speed, mix until the mixture looks like wet sand, 2 to 3 minutes. Scrape down the bottom and sides of the bowl and the paddle.

4. In a liquid measuring cup, whisk together the eggs, vanilla, and milk.

5. With the mixer on low speed, slowly pour in the egg mixture. Mix for 1 minute, until just incorporated. Do not overmix. Remove the bowl and paddle from the mixer. Scrape down the paddle, sides, and bottom of the bowl. Place the bowl back on the mixer, reinsert the paddle, and beat on medium speed for 1 minute.

6. Evenly divide the batter between the prepared pans. Bake for 40 to 45 minutes, or until the tops spring back when touched and a cake tester inserted in the centers comes out clean.

7. Let the cake cool in the pans for 30 minutes. Transfer the cakes to a cooling rack to cool completely.

8. To assemble and decorate the cake, place one layer top side up on a cake turner. Use an icing wand to evenly spread 1½ cups buttercream over the surface. Add the second cake layer top side up. Using an icing wand, spread the rest of the buttercream over the top and sides, smoothing with the wand to create smooth sides.

9. To create the little divots of caramel, as in the photo, press a small icing wand into the buttercream while spinning the cake tuner slowly, pressing and lifting as you go from the outside of the cake to the center, creating divots.

10. To fill the divots with caramel, place the caramel sauce in a squeeze bottle. Fill each divot with a small amount of caramel.

BANANA CHOCOLATE CHIP CAKE WITH NUTELLA BUTTERCREAM

Welcome to my version of a chocolate-hazelnut-banana sandwich. If you've never lucked into this combination during a late-night pantry raid, you're in for a treat. I fill and ice the banana cake with buttercream infused with the chocolate-hazelnut magic of Nutella. A crowning crosshatched drizzle of more Nutella gives it that wow factor.

MAKES two 9-inch layers;
serves 8 to 16

INGREDIENTS

3 cups (405g/14.3oz) all-purpose flour

½ cup (57.5g/2oz) cake flour

2 teaspoons baking powder

2 teaspoons baking soda

½ teaspoon salt

6 very ripe bananas (700g/24oz)

1 cup/2 sticks (226g/8oz) unsalted
    butter, at room temperature

1¼ cups (250g/8.8oz) granulated
    sugar

3 eggs

1½ teaspoons pure vanilla extract

1 cup (180g/6.3oz) semisweet
    chocolate chips

Nutella Buttercream (page 267)

½ cup (150g/5.3oz) Nutella,
    for garnish

½ cup (80g/2.8oz) mini chocolate
    chips, for garnish

1. Preheat the oven to 350°F. Grease and flour two 9-inch cake pans. Line the bottoms with rounds of parchment paper.

2. In a medium bowl, whisk together both flours, the baking powder, baking soda, and salt. Set aside.

3. Break the bananas into large pieces and place them in the stand mixer bowl. Use the paddle to beat on medium speed until pureed. Transfer to a bowl, scraping the mixer bowl clean, and set aside. (There's no need to clean the mixer bowl.)

4. In the stand mixer with the paddle, cream the butter and sugar on medium speed until light and fluffy, 3 to 5 minutes. Scrape down the bottom and sides of the bowl and paddle.

5. Add the eggs one at a time, beating well after each addition. Stop the mixer and scrape down the sides and bottom of the bowl and the paddle. Add the vanilla and mix. Add the pureed bananas and mix on low speed until combined. Remove the mixer bowl and scrape down the bottom and sides of the bowl and paddle.

6. Using a large rubber spatula, carefully fold in the flour mixture until no more streaks of flour remain. Gently fold in the chocolate chips.

7. Evenly divide the batter between the prepared pans. Bake for 38 to 40 minutes, or until the tops spring back when touched and a cake tester inserted in the center comes out clean.

8. Let the cakes cool in the pans for 30 minutes. Transfer the cakes to a cooling rack to cool completely.

9. To assemble and decorate the cake, place one cake layer top side up on a cake turner. Use an icing wand to evenly smooth 1 cup buttercream over the top. Add the second cake layer top side up. Using an icing wand, evenly spread the remaining buttercream over the top and sides. Place the ½ cup Nutella in a piping bag and drizzle in a crosshatch pattern over the top of the cake. Garnish the bottom and sides of the cake with mini chocolate chips.

THANKSGIVING CAKE
WITH CARAMEL SAUCE

After culinary school, I opened American Accent, a bakery/café in Brookline, Massachusetts, with my partner and friend, Stephanie Elkind. She's an amazing baker and chef with impeccable taste, as proven by this recipe of hers. Whenever I make this cake, filled with apples, cranberries, walnuts, and aromatic spices, it elicits raves. It's become a Thanksgiving tradition in my home. And it's actually very easy to adapt the recipe to whatever you have on hand— use pears instead of apples, figs instead of dates, pecans instead of walnuts. You don't even need a mixer, just two big bowls; and, if you have a scale, you won't need measuring cups either. If you love the cake, move on to the Apple Walnut Muffins (page 191) it inspired.

MAKES one very large, single layer 9-inch cake; serves 12 to 16

INGREDIENTS

FOR THE CAKE

3 cups (405g/14.3oz) all-purpose flour, plus 1 tablespoon for the raisins

2 teaspoons ground cinnamon

1 teaspoon baking soda

½ teaspoon grated nutmeg

½ teaspoon salt

½ cup (75g/2.6oz) raisins

3 eggs

1½ cups (312g/11oz) vegetable oil

2 teaspoons pure vanilla extract

2 cups (400g/14.2oz) granulated sugar

3 cups (405g/14.3oz) ½-inch-diced washed and unpeeled Granny Smith apples (about 3 medium apples)

1 cup (100g/3.5oz) fresh or frozen cranberries, chopped slightly in the food processor

½ cup (75g/2.6oz) diced dates

½ cup (60g/2.1oz) chopped walnuts (optional)

1. **MAKE THE CAKE:** Preheat the oven to 325°F. Grease and flour a 9-inch springform pan.

2. In a medium bowl whisk together 3 cups flour, cinnamon, baking soda, nutmeg, and salt. Set aside. Toss the raisins with the remaining 1 tablespoon flour. Set aside.

3. In a liquid measuring cup, whisk together the eggs, oil, and vanilla.

4. Place the sugar in a very large bowl and whisk in the egg mixture until smooth and creamy. Slowly fold in the flour mixture, stirring until incorporated. Scrape the bottom and sides of the bowl until no streaks of flour remain.

5. Using the same bowl that the flour was in, toss together the raisins, apples, cranberries, dates, and walnuts (if using) until evenly mixed. Using a large spoon, add the fruit to the batter and mix until evenly distributed throughout.

6. Spread the batter into the prepared pan. Bake for 1 hour 15 minutes to 1 hour 30 minutes, until a cake tester inserted in the center comes out clean. It can be difficult to know when this cake is done, as the cake creates a crust on the top while baking. You need to check the center with a cake tester several times. An extra 5 minutes in the oven to ensure the cake is done won't hurt it.

7. Place the pan on a cooling rack while preparing the glaze.

8. **MAKE THE GLAZE:** In a medium saucepan, stir together the butter, both sugars, cream, and vanilla. Bring to a boil and boil for 1 to 2 minutes, until the sugars are completely dissolved.

FOR THE GLAZE

6 tablespoons/¾ stick (85g/3oz) unsalted butter

6 tablespoons (75g/2.7oz) light brown sugar

6 tablespoons (75g/2.7oz) granulated sugar

6 tablespoons (90g/3.2oz) heavy cream

1 teaspoon pure vanilla extract

FOR THE SAUCE

1 cup (240g/8.5oz) heavy cream

9. Pour ⅓ cup of the glaze over the warm cake. Place the rest of the glaze in a covered container and store in the refrigerator until it's time to serve the cake.

10. Cool the cake completely in the pan for at least 1 hour. Once completely cool, remove the cake from the pan by running a small paring knife around the edges of the pan, then release the sides of the springform. Gently and carefully pull the pan away. Place the cake on a serving plate or platter. Cover with plastic wrap.

11. **MAKE THE SAUCE:** In a saucepan, combine the reserved glaze and cream and bring to a boil over medium-high heat. Cook and reduce until thickened, 5 to 10 minutes.

12. To serve, present the cake at the table with the sauce on the side. To cut the cake, use a serrated knife, cutting with a sawing motion to get a nice clean slice. This is a very moist cake. You can store this cake, covered, in a cake saver for 3 to 4 days.

PUMPKIN SPICE CAKE WITH CARAMEL CREAM CHEESE ICING

For this scrumptious cake, be sure to use fresh spices, ideally freshly ground, as it really makes a difference. The tang and light sweetness of the caramel cream cheese icing works well with the earthy pumpkin. Don't skip making the sugared cranberries; not only do they add a pop of color, they bring a sweet-tart burst to every slice.

MAKES three 9-inch layers; serves 12 to 16

INGREDIENTS

3 cups (405g/14.3oz) all-purpose flour

1 tablespoon baking powder

1 teaspoon baking soda

1 teaspoon salt

1 tablespoon ground cinnamon

2 teaspoons ground ginger

1 teaspoon ground allspice

½ teaspoon ground cloves

½ teaspoon grated nutmeg

2 cups/4 sticks (452g/16oz) unsalted butter, at room temperature

¾ cup (150g/5.3oz) granulated sugar

2¼ cups (450g/16oz) light brown sugar

1 tablespoon plus 1½ teaspoons grated orange zest

7 eggs

2¼ cups (540g/18oz) canned unsweetened pumpkin puree (preferably Libby's)

1 tablespoon pure vanilla extract

1½ cups (360g/12.7oz) buttermilk

1½ cups (225g/8oz) dried cranberries

Caramel Cream Cheese Icing (page 270)

Sugared Cranberries (optional; page 288), for garnish

1. Preheat the oven to 325°F. Grease and flour three 9-inch cake pans. Line the bottoms with rounds of parchment paper.

2. In a medium bowl, whisk together the flour, baking powder, baking soda, salt, cinnamon, ginger, allspice, cloves, and nutmeg. Set aside.

3. In a stand mixer with the paddle, cream the butter with both sugars until very light and fluffy, 4 to 5 minutes. Mix in the orange zest. Scrape down the bottom and sides of the bowl and the paddle.

4. With the mixer on medium speed, add the eggs one at a time, beating well after each addition. Scrape down the bottom and sides of the bowl. Add the pumpkin puree and vanilla and beat for 30 seconds, until well blended. Scrape down the bottom and sides of the bowl.

5. Reduce the mixer speed to low. Add the flour mixture in three additions, alternating with the buttermilk, beginning and ending with the dry ingredients. Remove the bowl from the mixer and scrape down the bottom and sides of the bowl. Using a large rubber spatula, fold in the dried cranberries.

6. Evenly divide the batter among the prepared pans. Bake for 40 to 45 minutes, or until a cake tester inserted in the center comes out clean.

7. Let the cakes cool in the pans for 30 minutes. Transfer the cakes to cooling racks to cool completely.

8. To assemble and decorate the cake, place a cake layer bottom side up on a cake turner. Use an icing wand to evenly spread a scant cup of the icing over the surface. Add a second cake layer top side up and spread a scant cup of icing over the surface. Add the final layer, top side up. Using an icing wand, spread the rest of the icing over the top and sides. To create the horizontal swipes effect shown in the photo, see Strawberry Cake with Strawberry Meringue Buttercream, page 34, step 4.

9. Evenly place 12 sugared cranberries on top of the cake and one in the center.

CHAPTER TWO

CUPCAKES

B aking is a science, but you don't have to be a scientist to make great cupcakes. They're also easier and quicker to make than cakes. That said, there is a certain mastery required to getting the perfect rise or crafting an icing that has just the right texture. After baking hundreds (if not thousands) of cupcakes over the years, I've stockpiled quite a few helpful tips and techniques, starting with "follow directions" and "be patient."

At Magnolia Bakery, our bakers turn out millions of cupcakes a year, the majority of which are decorated with our trademark signature swirl—which can take up to forty hours to perfect! But don't worry, I've made it easy for you to decorate beautiful cupcakes using some simple techniques.

Bake your way through this chapter and you'll surely emerge a cupcake master.

TIPS AND TECHNIQUES FOR PERFECT CUPCAKES

To evenly portion cupcakes, I prefer to use an ice cream scoop. A #20 scoop is exactly ¼ cup and is the perfect size for most cupcake recipes. If you don't have an ice cream scoop, the general rule of thumb is to fill your cupcake wells about halfway. You can use a ¼-cup dry measuring cup or place all the batter into a large resealable plastic bag, cut off about 1 inch at one corner, and squeeze the batter into each cupcake well, lifting the bag between cups.

Cupcakes can be affected by oven temperatures being off or uneven. Check your cupcakes about halfway through the baking time and rotate the pans front to back, top to bottom, if they are baking unevenly.

When checking your cupcakes for doneness, be sure to check the cupcakes in the center of the pan before pulling your pan out of the oven. A cake tester inserted in the center should come out clean, the cupcake should gently indent when pressed with your finger, and the room should smell like cake.

EVERYONE'S FAVORITE VANILLA CUPCAKES

This vanilla cupcake recipe uses the same ingredients and techniques as Everyone's Favorite Vanilla Cake (page 31). Try the variation with colorful confetti sprinkles (our Confetti Cake on page 33 reveals the confetti-filled interior).

MAKES 24 cupcakes

INGREDIENTS

3 cups (345g/12.2oz) cake flour

1¾ teaspoons baking powder

¼ teaspoon baking soda

½ teaspoon salt

1 cup (240g/8.5oz) whole milk

½ cup (115g/4oz) sour cream

1 cup/2 sticks (226g/8oz) unsalted butter, at room temperature

1½ cups (300g/10.6oz) granulated sugar

1¾ teaspoons pure vanilla extract

4 egg whites

Double recipe Magnolia Bakery Vanilla Buttercream (page 265)

½ cup 65g/2.3oz) confetti for decoration

FOR THE CONFETTI CUPCAKES

1 cup (130g/4.6oz) confetti sprinkles, plus another ½ cup (65g/2.30z) for decoration

1. Preheat the oven to 325°F. Line two 12-cup muffin tins with paper liners.

2. In a medium bowl, whisk together the flour, baking powder, baking soda, and salt. Set aside.

3. In a liquid measuring cup, whisk together the milk and sour cream until no lumps remain. Set aside.

4. In a stand mixer with the paddle, cream the butter, sugar, and vanilla on medium speed until light and fluffy, 3 to 5 minutes. Scrape the sides and bottom of the bowl and the paddle.

5. With the mixer on medium speed, slowly add the egg whites, a little at a time, beating until incorporated before adding more. Once the egg whites have been incorporated, stop the mixer and scrape down the sides and bottom of the bowl and the paddle.

6. With the mixer on low speed, add the flour mixture in three additions, alternating with the milk mixture, beginning and ending with the dry ingredients. Mix for about 15 seconds, just until incorporated.

7. Stop the mixer and remove the bowl. Scrape down the bowl and the paddle. (If you're making Confetti Cupcakes, add the confetti, place the bowl back on the mixer and mix for 20 to 30 seconds, until smooth and combined.)

8. Using a #20 scoop or a ¼-cup dry measuring cup, evenly scoop the batter into the prepared muffin cups.

9. Bake 20 to 22 minutes, or until the tops spring back when touched and a cake tester inserted into the centers comes out clean.

10. Let the cupcakes cool in the pan for 30 minutes. Transfer to a cooling rack to cool completely.

11. To decorate as in the photo, fill a piping bag with a Wilton #1M tip with vanilla buttercream and pipe a high rosette. (If making Confetti Cupcakes, finish with confetti sprinkles.)

STRAWBERRY CUPCAKES WITH STRAWBERRY MERINGUE BUTTERCREAM

I love to go berry-picking and always end up with way too many to eat, so I make this cupcake in June, when strawberries are at their peak. But thanks to the availability of frozen strawberries, we can re-create that summer pleasure any time! Just like the cake recipe from which it derives, this one maximizes strawberry flavor by using the berries three ways: in the batter, in the buttercream, and as a fresh garnish.

MAKES 24 cupcakes

INGREDIENTS

3 cups (345g/12.2oz) cake flour

1¾ teaspoons baking powder

¼ teaspoon baking soda

¾ teaspoon salt

¾ cup (170g/6oz) fresh strawberry puree (see Tip, page 34), or frozen, if fresh strawberries are not available

¾ cup (175g/6.2oz) sour cream

1 cup/2 sticks (226g/8oz) unsalted butter, at room temperature

1½ cups (300g/10.6oz) granulated sugar

1¾ teaspoons pure vanilla extract

4 egg whites

Strawberry Meringue Buttercream (page 272)

1 cup (175g/6.1oz) halved strawberries, for garnish (optional)

1. Preheat the oven to 325°F. Line two 12-cup muffin tins with paper liners.

2. In a medium bowl, whisk together the flour, baking powder, baking soda, and salt. Set aside.

3. In another medium bowl, whisk together the strawberry puree and sour cream until no lumps remain. Set aside.

4. In a stand mixer with the paddle, cream the butter, sugar, and vanilla on medium speed until light and fluffy, 3 to 5 minutes. Scrape down the sides and bottom of the bowl and the paddle.

5. With the mixer on medium speed, slowly add the egg whites, a little at a time, beating until incorporated before adding more. Once the egg whites have been added, stop the mixer and scrape down the sides and bottom of the bowl again.

6. With the mixer running on low speed, add all of the flour mixture. Mix for about 15 seconds, until just incorporated.

7. Add the strawberry/sour cream mixture and mix on low speed for about 10 seconds. Stop the mixer, scrape down the sides and bottom of the bowl again, folding a few times with a rubber spatula.

8. Using a #20 scoop or a ¼-cup dry measuring cup, evenly scoop the batter into the prepared muffin cups. Bake for 20 to 22 minutes, or until the tops spring back when touched and a cake tester inserted in the centers comes out clean.

9. Let the cupcakes cool in the pans for 30 minutes. Transfer to cooling racks to cool completely.

10. To decorate the top with a floral icing design, follow the step-by-step directions for Piping a Buttercream Rose on page 274.

SUPER-RICH CHOCOLATE CUPCAKES

If you've already tried our Super-Rich Chocolate Cake (page 39), you know why this cupcake recipe is an essential part of your arsenal. Rich in flavor and light as a feather, these cupcakes stay moist for days. The deep chocolate flavor works beautifully with several buttercreams and icings, including our chocolate buttercream, peanut butter buttercream, and caramel meringue buttercream.

MAKES 24 cupcakes

INGREDIENTS

2 cups plus 2 tablespoons (428g/15oz) granulated sugar

1¾ cups (237g/8.3oz) all-purpose flour

¾ cup plus 2 tablespoons (87g/3oz) unsweetened dark cocoa powder (22 to 24%), sifted

1½ teaspoons baking powder

½ teaspoon baking soda

1½ teaspoons salt

2 eggs

1 cup (240g/8.5oz) whole milk

½ cup (104g/3.6oz) vegetable oil

1 tablespoon pure vanilla extract

2 tablespoons instant espresso powder

¾ cup (180g/6.3oz) boiling water

Chocolate Buttercream (page 266)

White nonpareils, for decoration

1. Preheat the oven to 325°F. Line two 12-cup muffin tins with paper liners.

2. In a large bowl, whisk together the sugar, flour, cocoa, baking powder, baking soda, and salt. Set aside.

3. In a medium bowl, whisk together the eggs, milk, oil, and vanilla.

4. Whisk the egg mixture into the sugar-flour mixture just until incorporated. Scrape down the bowl with a rubber spatula.

5. Place the espresso powder and boiling water in a liquid measuring cup and whisk until dissolved. Carefully whisk into the cake batter until fully mixed. Scrape the bowl again.

6. Using a #20 scoop or a ¼-cup dry measuring cup, evenly scoop the batter into the prepared muffin cups. This batter is very loose and a bit messy. To get an even scoop, use your hand to level the batter and remove any excess from the bottom of the scoop. (You can also place the batter into a liquid measuring cup and fill each cupcake well halfway.)

7. Bake for 22 to 25 minutes, or until a cake tester inserted into the centers comes out clean.

8. Let the cupcakes cool in the pans for 30 minutes. Transfer to cooling racks to cool completely.

9. To decorate as in the photo, fill a piping bag with a Wilton #2A tip with chocolate buttercream and pipe onto the cupcakes. Sprinkle with chocolate cake crumbs or white nonpareils.

RAZZY CUPCAKES

This stunning raspberry jam–filled chocolate cupcake relies on a few components, all of which can be made ahead and assembled before serving. The chocolate ganache will hold in the refrigerator for a week. So, if you have a special occasion coming up and a busy week ahead, with just a little planning you can spread the steps out and still deliver an elaborate dessert.

MAKES 24 cupcakes

INGREDIENTS

24 Super-Rich Chocolate Cupcakes (page 79), prepared as directed through step 8

1½ cups (510g/18oz) raspberry jam

Chocolate Ganache (page 268), warm

½ recipe White Chocolate Raspberry Meringue Buttercream (page 272)

½ pint raspberries

1. Use the handle of a wooden spoon to poke a hole in the top of each cupcake. Fill a piping bag with the raspberry jam. Squeeze the bag until the jam comes to the top of the cupcake. Set aside.

2. Pour the warm ganache into a wide bowl. Dip the top of each cupcake into the warm ganache, twirling until coated. Place on a cooling rack to firm up.

3. Fit a piping bag with a Wilton #1M tip and fill with the buttercream. Pipe a rosette in the middle of the cupcake. Top with a fresh raspberry and serve.

COCONUT CUPCAKES WITH MARSHMALLOW MERINGUE ICING

With the addition of both shredded coconut and coconut milk, these cupcakes are like coconut ambassadors! I fill them with a sweet, chewy coconut filling and top with a marshmallow meringue icing, with even more (dyed) coconut for a truly showstopping cupcake.

MAKES 24 cupcakes

INGREDIENTS

2½ cups plus 2 tablespoons (301g/10.6oz) cake flour

1½ teaspoons baking powder

¼ teaspoon salt

1 cup/2 sticks (226g/8oz) unsalted butter, at room temperature

1½ cups (300g/10.6oz) granulated sugar

1 teaspoon pure vanilla extract

1 teaspoon grated lemon zest

2 eggs

2 egg yolks

1 cup (238g/8.4oz) full-fat coconut milk

2½ cups (250g/8.8oz) sweetened shredded coconut

Coconut Filling (page 286)

Gel food coloring

Marshmallow Meringue Icing (page 271)

1. Preheat the oven to 350°F. Line two 12-cup muffin tins with paper liners.

2. In a medium bowl, whisk together the flour, baking powder, and salt. Set aside.

3. In a stand mixer with the paddle, cream the butter and sugar on medium speed until light and fluffy, 3 to 5 minutes. Stop the mixer and scrape down the sides and bottom of the bowl and the paddle.

4. Beat in the vanilla and lemon zest until combined. Add the whole eggs and yolks one at a time, mixing after each addition until just incorporated. Scrape down the sides and bottom of the bowl. Reduce the mixer speed to low and add the flour mixture in three additions, alternating with the coconut milk, beginning and ending with the dry ingredients.

5. Scrape down the sides and bottom of the bowl and beat for 30 seconds.

6. Remove the bowl from the mixer. Using a large rubber spatula, fold in 1½ cups (150g/5.3oz) of the shredded coconut, just until incorporated.

7. Using a #20 scoop or a ¼-cup dry measuring cup, evenly scoop the batter into the prepared muffin cups. Bake for 20 to 22 minutes, or until a cake tester inserted in the centers comes out clean.

8. Let the cupcakes cool in the pans for 20 minutes. Transfer to cooling racks to cool completely.

9. To fill the cupcakes, fill a piping bag with the coconut filling. Use the handle of a wooden spoon to poke a hole in the top of each cupcake. Fill each cupcake with about 1 tablespoon of coconut filling. You can make the cupcakes ahead to this point and set aside, covered with plastic wrap, while making the marshmallow meringue icing.

10. To decorate as shown in the photo, divide the remaining 1 cup shredded coconut into four ¼- cup portions, dying each with your choice of food coloring (see How to Dye Coconut, page 289). Place each portion in its own shallow bowl. Use an icing wand to cover the cupcakes with icing. Carefully roll each cupcake in the dyed coconut, gently pressing the coconut on each cupcake to make sure it sticks.

S'MORES CUPCAKES

No campout is complete without the holy trinity of fire-roasted marshmallows, graham crackers, and Hershey's milk chocolate. This flavor combo conjures up a sweet childhood memory for so many people. At Magnolia Bakery, we take s'mores to another level with this cupcake filled with chocolate ganache, smothered in a marshmallow meringue icing, and swirled with more chocolate ganache. It's a trip down memory lane and a delicious classic in its own right. Because there are so many ingredients in this recipe, it's a good idea to start by getting everything set up and measured out first.

MAKES 24 cupcakes

INGREDIENTS

2¼ cups (304g/10.7oz) all-purpose flour

½ cup (55g/2.3oz) finely processed graham cracker crumbs

2 teaspoons baking powder

1 teaspoon salt

1 teaspoon ground cinnamon

1 cup/2 sticks plus 1 tablespoon (240g/8.5oz) unsalted butter, at room temperature

¾ cup (150g/5.3oz) granulated sugar

⅔ cup (133g/4.8oz) light brown sugar

½ cup (100g/3.5oz) honey

4 eggs

½ teaspoon pure vanilla extract

½ cup (120g/4.2oz) whole milk

Chocolate Ganache (page 268), at room temperature

½ recipe Marshmallow Meringue Icing (page 271)

1. Preheat the oven to 325°F. Line two 12-cup muffin tins with paper liners.

2. In a medium bowl, whisk together the flour, graham cracker crumbs, baking powder, salt, and cinnamon. Set aside.

3. In a stand mixer with the paddle, cream the butter, both sugars, and the honey on medium speed until very light and fluffy, 3 to 5 minutes. Scrape down the sides and bottom of the bowl and the paddle.

4. With the mixer on low, add the eggs, one at a time, mixing well after each addition. Add the vanilla and mix for 30 seconds. Scrape down the sides and bottom of the bowl and the paddle.

5. With the mixer on low, add the flour/graham cracker crumb mixture in three additions, alternating with the milk, beginning and ending with the dry ingredients, until just barely incorporated. Remove the bowl from the mixer. Finish mixing with a rubber spatula by folding and scraping the bowl until you no longer see streaks of flour. Scrape down the sides and bottom of the bowl.

6. Using a #20 scoop or a ¼-cup dry measuring cup, evenly scoop the batter into the prepared muffin cups. Bake for 25 to 28 minutes, or until the cupcakes spring back when touched and a cake tester inserted in the centers comes out clean.

7. Let the cupcakes cool in the pans for 30 minutes. Transfer to cooling racks to cool completely.

8. Fill a piping bag with 1½ cups of the ganache. Use the handle of a wooden spoon to poke a hole in the top of each cupcake. Fill each cupcake with about 1 tablespoon of ganache. You can make the cupcakes ahead to this point and set aside, covered with plastic wrap, while making the meringue icing.

9. Place the remaining ½ cup ganache in a heatproof glass bowl. Microwave in 30-second increments, stirring until the ganache is pourable but not hot. Pour the ganache into a plastic squeeze bottle or a plastic bag with a small hole cut in the tip.

10. To decorate as in the photo, use an icing wand to cover each cupcake with icing. Evenly drizzle each cupcake with the ganache, then use an icing wand to swirl the icing and ganache together to create streaks.

RED VELVET CUPCAKES

I love these red velvet cupcakes with whipped vanilla icing, but they are equally irresistible with cream cheese icing or our vanilla buttercream. Red velvet cupcakes have such a bright and beautiful color that they are a popular choice for brightening up a holiday table.

MAKES 24 cupcakes

INGREDIENTS

2 cups (400g/14.2oz) granulated sugar

3 tablespoons (23g/0.75oz) unsweetened dark cocoa powder (22 to 24%), sifted

3 cups (345g, 12oz) cake flour

1½ teaspoons baking soda

1½ teaspoons salt

¾ cup/1½ sticks (170g/6oz) unsalted butter, cut into 1-inch pieces, at room temperature (but still firm)

3 eggs

1½ cups (360g/12.7oz) buttermilk

1½ teaspoons cider vinegar

1½ teaspoons pure vanilla extract

2 tablespoons red food coloring

Whipped Vanilla Icing (page 270)

Shaved chocolate, for garnish

1. Preheat the oven to 350°F. Line two 12-cup muffin tins with paper liners.

2. In a stand mixer with the paddle, combine the sugar, cocoa, flour, baking soda, and salt. Mix on low for 1 minute.

3. Add all of the butter to the mixer bowl. Mix on low speed for 2 to 3 minutes, until the mixture resembles wet sand.

4. In a liquid measuring cup, whisk together the eggs, buttermilk, vinegar, vanilla, and red food coloring.

5. With the mixer on low speed, slowly pour in the egg-buttermilk mixture. Mix for 1 minute. Remove the bowl and paddle from the mixer and scrape down the sides, paddle, and bottom of the bowl. Place back on the mixer stand, reattach the paddle, and mix for 1 or 2 minutes more. Scrape down the sides and bottom of the bowl again.

6. Using a #20 scoop or a ¼-cup dry measuring cup, evenly scoop the batter into the prepared muffin cups. Bake for 20 to 25 minutes, or until a cake tester inserted into the centers comes out clean.

7. Let the cupcakes cool in the pans for 30 minutes. Transfer to cooling racks to cool completely.

8. Use an icing wand to spread the icing over the cupcakes until fully covered. Sprinkle with shaved chocolate, if using.

BANANA CUPCAKES

The fruity sweetness of banana is so versatile that these cupcakes pair well with a variety of icings. Try them with our Nutella Buttercream, as here, Chocolate Buttercream (page 266), Peanut Butter Buttercream (page 267), or Caramel Cream Cheese Icing (page 270). If you prefer to leave the icing off, they become the perfect morning muffin or afternoon snack.

MAKES 24 cupcakes

INGREDIENTS

6 very ripe bananas (700g/24oz)

3 cups (405g/14.3oz) all-purpose flour

½ cup (57.5g/2oz) cake flour

2 teaspoons baking powder

2 teaspoons baking soda

½ teaspoon salt

1 cup/2 sticks (226g/8oz) unsalted butter, at room temperature

1¼ cups (250g/8.8oz) granulated sugar

3 eggs

1½ teaspoons pure vanilla extract

½ recipe Nutella Buttercream (page 267)

1. Preheat the oven to 350°F. Line two 12-cup muffin tins with paper liners.

2. Break the bananas into large pieces and place them in the stand mixer bowl with the paddle. Beat on medium speed until pureed. Scrape the puree out of the mixer bowl into another bowl and set aside. (There's no need to clean the mixer bowl.)

3. In a medium bowl, whisk together both flours, baking powder, baking soda, and salt. Set aside.

4. In the stand mixer with the paddle, cream the butter and sugar on medium speed until light and fluffy, about 3 to 5 minutes. Scrape down the sides and bottom of the bowl and the paddle.

5. Add the eggs one at a time, beating well after each addition. Stop the mixer and scrape down the sides and bottom of the bowl. Mix in the vanilla. Add the mashed bananas and mix on low speed until combined. Remove the mixer bowl and scrape down the sides and bottom of the bowl and the paddle.

6. Using a large rubber spatula, carefully fold in the flour mixture with a rubber spatula. Do not overmix.

7. Using a #20 scoop or a ¼-cup dry measuring cup, evenly scoop the batter into the prepared muffin cups. Bake for 20 to 22 minutes, or until the tops spring back when touched and a toothpick inserted in the centers comes out clean.

8. Let the cupcakes cool in the pans for 20 to 30 minutes. Transfer to cooling racks to cool completely.

9. To decorate as in the photo, fit a piping bag with a Wilton #1M tip, fill with the buttercream, and pipe a flat rosette on the cupcake.

CARROT CUPCAKES

Jam-packed with fruit, nuts, and carrots, these flavorful cupcakes are great on their own or with a tangy smear of cream cheese icing. And they're a delicious way to sneak a lot of fiber into your diet!

MAKES 24 cupcakes

INGREDIENTS

2 cups (270g/9.6oz) all-purpose flour

1 teaspoon baking powder

1 teaspoon baking soda

1 teaspoon ground cinnamon

⅛ teaspoon grated nutmeg

½ teaspoon salt

2 cups (212g/7.5oz) lightly packed shredded carrots (about 3 large)

1 (8-ounce) can juice-packed crushed pineapple, drained

¾ cup (112g/3.9oz) raisins tossed with 1 tablespoon flour

¾ cup (90g/3.2oz) coarsely chopped toasted walnuts (see Tip, page 288), plus more for garnish

¾ cup (75g/2.6oz) sweetened shredded coconut

3 eggs

1¾ cups (350g/12.4oz) granulated sugar

1½ teaspoons pure vanilla extract

1 cup (208g/7.2oz) vegetable oil

Cream Cheese Icing (page 268)

1. Preheat the oven to 325°F. Line two 12-cup muffin tins with paper liners.

2. In a medium bowl, whisk together the flour, baking powder, baking soda, cinnamon, nutmeg, and salt. Set aside.

3. In another medium bowl, toss together the shredded carrots, pineapple, raisins, toasted walnuts, and coconut. Set aside.

4. In a stand mixer with the paddle, beat together the eggs and sugar on medium speed until light and thick, about 2 minutes. Add the vanilla and oil and beat well. Scrape down the sides and bottom of the bowl.

5. On low speed, gradually add the flour mixture, mixing until just barely incorporated. Remove the bowl from the mixer and scrape down the sides and bottom. Use a rubber spatula to fold and mix the batter until no streaks of flour remain.

6. Transfer to a large, wide bowl and fold in the carrot mixture.

7. Using a #20 scoop or a ¼-cup dry measuring cup, evenly scoop the batter into the prepared muffin cups. Bake for 22 to 24 minutes, or until a cake tester inserted in the centers comes out clean.

8. Let the cupcakes cool in the pans for 30 minutes. Transfer to cooling racks to cool completely.

9. To decorate as in the photo, fit a piping bag with a Wilton #1M tip, fill with the icing, and pipe a large rosette on the cupcakes. Sprinkle with toasted walnuts.

LEMON CUPCAKES WITH LEMON MERINGUE BUTTERCREAM

These delicate cupcakes are light, buttery, and infused with a wonderfully tangy lemon flavor that is further enhanced with the addition of our lemon meringue icing. Lemon fans will be in heaven!

MAKES 24 cupcakes

INGREDIENTS

2 cups (400g/15.5oz) granulated sugar

1 tablespoon grated lemon zest

3½ cups (402g/14oz) cake flour

1 tablespoon baking powder

¾ teaspoon salt

1 cup/2 sticks (226g/8oz) unsalted butter, cut into 8 chunks, at room temperature but firm

3 egg whites (85g/3oz)

1½ cups (370g/13oz) buttermilk

1 tablespoon fresh lemon juice

Lemon Meringue Buttercream (page 272)

½ cup (70g/2.4oz) yellow sprinkles

1. Preheat the oven to 325°F. Line two 12-cup muffin tins with paper liners.

2. In a stand mixer with the paddle, combine the sugar and lemon zest on medium speed. Mix for 1 minute, until fragrant. Add the flour, baking powder, and salt. Mix on low speed for 1 minute.

3. Add all the butter to the mixer and mix on low speed until the mixture resembles wet sand, 2 to 3 minutes.

4. In a liquid measuring cup, whisk together the egg whites, buttermilk, and lemon juice.

5. With the mixer on low speed, slowly pour in the egg white/buttermilk mixture. Mix for 1 minute. Scrape down the sides and mix again for 1 minute. Scrape down the sides and bottom of the bowl.

6. Using a #20 scoop or a ¼-cup dry measuring cup, evenly scoop the batter into the prepared muffin cups. Bake for 23 to 25 minutes, or until the cupcakes spring back when touched and a cake tester inserted in the centers comes out clean.

7. Let the cupcakes cool in the pans for 30 minutes. Transfer to cooling racks to cool completely.

8. To decorate as in the photo, fit a piping bag with a Wilton #104 tip and fill with the buttercream. Start with the wide end of the tip touching the center of the cupcake. While slowly twirling the cupcake, move the piping bag in and out, creating petals. Stagger the next row in the center of the one beneath it. Gently place a scant teaspoon of sprinkles in the center of the cupcake.

LEMON BLUEBERRY CUPCAKES WITH LEMON CREAM CHEESE ICING

We drop fresh blueberries onto our lemon cupcakes before they go into the oven. The blueberries burst, releasing their juices and flooding the cupcakes with intense blueberry flavor. No fresh blueberries? It works with frozen ones, too. This recipe tops the cupcakes with our lemon cream cheese icing, but also try them with Lemon Meringue Buttercream (page 272). Either way, they are deeply delicious.

MAKES 24 cupcakes

INGREDIENTS

2 cups (400g/15.5oz) granulated sugar

1 tablespoon grated lemon zest

3½ cups (402g/14oz) cake flour

1 tablespoon baking powder

¾ teaspoon salt

1 cup/2 sticks (226g/8oz) unsalted butter, cut into 1-inch pieces, at room temperature

3 egg whites (85g)

1½ cups (370g/13oz) buttermilk

1 tablespoon fresh lemon juice

1 cup (150g/5.7oz) fresh blueberries, rinsed and picked over for stems, plus more for garnish

1 tablespoon all-purpose flour

Lemon Cream Cheese Icing (page 269)

1. Preheat the oven to 325°F. Line two 12-cup muffin tins with paper liners.

2. In a stand mixer with the paddle, combine the sugar and lemon zest. Mix for 1 minute on medium speed until fragrant. Add the cake flour, baking powder, and salt. Mix on low speed for 1 minute.

3. Add all the butter to the mixer and mix on low speed until the mixture resembles wet sand, 2 to 3 minutes.

4. In a liquid measuring cup, whisk together the egg whites, buttermilk, and lemon juice.

5. With the mixer on low speed, slowly pour in the egg white/buttermilk mixture. Mix for 1 minute. Scrape down the sides and bottom and mix again for 1 minute. Scrape down the sides and bottom again. Remove the bowl from the mixer.

6. In a separate bowl, toss the blueberries in the all-purpose flour.

7. Using a #20 scoop or a ¼-cup dry measuring cup, evenly scoop the batter into the prepared muffin cups. Evenly distribute the flour-coated blueberries among the cupcakes. They will sink a little but that's okay.

8. Bake for 23 to 25 minutes, or until the cupcakes spring back when touched and a cake tester inserted in the centers comes out clean.

9. Let the cupcakes cool in the pans for 30 minutes. Transfer to cooling racks to cool completely.

10. To decorate as in the photo, fit a piping bag with a Wilton #199 tip and fill with the icing. Squeeze the bag while twirling the cupcake and the piping bag at the same time, circling in a counterclockwise motion until about 1 inch high. Set a blueberry on top for garnish.

PB&J CUPCAKES

I grew up at a time when kids still went home for lunch. My mother worked, but if my dad's schedule allowed, he would be home and make lunch. It was always hot dogs, cheese sandwiches, or—my favorite—peanut butter and jelly sandwiches. We had a huge grapevine in our backyard and every fall my mother would send us kids out to the vines with big brown paper bags to fill. We would spend the next few days making enough grape jelly to last us for the entire school year. I just had to create a cupcake that celebrates my eternal love for PB&J.

MAKES 24 cupcakes

INGREDIENTS

3 cups (405g/14.3oz) all-purpose flour

2 cups (400g/14.2oz) granulated sugar

1 cup (200g/7.1oz) light brown sugar

1 teaspoon baking powder

½ teaspoon baking soda

½ teaspoon salt

½ cup/1 stick (113g/4oz), unsalted butter, cut into 1-inch pieces, at room temperature

1½ cups (396g/8.5oz) Skippy creamy peanut butter

6 eggs

1¼ cups (360g/12.7oz) whole milk

2 teaspoons pure vanilla extract

1 cup (314g/11.2oz) grape jelly (preferably Welch's)

Peanut Butter Buttercream (page 267)

½ cup (70g/2.4oz) chopped peanuts, for garnish

1. Preheat the oven to 325°F. Line two 12-cup muffin tins with paper liners.

2. In a stand mixer with the paddle, combine the flour, both sugars, the baking powder, baking soda, and salt. Mix on low speed for 1 minute.

3. Add all of the butter and peanut butter to the mixer bowl. Carefully turn the mixer to low speed and mix until the mixture resembles wet sand, 2 to 3 minutes. Scrape down the sides and bottom of the bowl and the paddle. Mix again just until combined.

4. In a liquid measuring cup, whisk together the eggs, milk, and vanilla. With the mixer on low speed, slowly pour in the egg-milk mixture. Mix for 1 minute.

5. Remove the bowl and paddle from the mixer. Scrape down the sides and bottom of the bowl and the paddle. Place back on the mixer stand and reattach the paddle. Mix on medium speed for 1 minute, until fully combined.

6. Using a #20 scoop or a ¼-cup dry measuring cup, evenly scoop the batter into the prepared muffin cups. Bake for 22 to 25 minutes, or until the cupcakes spring back when touched and a cake tester inserted in the centers comes out clean.

7. Let the cupcakes cool in the pans for 30 minutes. Transfer to cooling racks to cool completely.

8. Use the handle of a wooden spoon to poke a hole in the top of each cupcake. Fill each cupcake with about 2 teaspoons grape jelly. The cupcakes can be made ahead to this point and covered with plastic wrap until just before serving time.

9. To decorate as in the photo, fit a piping bag with a Wilton #30 closed-star tip and fill with the buttercream. While evenly applying pressure, move the piping bag in and out and twirl the cupcake to create the ruffled flower look. Garnish with the chopped peanuts.

HARVEST APPLE CUPCAKES WITH CARAMEL MERINGUE BUTTERCREAM

If you've already made our delectable Apple Walnut Muffins (page 191), you will understand why I felt compelled to create an apple cupcake. They are chock-full of apple, so you get big chunks in every bite. I wanted that same fall combination of apples, cranberries, and spices, but I didn't think the big chunks would work well in a more delicate cupcake. I tried shredding the apples instead and it worked perfectly. Be sure to use Granny Smith apples or another tart, firm variety. The caramel meringue buttercream is a terrific match for these cupcakes, hinting at that other great fall flavor combo in caramel apples.

MAKES 24 cupcakes

INGREDIENTS

3 cups (405/14.4oz) all-purpose flour, plus 1 tablespoon for the raisins

2 teaspoons ground cinnamon

1 teaspoon baking soda

½ teaspoon grated nutmeg

½ teaspoon salt

3 eggs

1½ cups (312g/11oz) vegetable oil

2 teaspoons pure vanilla extract

2 cups (400g/14.2oz) granulated sugar

½ cup (75g/2.6oz) raisins

3 cups (405g/14.3oz) peeled and shredded Granny Smith apples (about 3 apples)

1 cup (100g/3.5oz) fresh or frozen cranberries, coarsely chopped

½ cup (58g/2oz) coarsely chopped pecans, lightly toasted (see Tip, page 288)

½ recipe Caramel Meringue Buttercream (page 272)

½ cup Candied Pecans (page 288), for garnish

1. Preheat the oven to 325°F. Line two 12-cup muffin tins with paper liners.

2. In a small bowl, whisk together the 3 cups flour, cinnamon, baking soda, nutmeg, and salt. Set aside.

3. In a liquid measuring cup, whisk together the eggs, oil, and vanilla.

4. Place the sugar in a very large bowl and whisk in the egg-oil mixture until smooth and creamy. Using a large rubber spatula, add the flour mixture to the sugar mixture and stir until incorporated. Scrape the sides and bottom of the bowl until no streaks of flour remain.

5. In a small bowl, toss the raisins with the remaining 1 tablespoon flour. In a large bowl, combine the shredded apples, cranberries, pecans, and raisins. Stir until thoroughly combined.

6. Using a large wooden spoon, add the fruit to the batter and mix until evenly distributed throughout.

7. Using a #20 scoop or a ¼-cup dry measuring cup, evenly scoop the batter into the prepared muffin cups. The muffin cups will be very full. Bake for 20 to 22 minutes, or until a tester inserted into the centers comes out clean.

8. Let the cupcakes cool in the pans for 30 minutes. Transfer to cooling racks to cool completely.

9. To decorate as in the photo, fill a piping bag with no tip with the buttercream. Pipe a large dollop in the center of the cupcake. Garnish with a candied pecan.

PUMPKIN SPICE CUPCAKES WITH MAPLE CREAM CHEESE ICING

Although pumpkin spice has been introduced into some questionable products (shampoo?!), this mix of aromatic spices remains one of my favorites. And with canned pumpkin always in stock, there's no reason these scrumptious cupcakes can't be enjoyed year-round.

MAKES 24 cupcakes

INGREDIENTS

1¾ cups (237g/8.4) all-purpose flour

1½ teaspoons baking soda

¼ teaspoon salt

1 teaspoon ground cinnamon

¼ teaspoon ground ginger

¼ teaspoon ground allspice

¼ teaspoon ground cloves

½ teaspoon grated nutmeg

¾ cup/1½ sticks (170g/6oz) unsalted butter, at room temperature but firm

½ cup (100g/3.5oz) granulated sugar

1 cup (200g/7.1oz) light brown sugar

1 teaspoon grated orange zest

3 eggs

1 cup (240g/8.5oz) canned unsweetened pumpkin puree (preferably Libby's)

1 tablespoon pure vanilla extract

⅔ cup (160g/5.6oz) buttermilk

⅔ cup (100g/3.5oz) dried cranberries

Maple Cream Cheese Icing (page 269)

1. Preheat the oven to 325°F. Line two 12-cup muffin tins with paper liners.

2. In a medium bowl, whisk together the flour, baking soda, salt, cinnamon, ginger, allspice, cloves, and nutmeg. Set aside.

3. In a stand mixer with the paddle, cream the butter, both sugars, and the orange zest on medium speed until very light and fluffy, about 4 to 5 minutes. Scrape down the sides and bottom of the bowl. Add the eggs, one at a time, beating well after each addition. Scrape down the sides and bottom of the bowl.

4. Add the pumpkin puree and vanilla and beat on low speed until well combined, about 30 seconds. Scrape down the sides and bottom of the bowl again.

5. On low speed, add the flour mixture in three additions, alternating with the buttermilk, beginning and ending with the dry ingredients. Scrape down the sides and bottom of the bowl once more.

6. Remove the bowl from the mixer and, using a large rubber spatula, fold in the dried cranberries.

7. Using a #20 scoop or a ¼-cup dry measuring cup, evenly scoop the batter into the prepared muffin cups. Bake for 20 to 22 minutes, or until the tops spring back when touched and a cake tester inserted in the centers comes out clean.

8. Let the cupcakes cool in the pans for 30 minutes. Transfer to cooling racks to cool completely.

9. Fill a piping bag with a Wilton #1M tip with the maple cream cheese icing and pipe a large rosette on the cupcake.

CHAPTER THREE

FROM THE COOKIE JAR

What is more homey and comforting than the smell of freshly baked cookies? Growing up, I loved the holiday season, a time of tradition and family togetherness. It also gave me a chance to perfect the art of baking cookies with the women I admired most. Some of my earliest memories are of making cut-out cookies with my great-grandmother. She would guide my hands as I rolled out the leftover scraps of sugar cookie dough that she would bake as a treat for me. Working in a bakery brings that special feeling back on a daily basis.

Cookie fads come and go, but the best recipes endure through it all. Those that never seem to change are the homestyle ones that can be easily grabbed from the cookie jar—Chocolate Chunks, Snickerdoodles, Thumbprints, and Gingersnaps, classics every one. In this chapter, I share recipes for those tried-and-true treats, some of them handed down by my family through the generations, as well as some perennial Magnolia Bakery favorites.

TIPS FOR PERFECT COOKIES EVERY TIME

The rules for baking cookies are the same as those for cakes and cupcakes. Proper measuring, timing, and oven temperatures are critical to the successful outcome of every batch.

CHILLING: If a recipe calls for chilling the dough for at least 30 minutes, never skip this important step. The gluten needs time to relax. It's better to chill up to 24 hours than not at all.

OVEN RACK: Bake your cookies on the center rack of the oven one sheet at a time, rotating the pan front to back halfway through baking time.

TIMING: Keep a close eye on your cookies—they can go from perfectly baked to overbaked in a minute. They also continue to bake on the pan after you remove them from the oven, so take the pan out just *before* you think the cookies are done.

COOLING: Unless otherwise stated, cool cookies on the pan for 5 to 10 minutes, then remove to a cooling rack to finish cooling completely.

STORAGE: Cookies should be stored in an airtight container between sheets of wax or parchment paper. When I was growing up, my mother would store cookies in a tin. To keep them fresh, she would add a slice of white sandwich bread. Overnight, the bread would get hard as a rock, keeping the cookies soft and delicious. She would do this every day for as many days as the cookies lasted.

CHOCOLATE CHUNK CARAMEL SEA SALT COOKIES

This is the best-selling cookie at Magnolia Bakery. We can't keep them in stock! They are big, soft, chewy, and sweet, loaded with caramel, and topped with a dash of sea salt.

MAKES 16 large cookies

INGREDIENTS

2¾ cups (372g/13.2oz) all-purpose flour

1 teaspoon baking soda

1 teaspoon baking powder

1 teaspoon salt

1¼ cups/2½ sticks (282g/10oz) unsalted butter, at room temperature

¼ cup (50g/1.8oz) granulated sugar

1¾ cups (350g/12.4oz) light brown sugar

2 eggs

2 teaspoons pure vanilla extract

2 cups (360g/12.8oz) semisweet chocolate chunks (from your favorite bar) or chips

16 Kraft caramel candies, each cut into 3 equal pieces

Flaked sea salt, preferably Maldon

TIP

Each cookie in this recipe has 3 pieces of caramel candy. Tempting as it is to add more, use restraint or the sweet stickiness will be overpowering.

1. In a medium bowl, whisk together the flour, baking soda, baking powder, and salt. Set aside.

2. In a stand mixer with the paddle, cream the butter and both sugars on medium speed until light and fluffy, 3 to 4 minutes. Scrape down the sides and bottom of the bowl.

3. Add the eggs, one at a time, mixing well after each addition. Scrape down the sides and bottom of the bowl. Add the vanilla and continue beating about 1 minute.

4. Reduce the mixer speed to low, gradually add the flour mixture, and mix until fully incorporated. Be sure not to overmix.

5. Remove the bowl from the mixer and fold in the chocolate chunks with a rubber spatula until just combined.

6. Line a baking sheet with parchment paper. Using a large (3-ounce) ice cream scoop, portion out 16 balls. Place on the prepared pan, cover with plastic wrap and refrigerate for 24 hours.

7. When ready to bake, preheat the oven to 325°F. Line two baking sheets with parchment paper.

8. Remove the cookies from the refrigerator, then arrange 6 cookies on each of two pans and 4 cookies on a third pan. Space them far enough part so that they won't spread into one another when baking. Let sit for 10 to 12 minutes before baking. Gently press the dough balls to flatten slightly before you put them in the oven.

9. Bake one sheet at a time. Transfer a pan to the oven and bake for 12 minutes. Remove the cookies from the oven and immediately place 3 small pieces of caramel candy on top of each cookie. Sprinkle with the sea salt flakes, rotate the pan front to back, and return the cookies to the oven. Bake for an additional 4 to 6 minutes, or until the middle is set and the cookies are lightly golden brown.

10. Let the cookies sit on the pan for 5 to 10 minutes, then transfer them to a cooling rack to cool completely. Store in an airtight container.

CHOCOLATE CHIP COOKIES

Easy-Bake Ovens came out just as I was turning seven. I was so excited when I got one for Christmas that year, I couldn't wait to make cookies for my dad. Our favorites were chocolate chip, and we could eat half the batter before they even went into the oven. This is where my journey to create the perfect chocolate chip cookie began. I like mine crispy on the bottom and edges, soft and chewy in the center. Adjusting the sugar ratios affects the ultimate texture. More brown sugar yields a chewier cookie; more white sugar yields a crisper cookie. Finding that perfect balance is where the magic lies. Here is my ultimate recipe.

MAKES 24 cookies

INGREDIENTS

2¼ cups (304g/10.7oz) all-purpose flour

1 teaspoon baking soda

½ teaspoon salt

½ cup/1 stick plus 2 tablespoons (141g/5oz) unsalted butter, at room temperature

¾ cup (150g/5.3oz) granulated sugar

¾ cup (150g/5.3oz) light brown sugar

2 eggs

¾ teaspoon pure vanilla extract

2 cups (360g/12.7 oz) semisweet chocolate chips or high-quality chocolate chunks from a bar

1. In a small bowl, whisk together the flour, baking soda, and salt. Set aside.

2. In a stand mixer with the paddle, cream the butter and both sugars for 2 minutes on medium speed. Scrape down the sides and bottom of the bowl and continue beating until light and fluffy, 2 to 4 minutes. Scrape down the sides and bottom of the bowl again.

3. Add the eggs, one at a time, mixing well after each addition. Beat in the vanilla. Scrape down the sides and bottom of the bowl.

4. Reduce the mixer speed to low and gradually add the flour mixture until fully incorporated. Be sure not to overmix. Remove the bowl from the mixer and fold in the chocolate chips with a rubber spatula until just combined.

5. Use a #40 (1-ounce) cookie scoop to portion the dough into 24 balls. Place on a baking sheet, wrap in plastic wrap and chill for at least 30 minutes and up to 24 hours.

6. When ready to bake, preheat the oven to 325°F. Line two baking sheets with parchment paper.

7. Remove the cookies from the refrigerator, then arrange 12 cookies on each of two pans. Space them far enough part so that they won't spread into one another when baking. Let sit for 10 to 12 minutes before baking. Gently press the dough balls to flatten slightly before you put them in the oven.

8. Bake one sheet at a time on the center rack for 10 to 12 minutes, or until lightly golden brown.

9. Let the cookies sit on the pan for 5 minutes, then transfer them to a cooling rack to cool completely. Store in an airtight container.

BROWN SUGAR COOKIES

Brown sugar cookies are a chewier version of our Chocolate Chip Cookies (page 106), minus the chocolate chips. I make them with equal amounts of brown and white sugar, which results in a chewier cookie with a more pronounced butterscotch flavor.

MAKES 24 cookies

INGREDIENTS

2 cups (270g/9.6oz) all-purpose flour

1 teaspoon baking soda

½ teaspoon salt

½ cup/1 stick plus 1 tablespoon (127g/4.5 oz) unsalted butter, at room temperature

⅔ cup (133g/4.7oz) granulated sugar

⅔ cup (133g/4.7oz) light brown sugar

2 eggs

¾ teaspoon pure vanilla extract

1. In a small bowl, whisk together the flour, baking soda, and salt. Set aside.

2. In a stand mixer with the paddle, cream the butter and both sugars on medium speed, scraping down the sides and bottom of the bowl after 2 minutes. Continue beating until light and fluffy, about 2 to 4 minutes. Scrape down the sides and bottom of the bowl again.

3. Add the eggs, one at a time, mixing well after each addition. Add the vanilla and mix until just incorporated. Scrape down the sides and bottom of the bowl.

4. Reduce the mixer speed to low and gradually add the flour mixture until fully incorporated. Be sure not to overmix. Remove the bowl from the mixer and scrape down the sides and bottom of the bowl again.

5. Line a baking sheet with parchment paper. Use a #40 (1-ounce) cookie scoop to portion the dough into 24 balls. Place a baking sheet and wrap in plastic wrap. Chill for at least 30 minutes and up to 24 hours (preferable).

6. When ready to bake the cookies, preheat the oven to 325°F. Line two baking sheets with parchment paper.

7. Arrange 12 cookies on each baking sheet. Let sit for 10 minutes before baking. Gently press the dough balls to flatten slightly.

8. Bake one sheet at a time. Transfer a pan to the oven and bake for 10 to 12 minutes, or until lightly golden brown. Let the cookies sit on the pan for 5 minutes, then transfer them to a cooling rack to cool completely.

9. Let the cookies sit on the pan for 5 minutes, then transfer them to a cooling rack to cool completely. Store in an airtight container.

CRACKED SUGAR COOKIES

Cracked sugar cookies get their name from the way the sugar topping makes them crack in the oven. They are a classic grab-and-go cookie-jar cookie that have been a staple at Magnolia Bakery for years. Because these do not require chilling, you can make this dough and have cookies in very short order, so they're ideal for an after-school treat or whenever you need dessert in a snap.

MAKES 24 cookies

INGREDIENTS

2½ cups (337g/12oz) all-purpose flour

1 teaspoon baking soda

½ teaspoon cream of tartar

½ teaspoon salt

1 cup/2 sticks (226g/8oz) unsalted butter, at room temperature (but still firm)

2 cups (400g/14.2oz) granulated sugar

4 egg yolks, lightly beaten

½ teaspoon pure vanilla extract

1. Preheat the oven to 325°F. Line two baking sheets with parchment paper.

2. In a small bowl, whisk together the flour, baking soda, cream of tartar, and salt. Set aside.

3. In a stand mixer with the paddle, cream the butter and 1½ cups (300g/10.6oz) of the sugar on medium speed. Scrape down the sides and bottom of the bowl and continue beating until light and fluffy, about 3 minutes.

4. Add the egg yolks and vanilla and mix well. Scrape down the sides and bottom of the bowl.

5. Reduce the mixer speed to low, gradually adding the flour until fully incorporated. Be sure not to overmix. Scrape down the sides and bottom of the bowl.

6. Place the remaining ½ cup (100g/3.5oz) sugar in a bowl. Using a #40 (1-ounce) cookie scoop, portion the dough into 24 balls and dip the tops into the sugar. Place 12 balls on each of the prepared baking sheets.

7. Bake one sheet at a time. Transfer a pan to the oven and bake for 10 to 12 minutes, or until lightly golden brown.

8. Let the cookies sit on the pan for 5 minutes, then transfer them to a cooling rack to cool completely. Store in an airtight container.

CONFETTI COOKIES

This variation on the Cracked Sugar Cookie (page 110) turns fun and festive with the simple addition to the dough of colorful confetti sprinkles.

MAKES 24 large cookies

INGREDIENTS

2½ cups (337g/12oz) all-purpose flour

1 teaspoon baking soda

½ teaspoon cream of tartar

½ teaspoon salt

1 cup/2 sticks (226g/8oz) unsalted butter, at room temperature (but still firm)

1½ cups (300g/10.6oz) granulated sugar

4 egg yolks, lightly beaten

½ teaspoon pure vanilla extract

½ cup (65g/2.3oz) confetti sprinkles

1. Preheat the oven to 325°F. Line two baking sheets with parchment paper.

2. In a small bowl, whisk together the flour, baking soda, cream of tartar, and salt. Set aside.

3. In a stand mixer with the paddle, cream the butter and sugar together on medium speed. Scrape down the sides and bottom of the bowl and continue beating until light and fluffy, about 3 minutes.

4. Add the egg yolks and vanilla and mix well. Scrape down the sides and bottom of the bowl.

5. Reduce the mixer speed to low and gradually add the flour mixture until fully incorporated. Be sure not to overmix. Scrape down the bottom and sides of the bowl. Add the confetti sprinkles and mix for 15 to 20 seconds, just until combined. Scrape down the bottom and sides of the bowl one last time.

6. Using a #40 (1-ounce) cookie scoop, portion the dough into 24 balls. Place 12 on each of the prepared baking sheets.

7. Bake one sheet at a time. Transfer a pan to the oven and bake for 10 to 12 minutes, or until lightly golden brown. They will continue to bake on the baking sheet when removed.

8. Let the cookies sit on the pan for 5 minutes, then transfer them to a cooling rack to cool completely.

PEANUT BUTTER REESE'S PIECES COOKIES

If a little of something is good, does that mean a lot is better? In the case of this cookie, the answer is a resounding YES! I adore loaded cookies, and this peanut butter version really holds up to a lot of special added ingredients. The texture is out of this world!

MAKES 24 cookies

INGREDIENTS

1¼ cups (170g/6oz) all-purpose flour

¾ teaspoon baking soda

½ teaspoon baking powder

¼ teaspoon salt

½ cup/1 stick (113g/4oz) unsalted butter, at room temperature

1 cup (266g/9.4oz) Skippy creamy peanut butter

½ cup (100g/3.5) light brown sugar

¾ cup (150g/5.3oz) granulated sugar

2 eggs

1 teaspoon pure vanilla extract

½ cup (90g/3.2oz) peanut butter chips

¾ cup (135g/4.8oz) semisweet chocolate chips

½ cup (110g/3.9oz) Reese's Pieces, roughly chopped

¼ cup (35g/1.2oz) chopped peanuts

1. In a small bowl, whisk together the flour, baking soda, baking powder, and salt. Set aside.

2. In a stand mixer with the paddle, cream the butter, peanut butter, and both sugars on medium speed until light and fluffy, about 4 minutes. Scrape down the sides and bottom of the bowl.

3. In a liquid measuring cup, whisk together the eggs and vanilla. Add to the mixer all at once and beat until combined.

4. Reduce the mixer speed to low and gradually add the flour mixture until just incorporated.

5. Remove the bowl from the mixer and use a rubber spatula to scrape down the paddle, sides, and bottom. Fold in the peanut butter chips, chocolate chips, Reese's Pieces, and peanuts until evenly distributed throughout the dough.

6. Line a baking sheet with parchment paper. Using a #40 (1-ounce) cookie scoop, portion out balls and place on a baking sheet. Wrap in plastic and refrigerate for at least 1 hour or up to 24 hours.

7. When ready to bake the cookies, preheat the oven to 325°F. Line two baking sheets with parchment paper.

8. Arrange 12 cookies evenly spaced on each baking sheet. Flatten them slightly.

9. Bake one sheet at a time. Transfer a pan to the oven and bake for 10 to 12 minutes, or until lightly golden brown and the center is just set.

10. Let the cookies sit on the pan for 10 minutes, then transfer them to a cooling rack to cool completely. Store in an airtight container.

GINGERSNAP COOKIES

More chewy than a classic gingersnap, these cookies have the perfect balance of warming spices and mellow sweetness. They have a long shelf life if kept in an airtight container, but they tend to get gobbled up pretty quickly!

MAKES 24 cookies

INGREDIENTS

2 cups (270g/9.6oz) all-purpose flour

1½ teaspoons baking soda

1½ teaspoons ground cinnamon

1½ teaspoons ground ginger

1 teaspoon ground cloves

⅛ teaspoon salt

1 cup (200g/7.1oz) light brown sugar

¼ cup (84g/3oz) molasses

¾ cup (155g/5.5oz) vegetable oil

1 egg

¼ cup (50g/1.8oz) granulated sugar

1. In a medium bowl, whisk together the flour, baking soda, cinnamon, ginger, cloves, and salt. Set aside.

2. In a large bowl, whisk together the brown sugar, molasses, vegetable oil, and egg.

3. Add the flour mixture to the brown sugar mixture. Using a wooden spoon, mix until combined; the dough will be dense and heavy. Cover with plastic wrap, pressing it directly on the surface of the dough. Refrigerate for at least 30 minutes and up to 24 hours.

4. When ready to bake the cookies, preheat the oven to 325°F. Line two baking sheets with parchment paper.

5. Place the granulated sugar in a small wide bowl. Using a #40 (1-ounce) cookie scoop, make uniform balls, then roll them in your palms until perfectly round. Roll the balls in the granulated sugar and place on the prepared baking sheets. Press down slightly.

6. Bake for 8 to 10 minutes; the cookies will be soft. Remove from the oven, let sit on the pan for 5 to 10 minutes, then transfer them to a rack to cool. The cookies will crisp up once cool. Store in an airtight container.

SNICKERDOODLES

Snickerdoodles are reminiscent of a sugar cookie, but softer and cakier. Rolled in spiced sugar, they crack a little bit, like our Cracked Sugar Cookies (page 110), but the coating gives them their own unique flavor. You can use cinnamon as called for, create a pumpkin spice version by adding grated nutmeg, ground allspice, and ground cloves to the sugar, or customize your own spice blend.

MAKES 30 cookies

INGREDIENTS

3 cups (405g/14.3oz) all-purpose flour

2 teaspoons cream of tartar

1½ teaspoons baking soda

¼ teaspoon salt

1 cup/2 sticks (226g/8oz) unsalted butter, at room temperature

2 cups (400g/14.2oz) granulated sugar

2 eggs

2 tablespoons whole milk

1 teaspoon pure vanilla extract

1 tablespoon ground cinnamon

1. In a medium bowl, whisk together the flour, cream of tartar, baking soda, and salt. Set aside.

2. In a stand mixer with the paddle, cream the butter and 1½ cups (300g/10.6oz) of the sugar on medium speed until light and fluffy, about 4 minutes, scraping down the sides and bottom of the bowl at least once.

3. Reduce the mixer speed to low and add the eggs, one at a time, mixing well after each addition. Add the milk and vanilla and mix until blended. Scrape down the sides and bottom of the bowl.

4. With the mixer speed still on low, gradually add the flour mixture until all the flour has been incorporated, making sure not to overmix. Remove the bowl from the mixer and scrape down the sides and bottom again.

5. Place the dough in a large bowl, cover with plastic wrap, and refrigerate for 1 hour before continuing.

6. When ready to bake the cookies, preheat the oven to 325°F. Line three baking sheets with parchment paper.

7. In a small bowl, whisk together the remaining ½ cup sugar with the cinnamon.

8. Using a #40 (1-ounce) cookie scoop, make 30 uniform balls, rolling them in between your palms until perfectly round. Roll each ball in the cinnamon sugar until thoroughly coated.

9. Place 10 sugared balls about 1 inch apart on each of the prepared pans.

10. Bake one sheet at a time. Transfer to the middle rack of the oven and bake for 12 to 14 minutes, rotating the pan front to back halfway through the baking time. Bake until just starting to lightly brown.

11. Let the cookies sit on the pan for 5 minutes, then transfer them to a cooling rack to cool completely. Repeat with the remaining pans. Store in an airtight container.

COCONUT MACAROONS

I have been making these cookies for so long I can't even remember the first time. Although they're not one of the recipes handed down from my grandmother, they have definitely become a family favorite. I love my macaroons on the chewy side with plenty of coconut. Inherently gluten-free, this versatile recipe can be easily customized with the addition of dried fruits and nuts—I suggest pistachios and cherries here—and a finishing drizzle of chocolate.

MAKES 24 macaroons

INGREDIENTS

4 cups (400g/14oz) sweetened shredded coconut

2 teaspoons pure vanilla extract

3½ tablespoons (46g/1.6oz) unsalted butter, melted

⅔ cup (133g/4.7oz) sugar

1½ cups (150g/5.3oz) chopped pistachios (optional)

1½ cups (200g/7.1oz) dried cherries, chopped (optional)

5 egg whites

½ cup (90g/3.2oz) semisweet chocolate chips, melted

1. Preheat the oven to 325°F. Line two baking sheets with parchment paper.

2. In a large bowl, thoroughly combine the coconut, vanilla, butter, and ⅓ cup (66g/2.3oz) of the sugar; the mixture will be light brown. If desired, stir in the pistachios and dried cherries. Set aside.

3. In a stand mixer with the whisk, whip the egg whites on medium speed until foamy and opaque.

4. Add the remaining ⅓ cup (66g/2.3oz) sugar in a slow, steady stream and continue whipping on medium speed until soft peaks are formed. Turn the mixer speed to high and whip for a few more seconds, until you have firm peaks.

5. Remove the bowl from the mixer. Using a spatula, gently fold the whipped whites into the coconut mixture. Do not overmix.

6. Use a #40 (1-ounce) cookie scoop to make 24 uniform balls. Place them on the prepared baking sheets, 2 to 3 inches apart.

7. Bake one sheet at a time. Transfer a pan to the middle rack of the oven and bake for 18 to 20 minutes, rotating the pan front to back once, until light brown.

8. Let the macaroons cool completely on the baking sheets. Use a piping bag to drizzle with the melted chocolate. Store in an airtight container.

BLACK AND WHITE COOKIES

<hr>

The iconic New York City black and white cookies aren't really cookies at all. They're made from a cake base, flipped over, and iced on the flat side with half white and half chocolate icing. Every corner deli in New York City carries a version finished with hard icing and wrapped in plastic. Make these yourself and see why they are a huge hit. Magnolia Bakery didn't have its own version until the summer of 2019, when Sony asked us to create one in honor of *Seinfeld*'s thirtieth anniversary. They were such a huge hit that they became a permanent item on our menu.

<hr>

MAKES 16 large cookies

INGREDIENTS

FOR THE COOKIES

1½ cups (202g/7.2oz) all-purpose flour

1 cup (115g/4oz) cake flour

1 teaspoon baking powder

1 teaspoon salt

1 cup/2 sticks (226g/8oz) unsalted butter, at room temperature

1 cup (200g/7.1oz) granulated sugar

2 eggs

1½ teaspoons pure vanilla extract

½ teaspoon grated lemon zest

½ cup (120g/4.2oz) whole milk

FOR THE WHITE GLAZE

2 cups (250g/8.8oz) powdered sugar, sifted

1½ tablespoons light corn syrup

¼ cup water

FOR THE CHOCOLATE GLAZE

2 cups (250g/8.8oz) powdered sugar, sifted

1½ tablespoons light corn syrup

¼ cup water

1 tablespoon unsweetened dark cocoa powder (22 to 24%)

1. Line three baking sheets with parchment paper.

2. In a medium bowl, whisk together both flours, the baking powder, and salt. Set aside.

3. In a stand mixer with the paddle, cream the butter on medium speed until light and fluffy, about 2 minutes. Add the granulated sugar and mix until light, pale, and fluffy, about 3 minutes. Scrape down the sides and bottom of the bowl.

4. On medium speed, add the eggs, one at a time, beating well after each addition. Add the vanilla and lemon zest and continue mixing for 1 minute. Scrape down the sides and bottom of the bowl and mix for another 30 seconds.

5. On low speed, add the flour mixture in three additions, alternating with the milk, beginning and ending with the dry ingredients. Scrape down the sides and bottom of the bowl and the paddle and mix for another 30 seconds. Do not overmix.

6. Using a #20 scoop or a ¼-cup measuring cup, scoop the batter onto the lined baking sheets, placing 5 on the first and second sheets, and 6 on the third. Flatten with an icing wand.

7. Preheat the oven to 325°F.

8. Bake for 10 minutes, rotate the pans front to back, and bake for another 8 minutes, or until the bottoms are slightly golden and the tops spring back to the touch. Do not overbake. The cookies should have very little color on the top.

9. Let the cookies sit on the pan for 10 to 15 minutes. Transfer to a cooling rack to cool completely before icing.

(continued)

Use an icing wand to scoop up a small amount of white glaze.

Tap the glaze down the middle of the cookie in a straight line.

Spread the glaze toward the outside of the cookie.

Clean the sides and place on a baking sheet to let the glaze set.

14a

Repeat steps 1–4 with the chocolate glaze.

14b

Let the cookies sit until the glaze is dry.

MAKE-AHEAD TIP

You can make the cookies 2 days ahead of time and wrap with plastic wrap as soon as they are cool, so they do not dry out.

10. **MAKE THE VANILLA GLAZE:** In a medium bowl, mix together the powdered sugar, corn syrup, and water. Whisk until the mixture is smooth and has the consistency of warm honey. Add more water if too thick.

11. **MAKE THE CHOCOLATE GLAZE:** In a medium bowl, mix together the powdered sugar, corn syrup, water, and cocoa. Whisk until the mixture is smooth and has the consistency of warm honey. Add more water if too thick.

12. Once the cookies are completely cool, flip them upside down so that the flat side is up.

13. Use the blade of an icing wand to scoop up a small amount of white glaze and "tap" the icing down the middle of the cookie in a straight line. Spread the icing toward the outside of the cookie and clean the sides. As you work, place each white-glazed cookie back on the baking sheet. Let set for 30 minutes, until the icing is firm.

14. Once the icing is set, repeat with the chocolate glaze. Let the cookies sit until the icing is dry, about 30 minutes. Wrap in plastic wrap to keep them fresh.

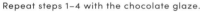

CRANBERRY WHITE CHOCOLATE CHUNK COOKIES

I graduated from culinary school in 1983, the same year that Maida Heatter's *Book of Great American Desserts* was published. This book became my bible. This recipe is inspired by her Chocolate Whoppers. I don't make them as big as she suggests, and I add white chocolate chips and dried cranberries to make them more festive.

MAKES 15 large or 30 small cookies

INGREDIENTS

1 cup (113g/4oz) unsweetened chocolate chunks

1½ cups (270g/9.6oz) semisweet chocolate chips

¾ cup/1½ sticks (170g/6oz) unsalted butter

½ cup (67g/2.4oz) all-purpose flour

½ teaspoon baking powder

1 teaspoon salt

4 eggs

1 tablespoon plus 1 teaspoon pure vanilla extract

1½ cups (300g/10.6oz) granulated sugar

4 teaspoons instant espresso powder

1½ cups (255g/9oz) white chocolate chips

1 cup (115g/4oz) coarsely chopped pecans, lightly toasted (see Tip, page 288)

1 cup (150g/5.3oz) dried cranberries

TIP
The chocolate mixture must be warm and pourable but not hot when added to the egg mixture. The batter must be scooped and baked right away. If you let the chocolate mixture cool too much before scooping, it will bake differently.

1. Preheat the oven to 325°F. Line two baking sheets with parchment paper.

2. Place the unsweetened chocolate, chocolate chips, and butter in a heatproof bowl and set over a saucepan of gently simmering water. Stir occasionally, until the chocolate and butter have melted. Remove from the heat and stir to be sure all the chocolate has melted and the mixture is smooth. (Alternatively, microwave in 30-second increments, stirring well after each.)

3. In a small bowl, whisk together the flour, baking powder, and salt. Set aside.

4. In a stand mixer with the whisk, beat the eggs, vanilla, sugar, and espresso powder on medium speed until very light in color, about 4 minutes.

5. Add the melted chocolate/butter mixture and mix on low speed until just combined, about 30 seconds. Scrape down the sides and bottom of the bowl.

6. Remove the bowl from the mixer. Using a rubber spatula, fold in the flour mixture. Gently fold in the white chocolate chips, pecans, and dried cranberries.

7. Using a #20 scoop or a ¼-cup dry measuring cup or, for small cookies, use a #40 (1-ounce) cookie scoop to scoop the batter onto the prepared baking sheets 2 inches apart.

8. Transfer two pans to the oven and bake for 24 to 26 minutes for large cookies and 15 to 16 minutes for small ones, rotating top to bottom, front to back halfway through the baking time. The cookies will have a beautiful sheen and a cracked surface.

9. Let the cookies cool completely on the pan before placing on a cooling rack. Store in an airtight container.

CRINKLE COOKIES

Similar in texture to a chewy brownie, these cookies have a deep fudgy flavor that relies on the best quality 22 to 24% unsweetened dark cocoa, such as Valrhona or Guittard. Coated in powdered sugar, the cookies spread and crack as they bake, revealing a tempting dark interior. Although I've always associated them with the holidays, they are a coveted year-round staple at Magnolia Bakery.

MAKES 36 cookies

INGREDIENTS

2 cups (270g/9.6oz) all-purpose flour

2 teaspoons baking powder

½ teaspoon salt

1 cup (120g/4.2oz) unsweetened dark cocoa powder (22 to 24%), sifted

2 cups (400g/14.2oz) granulated sugar

½ cup (104g/3.6oz) vegetable oil

4 eggs

2 teaspoons pure vanilla extract

2 cups (250g/8.8oz) powdered sugar, sifted

1. In a medium bowl, whisk together the flour, baking powder, and salt.

2. In another medium bowl, whisk together the cocoa, granulated sugar, and oil. Whisk in the eggs, one at a time, then add the vanilla. With a rubber spatula, stir the flour mixture into the cocoa mixture. Cover the bowl with plastic wrap and refrigerate for at least 30 minutes and up to 1 hour.

3. Preheat the oven to 325°F. Line three baking sheets with parchment paper.

4. Place the sifted powdered sugar in a large bowl.

5. Using a #40 (1-ounce) cookie scoop, make uniform balls, then roll them in your palms until perfectly round. Drop the dough balls, a few at a time, in the powdered sugar, tossing until completely coated, then roll them a second time in the sugar.

6. Evenly space 12 cookies about 2 inches apart on the lined baking sheets. Bake one sheet at a time on the center rack for 10 to 12 minutes. The cookies should crack on top and just start to set. Do not overbake.

7. Let the cookies sit on the baking sheet for 5 to 10 minutes, then transfer them to a cooling rack to cool completely.

8. Store in an airtight container with parchment paper between the layers.

GRANDMA'S THUMBPRINTS
WITH VARIATIONS

This recipe has been handed down in my family for generations. When I was a little girl, my grandmother would host a December cookie-making day with my great-grandmother, mother, aunt, and me. We would spend the day baking batches of cookies and making holiday candy. At the end of the day, everyone went home with cookie canisters overflowing with treats. This dough is so versatile it can be turned into plain thumbprints, or filled with raspberry jam or buttercream, or even round snowballs rolled in powdered sugar.

MAKES 32 cookies

INGREDIENTS

2 cups (230g/8.1oz) coarsely chopped pecans

2 cups (270g/9.5oz) all-purpose flour

¾ teaspoon salt

1 cup/2 sticks (226g/8oz) unsalted butter, at room temperature

⅓ cup (66g/2.3oz) granulated sugar

1½ teaspoons pure vanilla extract

Jam, buttercream, or powdered sugar for variations (see page 132 for recipes)

1. Line three baking sheets with parchment paper. Set aside.

2. In a food processor, finely grind 1 cup (115g/4.1oz) of the pecans with ¼ cup (34g/1.2oz) of the flour until it is the texture of coarse cornmeal, 10 to 15 seconds. Transfer to a medium bowl. Coarsely grind the remaining pecans in the food processor, about 5 seconds, then transfer to the bowl with the pecan-flour mixture. Stir in the remaining 1¾ cups (236g/8.3oz) flour and the salt.

3. In a stand mixer with the paddle, cream the butter and granulated sugar on medium speed until light and fluffy, about 4 minutes. Scrape down the sides and bottom of the bowl. Beat in the vanilla. Reduce the mixer speed to low and slowly add in the pecan-flour mixture until combined, about 30 seconds. Scrape the bowl and paddle and continue to beat on low speed until the dough just comes together, about 10 seconds.

4. Using a #40 (1-ounce) cookie scoop, make 32 balls, rolling them in between your palms until perfectly round. Place no more than 12 balls on each prepared baking sheet, spaced about 1 inch apart. If making thumbprint cookies, use your thumb or the back of a measuring teaspoon to create an indent in the center of each cookie. Place the baking sheets in the refrigerator for 30 minutes to 1 hour.

5. When ready to bake the cookies, position the oven racks in the upper-middle and lower-middle positions and preheat the oven to 325°F.

6. Transfer two pans to the oven and bake for 14 to 16 minutes, rotating top to bottom, front to back halfway through the baking time, until the bottoms are lightly golden brown.

7. Let the cookies sit on the baking sheets for 5 to 10 minutes, unless filling with jam as described on page 132, then transfer to a cooling rack to cool completely. Store in an airtight container.

(continued)

JAMMY THUMBPRINTS: Bake the thumbprints as directed. As soon as the cookies come out of the oven, spoon about ½ teaspoon raspberry jam into the indents. (You will need a total of 1 cup/340g/12oz jam.) Let sit on the baking sheets for 15 minutes before transferring to a cooling rack to cool completely.

BUTTERCREAM-FILLED THUMBPRINTS: Bake and cool the cookies as directed. Make 2 cups vanilla buttercream, divide it into small batches, then tint each as desired (see page 265). Once the cookies are completely cool, fill the indents with the buttercream and decorate.

SNOWBALLS: Make and form the dough into round balls (do not indent them). Bake as directed. Meanwhile, place 1½ cups (187g/6oz) powdered sugar, sifted, in a bowl. When the cookies come out of the oven and have cooled on the pan for about 15 minutes, they should be cool enough to roll in the sugar. (They should not be hot when they are rolled in the sugar or the sugar will melt.) Gently place the balls one at a time into the bowl of powdered sugar, rolling them around until completely covered.

Place on a cooling rack to cool completely. Store in an airtight container with wax paper between the layers. Before serving, dust with more powdered sugar.

HOLIDAY SPRITZ COOKIES

These adorable cookies are traditional holiday treats in Scandinavia. They are made with a simple butter dough that is extruded through a cookie press—an inexpensive baking tool that comes with die plates in different shapes. (Kids will enjoy helping!) You will definitely want to double the recipe so you can gift these to everyone you know, perhaps stacked in glass jars and tied with ribbon. I like to use three or four different gel food colors, and also colored sanding sugar, to create a festive plate.

MAKES 75 to 85 cookies
(depending on cookie-press die used)

INGREDIENTS

2¼ cups (304g/10.7oz) all-purpose flour

½ teaspoon ground cardamom

¼ teaspoon salt

1 cup/2 sticks (226g/8oz) unsalted butter, at room temperature

½ cup (100g/3.5oz) granulated sugar

1 egg

1 teaspoon pure vanilla extract

Gel food coloring of choice

3 tablespoons white sanding sugar

1. Preheat the oven to 350°F. Assemble your cookie press.

2. In a medium bowl, whisk together the flour, cardamom, and salt. Set aside.

3. In a stand mixer with the paddle, cream the butter and granulated sugar on medium speed until light and fluffy, about 3 minutes. Add the egg and vanilla and mix thoroughly. Scrape down the sides and bottom of the bowl.

4. On low speed, add the flour mixture and mix until incorporated and no streaks of flour remain, about 10 seconds.

5. Portion out into separate bowls the amount of dough you want to color. Add the desired food coloring and mix until combined. If you want to make several colors divide the dough into 3 to 4 equal parts. I used plain, pink, and blue, as shown on page 135.

Add tiny drops of gel food coloring for pastel colors.

(continued)

Form the dough into cylinder-shaped pieces.

Make sure the disk lies flat inside the barrel of the cookie press.

Use a clean, grease-free, unlined baking sheet.

Quickly pull the press straight up and away from the cookie.

6. Gently form portions of the dough into cylinder-shaped pieces to fit into the cookie press.

7. Don't overload the press with dough; leave at least an inch of space near the end of cylinder. If you don't, it'll be difficult to press out the cookies. It's also important that the disk you place inside the barrel lies flat.

8. Set out a clean, grease-free, and unlined baking sheet. It's very important that your baking sheet be clean and grease-free or the cookies won't stick. Place the end of the cookie press firmly onto the pan and pull the trigger 1 or 2 times.

9. Once you feel the dough sticking to the sheet, quickly pull the press straight up and away from the cookie. It may take you a few tries to get the hang of it. It's fine; you can reuse the dough. Space cookies 2 inches apart. You can get 12 to 18 cookies per pan, depending on the size.

10. Sprinkle generously with the white sanding sugar to finish.

11. Bake one sheet at a time. Transfer to the oven and bake for about 10 minutes, or until barely golden on the bottom.

12. Let the cookies sit on the pan for 5 minutes, then gently transfer to a cooling rack to cool completely. Be sure to thoroughly clean the baking sheet before using again. Store in airtight containers.

CUT-OUT SUGAR COOKIES

When my kids were little, I hosted cookie-decorating parties at our house to carry on the family tradition started by my great-grandmother. I would begin a week ahead of time: making the dough one night, cutting out the cookies the next, and making the buttercream on the third night. Moms and kids alike loved making their own custom creations from the huge selection of cut-out cookies I would provide. Everyone would get a tray to place their cookies on and then choose from a wide variety of buttercream colors, sprinkles, and candies. When you do this, your house *will* be a mess—with sprinkles and crumbs all over the floor—but the wonderful memories and sweet companionship are well worth it.

MAKES forty 2½-inch round cookies

INGREDIENTS

3 cups (405g/14.3oz) all-purpose flour

½ teaspoon baking soda

¾ teaspoon salt

1 cup/2 sticks (226g/8oz) unsalted
    butter, at room temperature

1 cup (200g/7.1oz) granulated sugar

2 eggs

2 teaspoons pure vanilla extract

Magnolia Bakery Vanilla Buttercream
    (page 265), for decorating

Sprinkles, for decorating

1. In a medium bowl, whisk together the flour, baking soda, and salt. Set aside.

2. In a stand mixer with the paddle, cream the butter on medium speed for 1 minute.

3. On low speed, gradually add the sugar and beat until smooth and creamy, 2 to 3 minutes. Add the eggs, one at a time, mixing thoroughly after each addition. Scrape down the sides and bottom of the bowl. Add the vanilla and continue to mix on low speed for another minute.

4. Add the flour mixture and increase the speed to medium. Beat until smooth. If the dough is sticky, add an additional tablespoon or two of flour, 1 tablespoon at a time.

5. Remove the dough from the mixer bowl. Form into three equal-size balls (they should each weigh about 10 ounces). Wrap the balls in plastic wrap, pressing into a flat disc, and refrigerate for at least 1 hour and up to 2 days.

6. When ready to bake, preheat the oven to 325°F. Line two baking sheets with parchment paper.

7. Remove one ball from the refrigerator and let it sit for about 5 minutes, until pliable. Knead 4 or 5 times to soften. (Keep the remaining dough refrigerated until you're ready to work with it.) Roll the dough out on a lightly floured surface to a ¼-inch thickness. Work quickly so the dough doesn't get too soft.

8. Using a 2½-inch round cookie cutter, carefully cut out cookies. You can reroll the scraps to cut out more cookies. Use a metal spatula to transfer them from your work surface to one of the lined baking sheets, spacing the cookies 1 inch apart.

9. Bake one sheet at a time. (While the first sheet is baking you can set up the second sheet.) Transfer to the oven and bake for 10 to 12 minutes, or until the cookies puff up slightly and just begin to lightly brown on the bottom. Repeat with the remaining pan.

10. Let the cookies sit on the pan for 5 to 10 minutes, then transfer them to a cooling rack to cool completely.

11. Decorate with vanilla buttercream in assorted colors, as well as sprinkles.

12. Stored in an airtight container, they will keep for up to 5 days. Un-iced cookies freeze beautifully for up to 2 months.

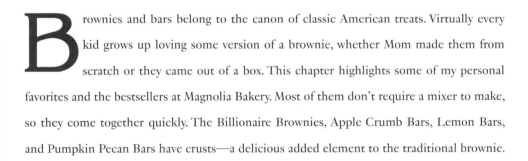

CHAPTER FOUR

BROWNIES & BARS

Brownies and bars belong to the canon of classic American treats. Virtually every kid grows up loving some version of a brownie, whether Mom made them from scratch or they came out of a box. This chapter highlights some of my personal favorites and the bestsellers at Magnolia Bakery. Most of them don't require a mixer to make, so they come together quickly. The Billionaire Brownies, Apple Crumb Bars, Lemon Bars, and Pumpkin Pecan Bars have crusts—a delicious added element to the traditional brownie.

PERFECT BARS EVERY TIME

Lining a baking pan with parchment paper or foil and leaving an overhang eliminates the possibility that your bars will stick to the bottom of the pan. An overhang makes removing them from the pan and cutting attractive bars of equal portions easy every time.

LINING THE PAN

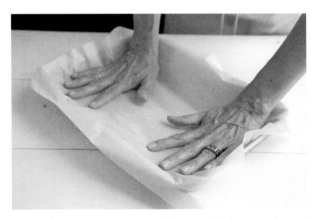

Butter the pan, or use nonstick spray, being sure to get into the corners. Line the pan evenly with a piece of foil or parchment paper a couple of inches larger than the pan on all sides to create an overhang.

Be sure to press the paper down into the bottom of the pan while pushing the paper into the corners.

REMOVING BARS FROM A PAN

Once the bars have cooled completely, firmly grasp the ends of the liner to pull them out of the pan. Set them on a cutting board and cut them into equal portions.

CUTTING THE PERFECT BARS

When using a 9 × 13-inch pan, you can cut 12, 16, or 24 bars. It all depends on what size you prefer. With an 8 x 8-inch pan, cut into equal size pieces. The richer the bar, the smaller each piece should be. With a chef's knife, pressing down firmly and cleanly, score the bars in a 3 × 4 grid to get 12 pieces, a 4 × 4 grid for 16, or a 4 × 6 grid for 24 pieces. Then, use a small square metal spatula to separate each bar. If you are cutting bars with nuts or a firm crust, such as the Pumpkin Pecan Bars (page 163), use a serrated knife with a slow sawing motion and cut through the nuts first before cutting through the entire bar.

DOUBLE-FUDGE BROWNIES

Over a lifetime of baking brownies, I finally figured out that there is no one ideal. Taste is subjective: Some people like them soft and chewy, some adore the crispy edges, some prefer the cake-like kind with walnuts, and then there is me. I like my brownies soft and chewy in the center, a little crispy on the top, dense and fudgy throughout—never, ever cake-like!—and always without nuts.

The intensity of the chocolate flavor plays a huge part. I prefer it rich and very dark, so I use both an unsweetened dark cocoa powder (22 to 24%) *and* semisweet chocolate chips. As with all cakes and brownies, the better the cocoa, the richer the flavor and texture will be.

MAKES one 9 × 13-inch pan; 12, 16, or 24 brownies

INGREDIENTS

1 cup (135g/4.8oz) all-purpose flour

½ cup (60g/2.15oz) unsweetened dark cocoa powder (22 to 24%), sifted

½ teaspoon baking powder

½ teaspoon salt

2 cups (400g/14.2oz) granulated sugar

1 cup/2 sticks (226g/8oz) unsalted butter, melted and cooled to room temperature

2 teaspoons pure vanilla extract

4 eggs

1 cup (180g/6.3oz) semisweet chocolate chips

1. Position an oven rack in the center of the oven and preheat the oven to 325°F. Grease a 9 × 13-inch pan with nonstick spray or butter, then line it with parchment paper or foil, leaving overhang on the sides (see Lining the Pan, page 141).

2. In a small bowl, whisk together the flour, cocoa, baking powder, and salt.

3. In a large bowl, whisk together the sugar, melted butter, and vanilla until creamy. Whisk the eggs into the butter and sugar mixture, one at a time, until creamy. Add the flour mixture and whisk together until just combined. Using a large rubber spatula, fold the chocolate chips into the batter.

4. Pour the batter into the prepared pan. Using an offset spatula, spread the batter evenly, getting into the corners.

5. Bake for 25 to 28 minutes, or until a cake tester inserted in the center comes out slightly wet, with moist crumbs attached.

6. Let the brownies cool completely in the pan on a cooling rack. Remove them from the pan by lifting the sides of parchment or foil. Cut them to your desired size (see page 141).

7. Store in an airtight container for up to 3 days. These brownies also freeze beautifully for up to 1 month (if you can keep them that long)!

BILLIONAIRE BROWNIES

A layer of buttery shortbread smothered in decadent caramel and topped with luxurious ganache—these are definitely rich enough for a billionaire! I decided to take these one step further and combine them with my brownie recipe for the ultimate treat. A brown sugar shortbread crust is covered with homemade caramel sauce and topped with brownie batter before baking. Once cooled, it gets drizzled with even more caramel. If you really want to live dangerously, add a scoop of ice cream and a little more caramel!

MAKES one 9 × 13-inch pan;
12, 16, or 24 bars

INGREDIENTS

FOR THE BROWN SUGAR SHORTBREAD BASE
Brown Sugar Shortbread Crust
(page 282)

1 cup (300g/10.6oz) Caramel Sauce
(page 287), or store-bought

FOR THE BROWNIE LAYER
Double-Fudge Brownies (page 143)

1. Bake and cool the shortbread crust as directed.

2. Leave the oven on at 325°F. Let the shortbread cool. The crust can be made ahead and wrapped in plastic wrap for up to 3 days.

3. Once the shortbread has cooled, drizzle the caramel sauce over it. Using an offset spatula, spread the caramel evenly on top of the shortbread.

4. Make the Double-Fudge Brownie recipe.

5. Using a #20 scoop or a ¼ cup measuring cup, drop dollops of the brownie batter evenly over the caramel sauce. Then, with an offset spatula, spread the batter evenly on top of the shortbread layer.

6. Return the pan to the oven and bake the brownies for 26 to 30 minutes, or until a cake tester inserted into the center comes out with thick, moist crumbs.

7. Let the brownies cool completely in the pan. Remove them from the pan by lifting the sides of the parchment or foil. These bars are very rich; you may want to cut into small pieces!

BROWN BUTTER CHOCOLATE CHUNK BLONDIES

Blondies remind me of the chocolate-chip-cookie pie my mother made when I was a kid. It seemed so innovative at the time. My favorite part was the soft, chewy center reminiscent of my favorite chocolate chip cookies. Over time, I worked out my preferred ratio of white sugar to brown sugar—which in the end became no white sugar at all—to ensure the chewiest blondie. Next was determining what type of chocolate to use. This version uses one that is not too dark but still offers up a distinct flavor. As always, the best quality ingredients ensure the most delicious results.

MAKES one 9 × 13-inch pan
(cut into 12, 16, or 24 pieces)

or an 8 × 8 inch pan
(cut into 16 pieces for rich, thick, small bites)

INGREDIENTS

1 cup/2 sticks (226g/8oz) unsalted butter, browned and cooled to room temperature

2 cups (270g/9.6oz) all-purpose flour

1¼ teaspoons baking powder

½ teaspoon salt

1¾ cups (350g/12.4oz) light brown sugar

1 teaspoon pure vanilla extract

2 eggs

1 cup (180g/6.3oz) semisweet chocolate chunks or chips

1. Position an oven rack in the center of the oven and preheat the oven to 325°F. Grease a 9 × 13-inch or an 8 × 8-inch pan with nonstick spray or butter, then line it with parchment paper or foil, leaving overhang on the sides (see Lining the Pan, page 141).

2. Before starting to make your blondies, make sure your browned butter has cooled to room temperature.

3. In a medium bowl, whisk together the flour, baking powder, and salt. Set aside.

4. In a large bowl, combine the brown sugar, melted browned butter, and vanilla. Whisk together until creamy. Add the eggs and mix thoroughly until creamy again. Add the flour mixture and whisk together until combined. Using a rubber spatula, fold in the chocolate chunks or chips.

5. Pour the batter into the prepared pan. Using an offset spatula, spread the batter evenly, getting into the corners.

6. Bake until a cake tester inserted into the center comes out clean: 25 to 28 minutes for the 9 × 13-inch pan; 40 to 45 minutes for the 8 × 8-inch pan. Rotate the pan front to back at least once during baking.

7. Let the blondies cool completely in the pan on a cooling rack. Remove them from the pan by lifting the sides of parchment or foil. Cut them to your desired size (see page 141).

8. Store covered for up to 3 days. You can also freeze the bars, individually wrapped, for up to 1 month.

MARBLE CREAM CHEESE BROWNIES

This gloriously marbled combination of brownie and cheesecake is an inspired one. Insanely rich, moist, and dense, these bars are nothing short of heavenly. I like to serve them cold, straight from the refrigerator, but they sell too quickly for this at Magnolia Bakery. At home, if my family hasn't eaten them in one sitting, I hide them in the back of the fridge and sneak little slivers every day.

MAKES one 9 × 13-inch pan; 12, 16, or 24 bars

INGREDIENTS

FOR THE BROWNIE LAYER

1¼ cups (225g/8oz) semisweet chocolate chips

¾ cup/1½ sticks (170g/6oz) unsalted butter, cut into ½-inch pieces

½ cup (68g/2.4oz) all-purpose flour

2 tablespoons (22g/3oz) unsweetened dark cocoa powder (22 to 24%), sifted

4 eggs

1¾ cups (350g/12.4oz) granulated sugar

4 teaspoons pure vanilla extract

½ teaspoon salt

FOR THE CREAM CHEESE LAYER

¾ cup (169g/5.9oz) full-fat cream cheese (preferably Philadelphia brand), at room temperature

¼ cup (50g/1.8oz) granulated sugar

¼ teaspoon salt

½ teaspoon pure vanilla extract

1 egg

1 teaspoon fresh lemon juice

2 tablespoons (30g/1oz) sour cream

1. **MAKE THE BROWNIE LAYER:** Position an oven rack in the center of the oven and preheat the oven to 350°F. Grease a 9 × 13-inch pan with nonstick spray, then line it with parchment paper or foil, leaving overhang on the sides (see Lining the Pan, page 141).

2. Place the chocolate and butter in a heatproof bowl and set over a saucepan of gently simmering water (do not let the bowl touch the water). Stir occasionally until the chocolate and butter are melted together but not hot. (Alternatively, microwave the butter and chocolate in 30-second increments, stirring well after each, until smooth but not hot.) Set aside. Cool to room temperature.

3. In a small bowl, whisk together the flour and cocoa.

4. In a stand mixer with the whisk, whisk the eggs and sugar together on medium speed until very thick, about 4 minutes. Add the chocolate-butter mixture to the bowl along with the vanilla and salt. Mix on medium speed until thoroughly combined. Scrape down the sides and bottom of the bowl. Remove the bowl from the mixer and fold in the flour-cocoa mixture. Set aside while you make the cream cheese layer.

5. **MAKE THE CREAM CHEESE LAYER:** In a medium bowl, with a hand-held mixer, beat the cream cheese, sugar, salt, and vanilla on medium speed until light and fluffy, about 3 minutes. Scrape down the sides and bottom of the bowl. Add the egg, mixing just until combined. Add the lemon juice and sour cream. Mix on medium speed for about 1 minute, until thoroughly mixed. Thoroughly scrape down the bowl again.

6. Place the cream cheese batter in a piping bag and cut a hole in the tip. Use half the mixture to evenly pipe strips over the bottom of the pan.

7. Pour in the brownie batter and use an offset spatula to evenly spread over the cream cheese layer.

8. Evenly pipe the remaining cream cheese mixture in strips over the brownie layer.

Piping the cream cheese mixture in strips over the brownie layer.

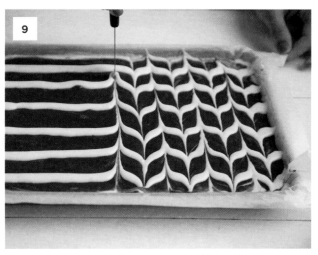

Using a small paring knife to create a marbling effect.

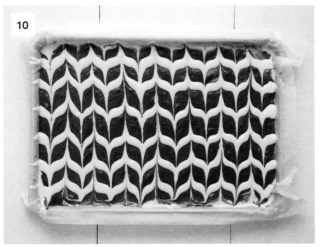

The full marbled effect.

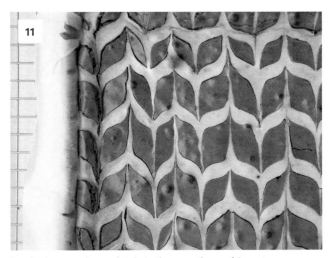

Let the bars cool completely in the pan, then refrigerate.

9. With a small paring knife, evenly pass from front to back through all the layers, creating a marbling effect.

10. Bake for 30 to 35 minutes, or until a cake tester inserted into the center comes out with thick, moist crumbs.

11. Let the bars cool completely in the pan on a cooling rack, then refrigerate until firm, 2 to 3 hours.

12. Remove the brownies by lifting the sides of the parchment or foil. Cut them to your desired size (see page 141). If not serving immediately, keep refrigerated. These are great served cold or at room temperature.

MAGIC COOKIE BARS—TWO WAYS!

Magic Cookie Bars are the most-requested bar at Magnolia Bakery. You may know this as a Hello Dolly Bar or 7-Layer Bar, but by any other name it's still as sweet. Start with the graham cracker crust and add as many of these layers as you like: chocolate chips, white chocolate chips, butterscotch chips, nuts, and coconut. The final touch is to smother it all with sweetened condensed milk. At Magnolia Bakery, we leave out the butterscotch and white chocolate chips in order to showcase the dark chocolate.

These bars are sweet, crunchy, rich, chocolatey, and totally addictive. I played around with the original recipe and created a new version with dried cherries, white chocolate chunks, and pistachios that makes a gorgeous addition to a holiday dessert tray.

MAKES 12 bars

INGREDIENTS

FOR THE CRUST

¾ cup (170g/6oz) unsalted butter, melted

2¼ cups (225g/8oz) graham cracker crumbs

FOR THE TOPPING

1 cup (120g/4.2oz) walnuts, toasted (see Tip, page 288) and chopped

1 cup (180g/6.3oz) semisweet chocolate chips

3 cups (300g/10.6oz) lightly packed sweetened shredded coconut

2¼ cups (641g/20.3oz) sweetened condensed milk

1. **MAKE THE CRUST:** Position an oven rack in the center of the oven and preheat the oven to 325°F. Grease a 9 × 13-inch pan with nonstick spray or butter, then line it with parchment paper or foil, leaving overhang on the sides (see Lining the Pan, page 141).

2. In a small bowl, combine the melted butter and graham cracker crumbs, mixing until thoroughly combined. Spread the crumbs into the prepared pan and press firmly with the bottom of a 1-cup measuring cup or use an offset spatula to evenly distribute.

3. Bake for 10 minutes to set, remove from the oven, and cool completely. The crust can be made ahead and wrapped in plastic wrap for up to 3 days.

4. **MAKE THE TOPPING:** Evenly layer the nuts and then the chocolate chips over the crust. Cover with coconut, making sure to fully cover the chips and nuts.

5. Carefully and evenly pour the sweetened condensed milk over the top of the coconut. An easy way to do this is to pour the sweetened condensed milk into a piping bag with no tip. Cut a ½-inch hole in the end and slowly and evenly drizzle it over the coconut.

6. Make sure to get into the corners and edges of the pan, or the bars will dry out in the oven. Avoid spilling the condensed milk over the edges so it doesn't burn in the oven.

7. Let the condensed milk set and seep into the topping for 30 minutes before placing into the oven. Meanwhile, preheat the oven again to 325°F.

8. Transfer the pan to the oven and bake for 25 to 28 minutes, rotating the pan front to back halfway through, until the coconut on the top is evenly golden brown.

(continued)

Pressing the graham cracker crust firmly into the prepared pan.

Piping the condensed milk over the coconut.

9. Let the bars cool completely in the pan on a cooling rack. Remove them from the pan by lifting the sides of the parchment or foil. Score the bars in a 3 × 4 grid (for 12 bars). Using a serrated knife, slice through the bars with a sawing motion until completely cut through.

10. If not devouring the bars immediately, individually wrap them tightly in foil and store them for up to 1 week in the refrigerator. They are equally good when cut into bite-sized pieces and frozen. Enjoy them straight from the freezer!

VARIATION

Follow the directions above and layer the ingredients on the cooled crust in this order:

1 cup (150g/5.3oz) pistachios, roughly chopped

½ cup (75g/2.65oz) dried cherries, roughly chopped

1 cup (150g/5.3oz) white chocolate chunks or chips

3 cups (300g/10.6oz) shredded, sweetened coconut, lightly packed

2¼ cups (641g/20.3oz) sweetened condensed milk

LINZER BARS

Adapted from a traditional Austrian holiday torte, Linzer cookies always combine a nutty crust with fruit preserves. For Magnolia Bakery, I wanted to make something homier, without any fussy rolling or cutting of dough. In this recipe, you simply press the dough into a pan and scatter more of it on top of the jam to create a crumb crust. Use the best raspberry jam you can find—I recommend the Bonne Maman brand.

MAKES one 9 × 13-inch pan; 12, 16, or 24 bars

INGREDIENTS

2½ cups (337g/12oz) all-purpose flour

2 cups (240g/8.4oz) blanched almonds, ground

1¼ teaspoons baking powder

¾ teaspoon salt

1½ teaspoons ground cinnamon

1 cup/2 sticks (226g/8oz) unsalted butter, at room temperature

1⅓ cups (167g/5.3oz) powdered sugar, sifted

⅓ cup (66g/2.3oz) granulated sugar

1 egg

1 egg yolk

1¼ teaspoons pure vanilla extract

½ teaspoon almond extract

1 tablespoon grated lemon zest

1¼ cups (411g/14.5oz) raspberry jam

Powdered sugar, for dusting

1. Position an oven rack in the center of the oven and preheat the oven to 350°F. Grease a 9 × 13-inch pan with nonstick spray or butter, then line it with parchment paper or foil, leaving overhang on the sides (see Lining the Pan, page 141).

2. In a small bowl, whisk together the flour, ground almonds, baking powder, salt, and cinnamon. Set aside.

3. In a stand mixer with the paddle, cream the butter on medium speed. Add both sugars and beat until light and fluffy, about 5 minutes. Occasionally scrape down the sides and bottom of the bowl.

4. Add the whole egg, egg yolk, vanilla, almond extract, and lemon zest and mix well. Add the ground almond/flour mixture and combine until just blended. Scrape down the bottom and sides of the bowl.

5. Divide the dough in half, reserving half of the dough for the crumb topping.

6. Evenly press half of the dough into the bottom of the prepared pan.

7. Bake for 15 minutes, or until lightly golden brown. Remove the crust from the oven. Using an offset spatula, spread the jam over the crust.

8. Evenly scatter the reserved dough in medium to large clumps all over the jam.

9. Return to the oven and bake for 23 to 25 minutes, or until the crumbs are golden.

(continued)

Spreading the jam over the crust.

Scattering clumps of the reserved dough over the jam.

10. Let the bars cool completely in the pan on a cooling rack.

11. Remove them from the pan by lifting the sides of the parchment or foil. Place on a cutting board and cut into 12, 16, or 24 bars. Dust with powdered sugar (see Note).

> **NOTE**
>
> If you plan to serve these bars at a later time, do not dust with powdered sugar. They can be sealed in a plastic container or tin for up to 3 days or wrapped well and frozen for up to 1 month. Sprinkle with powdered sugar just before serving.

LEMON BARS WITH A SHORTBREAD COOKIE CRUST

I discovered lemon bars when I moved to the East Coast. What hooked me was the flaky shortbread crust, which reminded me of the beloved Salerno butter cookies of my childhood. For this recipe, I found the perfect ratio of buttery crust to bright lemon curd. At Magnolia Bakery, we make these bars in small batches for maximum freshness, but they're never in stock for long.

MAKES one 9 × 13-inch pan
cut into 12 bars

INGREDIENTS

FOR THE CRUST
Shortbread Cookie Crust
(page 282)

FOR THE FILLING
2 cups (400g/14.2oz) granulated
sugar

2 teaspoons grated lemon zest

4 eggs

½ cup (112g/3.9oz) fresh lemon juice,
strained

¼ cup (34g/1.2oz) all-purpose flour

1 teaspoon baking powder

FOR SERVING
½ cup (62g/2oz) powdered sugar,
sifted

1 pint raspberries (optional)

1. Bake the shortbread cookie crust as directed.

2. Meanwhile, prepare the filling: In a medium bowl, combine the granulated sugar and lemon zest and rub the sugar and zest together with your hands until the zest is fully coated and aromatic. Add the eggs and whisk until well combined. Add the lemon juice and whisk again. Finally, add the flour and baking powder and continue whisking for another minute until light and creamy.

3. Pour the mixture on top of the crust while the crust is still warm from the oven. Return to the oven and bake for 22 to 25 minutes, rotating the pan front to back halfway through, until the filling is set and jiggles just ever so slightly when the pan is moved. If you are not sure if the bars are done, poke a small hole in the center of the pan to check the filling. It should be set and not move.

4. Let the bars cool in the pan on a cooling rack for at least 1 hour. Refrigerate for 2 hours before cutting.

5. **TO SERVE:** Gently lift the lemon bars out of the pan using the long edges of the parchment or foil and place on a cutting board. Run a large, sharp knife under hot water for a moment, then completely dry the knife. This will help keep the bars from sticking to the knife.

6. Carefully score the bars in a 3 × 4 grid (for 12 bars) and then cut through the bars in one clean cut for each score. You may need to heat and clean the knife between cuts if the filling sticks. Once you have completely cut the bars, dust generously with powdered sugar. Using a small spatula, remove the bars from the parchment and place on a serving tray.

7. If serving as a plated dessert, they are so pretty with a few raspberries added on top of the lemon curd. Use as few or as many as you like.

8. If not serving right away, keep in the refrigerator. These are best if served the same day.

CHOCOLATE PEANUT BUTTER NO-BAKE BARS

I absolutely adore peanut butter—and there's no better partner for it than chocolate. My husband is from Ohio, where the state confection is called a buckeye, named for the state tree. It's a peanut butter fudge ball partially dipped in chocolate, with a circle of peanut butter peeking out on top. Whenever I made these, they would be so popular with friends and family that I decided to create a bar version for Magnolia Bakery. This recipe is so easy, as it requires no baking and has only six ingredients, including graham cracker crumbs for added texture.

MAKES one 9 × 13-inch pan; 12, 16, or 24 bars

INGREDIENTS

FOR THE BARS

¾ cup/1½ sticks (170g/6oz) unsalted butter, at room temperature

1¼ cups (330g/11.6oz) Skippy creamy peanut butter

1 teaspoon pure vanilla extract

1 cup (125g/4.4oz) powdered sugar, sifted

3 cups (330g/11.6oz) graham cracker crumbs

FOR THE TOPPING

¾ cup (200g/7oz) Skippy creamy peanut butter

2 cups (360g/12.7oz) semisweet chocolate chips

1. **MAKE THE BARS:** Butter a 9 × 13-inch baking pan, then line it with parchment paper or foil, leaving overhang on the sides (see Lining the Pan, page 141).

2. In a stand mixer with the paddle, cream the butter for about 1 minute. Add the peanut butter and vanilla. Continue beating on medium speed until creamy. Scrape down the bottom and sides of the bowl. Add the powdered sugar and continue beating until creamy. Scrape down the sides and bottom of the bowl again. Add the graham cracker crumbs and mix until thoroughly combined. Scrape down the paddle, bottom, and sides of the bowl once more.

3. Spread the mixture evenly into the prepared pan, being sure to get into the corners. Use an offset spatula to smooth out the surface. Place in the refrigerator while you prepare the chocolate topping.

4. **MAKE THE TOPPING:** Place the peanut butter and chocolate chips in a small heatproof bowl and set over a saucepan of gently simmering water. Stir constantly until smooth. (Alternatively, microwave the chocolate and peanut butter in 30-second increments, stirring well after each.) Pour the melted chocolate/peanut butter mixture over the crust. Using an offset spatula, evenly spread the chocolate over the bars.

5. Refrigerate for at least 1 hour, or until the chocolate is firm. Remove the bars from the pan by lifting the sides of the parchment or foil. Cut into 12, 16, or 24 bars.

6. Cover with plastic wrap and store in the refrigerator. The bars can be served chilled or at room temperature. Keep refrigerated until serving.

APPLE CRUMB BARS

A cross between an apple pie and a New York–style apple crumb cake, this bar has big, crunchy crumbs and tender, toothsome apples. I like to use Golden Delicious apples because they have a beautifully sweet-tart flavor and are crisp enough to hold their shape. This is actually an assembly of three different recipes, each of which you can make ahead of time. For a smaller crowd, you can also easily cut all the recipes in half and bake in an 8 × 8-inch pan. Use a pretty dish to serve these bars tableside, either straight from the refrigerator or warm with fresh whipped cream and/or vanilla ice cream.

MAKES one 9 × 13-inch pan;
12 to 16 bars

INGREDIENTS
Brown Sugar Shortbread Crust
(page 282)

Apple Filling (page 285), at room
temperature

Cinnamon Crumb Topping (page 284)

1. Bake the shortbread crust, apple filling, and crumb topping as directed.

2. Preheat or adjust the oven to 350°F.

3. Evenly spread the apple filling onto the cooled crust. Squeeze the crumb topping in your fist to make large chunks and drop them on top of the filling.

4. Transfer to the oven and bake for 30 to 35 minutes, or until the crumb topping is golden brown and the apple filling is warm.

5. Let cool in the pan on a cooling rack for 2 hours, or until completely set.

6. Remove the bars from the pan by lifting the foil or parchment sides and carefully place on a cutting board. Cut into a 3 × 4 grid (for 12 bars) or a 4 × 4 grid (for 16 bars). Use a serrated knife and cut the bars using a sawing motion. You want to keep those crumbs intact.

7. You can store these in the refrigerator for up to 2 days and serve chilled. To serve warm, reheat at 375°F for 10 to 15 minutes, until the crumbs are crispy.

PUMPKIN PECAN BARS

The perfect marriage of pumpkin pie and pecan pie, these sweet, nutty bars make a welcome addition to any holiday dessert table. For a special presentation, serve them warm with a scoop of vanilla ice cream and a dollop of whipped cream.

MAKES one 9 × 13-inch pan; 24 bars

INGREDIENTS

Brown Sugar Shortbread Crust
    (page 282)

FOR THE FILLING

6 eggs

¾ cup (150g/5.3oz) granulated sugar

¾ cup (150g/5.3oz) light brown sugar

1 (15-ounce) can unsweetened
    pumpkin puree (preferably Libby's)

1 cup (300g/10.6oz) dark maple syrup

½ cup (140g/4.9) light corn syrup

1 teaspoon ground cinnamon

½ teaspoon salt

¼ teaspoon ground cloves

¼ teaspoon grated nutmeg

3 cups (300g/10.6oz) pecan halves

1. Bake the shortbread crust as directed.

2. **MAKE THE FILLING:** In a large bowl, whisk together the eggs and both sugars until combined. Mix in the pumpkin puree, maple syrup, corn syrup, cinnamon, salt, cloves, and nutmeg until combined. Stir in the pecans. Note: Do not add the pecans until just before adding the filling to the pan or they will settle.

3. Pour the filling over the hot crust, return the pan to the oven, and bake for 34 to 36 minutes, or until the filling is completely set.

4. Let cool completely in the pan on a cooling rack. Carefully pick up the ends of the parchment paper or foil and lift the bars out of the pan. With a serrated knife, cut into a 4 × 6 grid (for 24 bars), slowly cutting and using a gentle sawing motion until you completely cut through the pecans, then press down firmly to cut all the way through to the crust.

CHAPTER FIVE

PIES & CRISPS

My mother made the most beautiful pies using tools that fascinated me, including a glass rolling pin filled with ice cubes. She always let me bake the leftover scraps of pie dough topped with a little cinnamon sugar. It's no mystery where my obsession with pie began.

I moved to New York in the summer of 1987 to be the private chef for a famous designer and his newlywed wife while they summered in East Hampton. In addition to preparing meals for the couple and their guests, my role included making sure there were always freshly baked pies, cookies, and bread on the counter. With the bounty of seasonal fruits available in the Hamptons, I was in heaven. I baked at least five pies a week: strawberry, blueberry, peach, and every combination that came to mind. That summer, I perfected my pie skills. I include some helpful tips in this chapter, but for a more comprehensive step-by-step tutorial see Crumbs and Crusts (page 276).

Here are some quick tips to get you started. If your dough is always cold, it will bake up perfectly flaky and delicious every time:

- Make sure your ingredients are cold, even the flour.
- If your hands are warm, run them under cold water.
- Handle the dough gently, work quickly, and don't stretch your dough when rolling it out.
- Chill the dough in the pan before adding filling.

THE PERFECT PAN FOR PIES

Use metal or aluminum pie pans. Your pies will cook more evenly and the bottom crust will bake through and not be soggy.

DOUBLE-CRUST APPLE PIE

I've spent the better part of my adult life perfecting my apple pie recipe. Finding the right types of apple and the perfect ratio for them was a real quest. My secret is to always use three firm, tart Granny Smiths among a total of 3 to 4 pounds of apples. A little butter added to the filling contributes an extra richness that goes a long way.

MAKES one 9-inch pie

INGREDIENTS

¾ cup (150g/5.3oz) light brown sugar

¼ cup (50g/1.8oz) granulated sugar

3 tablespoons (22g/0.75oz) cornstarch

1 teaspoon ground cinnamon

⅛ teaspoon grated nutmeg

4 Golden Delicious apples

3 Granny Smith apples

1 tablespoon fresh lemon juice

2 discs Magnolia Bakery's Classic Pie Dough (page 281), rolled out (see Note)

1 egg white

1 teaspoon water

1 tablespoon unsalted butter, cut into small pieces

1 tablespoon granulated sugar, for garnish

½ teaspoon ground cinnamon, for garnish

1. Position an oven rack in the center of the oven and preheat the oven to 425°F. Line a baking sheet with foil.

2. In a small bowl, whisk together both sugars, the cornstarch, cinnamon, and nutmeg. Set aside.

3. Peel, core, and cut the apples into ¼- to ½-inch slices and place in a large bowl; sprinkle with the lemon juice. You should end up with about 8 cups of sliced apples (1 kg or 2 pounds).

4. Fit the bottom crust into a 9-inch pie pan and trim to a ½-inch overhang.

5. In a small bowl, whisk the egg white and water. Brush the inside of the pie shell with the egg wash. This helps to seal the crust, preventing it from getting soggy.

6. Toss the apples with the sugar mixture until thoroughly coated. Place in the prepared pie shell. Make sure there are no large air gaps in the apples; you may need to push some of the slices around until the pie is evenly filled. Dot with the small pieces of butter.

7. Place the rolled-out top crust over the apples, pressing the crust along the rim of the pan to seal it to the bottom crust. Using a paring knife or kitchen shears, trim the excess dough to ½ inch, then fold the top crust under the bottom crust.

8. To seal, dip a 4-tined fork in flour and press into the dough on the edges of the pan, working your way around the pie.

9. With a small knife trim the dough flush against the rim. Make several slashes through the dough near the top crust to allow the steam to escape. In a small bowl, mix the sugar and cinnamon. Brush the dough lightly with more of the egg wash and evenly sprinkle with the cinnamon-sugar.

10. Place the pie on the foil-lined baking sheet. Bake for 45 minutes to over 1 hour, rotating the pie front to back halfway through the baking time. To test for doneness, poke a small paring knife through one of the slits in the middle of the pie; the apples should

be tender but not mushy and the juices should bubble a little. Starting at 45 minutes, keep a close eye on your pie. You may need to cover the pie with foil or a pie shield if it starts to brown too quickly. Your crust should be a dark golden brown but not burned.

11. Place on a cooling rack for at least 1 hour. This pie needs time to set before serving or the juices will spill out when you cut into it.

APPLE CRUMB PIE

As with any great story, the key to a compelling recipe is specificity. For this pie, the apple filling needs to be sweet, not tart, and not too soft. The crumb topping has to have big, clumpy chunks. I like to serve it still warm from the oven so that my vanilla ice cream melts and drips down through the crumbs.

MAKES one 9-inch pie

INGREDIENTS

2 tablespoons (16g/2.4oz) all-purpose flour

¾ cup (150g/5.3oz) granulated sugar

¼ cup (50g/1.8oz) light brown sugar

1 teaspoon ground cinnamon

⅛ teaspoon grated nutmeg

8 Golden Delicious apples, peeled, cored, and cut into ½-inch chunks

1 (9-inch) Magnolia Bakery's Classic Pie Dough (page 281), parbaked

2½ cups (½ recipe) Cinnamon Crumb Topping (page 284)

1. Position an oven rack in the center of the oven and preheat to 425°F. Line a baking sheet with foil.

2. In a small bowl, whisk together the flour, both sugars, the cinnamon, and nutmeg.

3. Place the apple pieces in a large bowl. You should end up with about 8 cups of cut apples (1kg/2lbs). Toss the apples with the sugar mixture until thoroughly coated. Place in the parbaked crust.

4. Cover the apples with large clumps of the crumb mixture by pinching the crumb topping with your fingers.

5. Place the pie on the lined baking sheet. Bake for 45 to 55 minutes, or until the apples are just tender and the crumbs are toasted. At 45 minutes, keep a close eye on the pie. You may need to cover the crust with foil or a pie shield if it starts to brown too quickly.

6. Place on a cooling rack for at least 1 hour. This pie is great served warm. To reheat, place in a 350°F oven for 15 to 20 minutes.

BLUEBERRY CRUMB PIE

When the farmers' markets are filled with seasonal fruit, blueberries are the shining star. Nothing says summer like a big blueberry pie. The blueberries cook down to a smooth texture, and the crumb topping is a lovely, crunchy counterpoint.

MAKES one 9-inch pie

INGREDIENTS

6 cups (960g/32.5oz) fresh blueberries, rinsed and picked over for stems

1 teaspoon grated lemon zest

¼ cup (30g/1oz) cornstarch

¾ cup (150g/5.3oz) granulated sugar

¼ teaspoon ground cinnamon

1 teaspoon fresh lemon juice

1 (9-inch) Magnolia Bakery's Classic Pie Dough (page 281), parbaked, cooled

2½ cups (½ recipe) Cinnamon Crumb Topping (page 284)

1. Position an oven rack in the center of the oven and preheat to 425°F. Line a baking sheet with foil.

2. Place the blueberries in a large bowl. In a small bowl, whisk together the lemon zest, cornstarch, sugar, and cinnamon.

3. Gently mix the blueberries with the sugar mixture and lemon juice. Place the berries in the parbaked crust.

4. Cover the blueberries with large clumps of the crumb mixture by pinching the crumb topping with your fingers.

5. Bake for 20 minutes. Reduce the oven temperature to 350°F and bake for 30 to 40 minutes more, or until the juices have thickened and are bubbling through the crumbs. If the crumbs begin to darken too quickly, cover the top with foil and continue baking.

6. Place on a cooling rack for at least 1 hour before serving.

APPLE CRISP

Make the apple filling and crumb topping ahead of time, and this becomes the quickest dessert to throw together. Assemble and bake it before dinner and it will be ready when it's time for dessert.

MAKES one 9-inch baking dish; serves 6 to 8

INGREDIENTS

Butter, for the baking dish

Apple Filling (page 285)

Streusel Crumb Topping for Crisps (page 284)

1. Position an oven rack in the center of the oven and preheat to 350°F. Butter a decorative 9-inch baking dish.

2. Place the apple filling in the buttered dish. Pinch the streusel with your fingers to create large crumbs. Spread these crumbs over the filling.

3. Bake for 30 to 40 minutes, or until the filling is heated through and bubbling and the streusel is lightly browned and crisp.

4. Place on a cooling rack and cool for 15 minutes. Serve warm with ice cream and/or whipped cream.

BLUEBERRY-RASPBERRY CRISP

The best time to make this crisp is when blueberries and raspberries are in season. Buy them at a local farmer's market or, better yet, go to a pick-your-own. That said, frozen berries work almost as well, especially since they're usually preserved at the height of their flavor. You can use any combination of berries or quick-cooking fruits such as peaches or plums. Serve the crisp warm with ice cream or whipped cream.

MAKES one 9-inch baking dish; serves 6 to 8

INGREDIENTS

4 cups (640g/22.8oz) fresh blueberries, rinsed and picked over for stems

4 cups (533g/18.7oz) fresh raspberries

½ cup (100g/3.5oz) granulated sugar

¼ cup (30g/1oz) cornstarch

1 teaspoon grated lemon zest

½ teaspoon salt

¼ teaspoon ground cinnamon

⅛ teaspoon grated nutmeg

Streusel Crumb Topping for Crisps (page 284)

1. Position an oven rack in the center of the oven and preheat to 350°F. Butter a 9-inch round baking pan and place on a foil-lined baking sheet.

2. In a large bowl, gently toss together the blueberries and raspberries. In a separate bowl, whisk together the sugar, cornstarch, lemon zest, salt, and spices. Gently toss with the fruit, being careful not to crush the raspberries.

3. Place the fruit mixture in the baking pan. Loosely cover with foil, transfer to the oven, and bake for 30 minutes while you prepare the streusel topping, if you haven't already.

4. After the first 30 minutes, remove the foil and cover the fruit with the streusel topping, spreading evenly but not too close to the edge. You want to still be able to see the fruit peeking through.

5. Bake for another 30 minutes, or until the crisp is lightly browned and the fruit juices are bubbling around the edges.

6. Cool for 30 minutes to 1 hour before serving. Serve warm.

PECAN PIE

This pecan-loaded pie is quick and easy and doesn't require a mixer to make! This is a custard pie and must bake long enough for the custard to set, but not so long that it will curdle or crack. With all those pecans on top, it can be hard to tell when it's done, but we've included some techniques to ensure that your pie comes out perfectly. I like a deep, rich flavor, so I use dark corn syrup; if you prefer a lighter flavor use half light and half dark corn syrup, or all light.

MAKES one 9-inch pie

INGREDIENTS

3 eggs

1 cup (200g/7.1oz) light brown sugar

4 tablespoons/½ stick (60g/2.1oz) unsalted butter, melted

1 cup (337g/11.9oz) dark corn syrup (preferably Karo)

1¼ teaspoons pure vanilla extract

½ teaspoon salt

2 cups (230g/8.1oz) coarsely chopped pecans, lightly toasted (see Tip, page 288)

1 (9-inch) Magnolia Bakery's Classic Pie Dough (page 281), parbaked

24 mammoth pecan halves, for decoration

Fresh whipped cream, for serving

1. Position an oven rack in the center of the oven and preheat to 350°F. Line a baking sheet with foil.

2. In a large bowl, whisk the eggs until thick and light in color. Add the brown sugar and mix until incorporated. Add the melted butter and mix just until combined. Add the dark corn syrup, vanilla, and salt, stirring until thoroughly combined.

3. Spread the chopped toasted pecans in the pie shell. Place the pie on the lined baking sheet. Very slowly pour the filling into the crust. The pecans will rise to the top as you pour in the filling. Decoratively arrange the mammoth pecan halves atop the pie.

4. Bake for 45 to 55 minutes, or until the custard is set. (If the crust or pecans begin to darken before your custard is set, cover the top with a piece of foil or a pie shield.) To test for doneness, the center of the custard should just barely jiggle when you shake the pan. If you are not certain, stick an instant-read thermometer in the center of the pie to confirm that the internal temperature is at least 190 to 195°F; if not, continue baking another 3 to 5 minutes, or until the center is no longer too jiggly.

5. Transfer to a cooling rack to cool completely, at least 4 hours. Serve with fresh whipped cream.

BLACK BOTTOM PECAN PIE

A twist on the Thanksgiving classic, this pie is a bit more decadent thanks to the addition of chocolate. Fresh whipped cream or vanilla ice cream make the perfect accompaniment.

MAKES one 9-inch pie

INGREDIENTS

⅔ cup (120g/4.2oz) semisweet chocolate chips

2 tablespoons unsalted butter

¼ cup (58g/2oz) hot coffee, preferably instant espresso

3 eggs

1 cup (200g/7.1oz) light brown sugar

½ cup (168g/6oz) dark corn syrup (preferably Karo)

1¼ teaspoons pure vanilla extract

½ teaspoon salt

1½ cups (173g/6.1oz) coarsely chopped pecans, lightly toasted (see Tip, page 288)

1 (9-inch) Magnolia Bakery's Classic Pie Dough (page 281), parbaked

1. Position an oven rack in the center of the oven and preheat to 350°F. Line a baking sheet with foil.

2. Place ⅓ cup (60g/2.1oz) of the chocolate chips and the butter in a small glass bowl. Microwave for 20 seconds, then stir with a rubber spatula to combine. If there are still large pieces of chocolate, microwave for another 10 seconds. Stir in the espresso and mix to blend.

3. In a large bowl, whisk the eggs until thick and pale. Add the brown sugar and mix until incorporated, being careful not to overmix. Add the dark corn syrup, vanilla, and salt, stirring until thoroughly combined.

4. Spread the chopped toasted pecans in the parbaked pie crust. Place the pie on the lined baking sheet. Very slowly pour the filling into the pie shell. The pecans will rise to the top as you pour in the filling.

5. Bake for 45 to 55 minutes, or until the custard is set. (If the crust or pecans begin to darken before your custard is set, cover the top with a piece of foil or a pie shield.) To test for doneness, the center of the custard should just barely jiggle when you shake the pan. If you are not certain, then stick an instant-read thermometer in the center of the pie to confirm that the internal temperature is at least 190 to 195°F; if not, continue baking another 3 to 5 minutes, or until the center is no longer too jiggly.

6. Transfer to a cooling rack to cool completely, at least 4 hours.

7. The pie can be made 2 days ahead and refrigerated. Bring to room temperature before serving.

8. When ready to serve, place the remaining ⅓ cup (60g/2.1oz) chocolate chips in a small glass bowl. Microwave in 10-second increments, stirring after each, until melted and smooth. Transfer the melted chocolate to a piping bag or small plastic bag. Cut a small hole in the corner. Drizzle the chocolate on top of the pie, creating a crosshatch pattern. Let set.

PUMPKIN PIE <small>WITH</small> PRALINE TOPPING

Pumpkin pie is a good starter pie for anyone new to baking a cooked custard. This filling is very easy to make, and the addition of a crunchy praline topping elevates this classic.

MAKES one 9-inch pie

INGREDIENTS

FOR THE PRALINE TOPPING

1 cup (115g/4oz) coarsely chopped pecans

½ cup (100g/3.5oz) dark brown sugar

1 teaspoon salt

2 teaspoons dark corn syrup (preferably Karo)

1 teaspoon pure vanilla extract

FOR THE FILLING

⅔ cup (133g/4.7oz) granulated sugar, plus 2 teaspoons for sprinkling

1¼ teaspoons ground cinnamon

¾ teaspoon grated nutmeg

½ teaspoon ground cloves

4 eggs

2 cups (480g/17oz) canned unsweetened pumpkin puree (preferably Libby's)

⅓ cup (107g/3.5oz) dark maple syrup

½ cup (120g/4.2oz) whole milk

¼ cup (60g/2.1oz) heavy cream

¼ cup/½ stick (56g/2oz) unsalted butter, melted

1 (9-inch) Magnolia Bakery's Classic Pie Dough (page 281), parbaked

1. Position an oven rack in the center of the oven and preheat to 425°F. Line a baking sheet with foil.

2. **MAKE THE TOPPING:** In a small bowl, toss together the pecans, brown sugar, and salt. Add the corn syrup and vanilla, mixing to ensure that the ingredients are well blended.

3. **MAKE THE FILLING:** In a small bowl, whisk together the ⅔ cup granulated sugar, the cinnamon, nutmeg, and cloves.

4. In a stand mixer with the whisk, lightly whisk the eggs on low speed until combined. Add the sugar mixture and whisk until smooth. Scrape down the bottom and sides of the bowl. Add the pumpkin puree, maple syrup, milk, and cream. Whisk until combined. Remove the bowl from the mixer and slowly whisk in the melted butter by hand until combined.

5. Place the parbaked crust on the lined baking sheet. Pour the filling into the pie crust.

6. Bake for 15 minutes. Rotate the pan front to back and reduce the oven temperature to 350°F. Bake for an additional 35 to 40 minutes, or until a knife inserted just off center comes out clean and the center of the pie just barely jiggles. Use an instant-read thermometer to confirm that the internal temperature is 175 to 180°F. Be careful not to overbake your pie, as it will crack on the top. Scatter handfuls of the praline topping evenly over the puffed pumpkin filling and sprinkle lightly with the remaingin 2 teaspoons granulated sugar.

7. Return to the oven and bake for 10 to 12 more minutes, or until the pecans are fragrant and the topping is bubbling around the edges.

8. Turn the oven off, crack open the door, and let the pie sit in the oven for another 10 to 15 minutes. This will ensure that your pie doesn't crack or shrink away from the crust.

9. Cool completely on a cooling rack for at least 4 hours before serving.

10. It is not necessary to store your pie in the refrigerator; however, if you do, be sure it is completely cool first. Bring to room temperature before serving.

CHOCOLATE FUNNY CAKE PIE

I was recently looking through my recipe clipping collection and came upon this recipe, which I recall making back in the 1980s. It's an unusual combination of cake and pie. You make a vanilla batter and a chocolate batter, pour them into a pie crust, and watch the magic happen as the two meld during baking. The chocolate cake sinks to the bottom, creating a fudgy layer, while the vanilla cake sits on top. I updated the original recipe to specify a high-quality chocolate, more vanilla, and a little espresso powder to enhance the chocolate flavor. Serve with a dollop of whipped cream.

MAKES one 9-inch pie

INGREDIENTS

FOR THE VANILLA BATTER

1 cup (135g/4.8oz) all-purpose flour

1 teaspoon baking powder

½ teaspoon salt

½ cup (120g/4.2oz) whole milk

1 egg

1 teaspoon pure vanilla extract

¼ cup/½ stick (56g/2oz) unsalted
    butter, at room temperature

1 cup (200g/7.1oz) granulated sugar

FOR THE CHOCOLATE BATTER

¼ cup (30g/1oz) unsweetened dark
    cocoa powder (22 to 24%), sifted

½ cup (100g/3.5oz) granulated sugar

1 teaspoon espresso powder

6 tablespoons hot water

½ teaspoon pure vanilla extract

1 (9-inch) Magnolia Bakery's Classic
    Pie Dough (page 281), parbaked

1. Position a rack in the center of the oven and preheat to 350°F.

2. **MAKE THE VANILLA BATTER:** In a small bowl, whisk together the flour, baking powder, and salt. In a liquid measuring cup, whisk together the milk, egg, and vanilla.

3. In a stand mixer with the paddle, cream the butter and sugar together until light and fluffy. Scrape down the bottom and sides of the bowl. Add the flour mixture in three additions, alternating with the milk mixture, beginning and ending with the flour. Stop the mixer and scrape down bottom and sides of bowl. Set aside.

4. **MAKE THE CHOCOLATE BATTER:** In a small bowl, whisk together the cocoa, sugar, and espresso powder. Gradually whisk in the water and vanilla until smooth.

5. Pour the vanilla batter into the parbaked crust. Carefully and slowly pour the chocolate batter over the vanilla.

6. Bake for 45 to 50 minutes, or until a cake tester inserted in the center comes out clean.

7. Let cool completely before serving.

CHAPTER SIX

MUFFINS & COFFEE CAKES

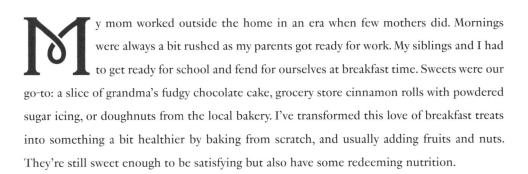

My mom worked outside the home in an era when few mothers did. Mornings were always a bit rushed as my parents got ready for work. My siblings and I had to get ready for school and fend for ourselves at breakfast time. Sweets were our go-to: a slice of grandma's fudgy chocolate cake, grocery store cinnamon rolls with powdered sugar icing, or doughnuts from the local bakery. I've transformed this love of breakfast treats into something a bit healthier by baking from scratch, and usually adding fruits and nuts. They're still sweet enough to be satisfying but also have some redeeming nutrition.

BERRY-BUTTERMILK CRUMB MUFFINS

This recipe is versatile and can be thrown together with ingredients you most likely always have on hand. You can use any quick-cooking berries, such as raspberries or blueberries, or soft fruit such as peaches, when in season. The crumb adds a light crunch and sweetness that really make the muffin. You can freeze any leftover crumb or use it to top cakes or fruit crisps.

MAKES 15 muffins

INGREDIENTS

2½ cups (337g/12oz) all-purpose flour

1 teaspoon baking powder

1 teaspoon baking soda

½ teaspoon salt

1 egg

½ cup (104g/3.6oz) vegetable oil

1¼ cups (250g/8.8oz) light brown sugar

1 teaspoon pure vanilla extract

1 cup (242g/8.5oz) buttermilk

1½ cups (200g/7oz) fresh raspberries, 1½ cups (240g/8.5oz) fresh blueberries, rinsed and picked over for stems, or 1½ cups (307g/10.8oz) peeled peaches, cut into large chunks

Cinnamon Crumb Topping (page 284)

1. Preheat the oven to 350°F. Line 15 cups of two muffin tins with paper liners or coat with nonstick spray.

2. In a small bowl, whisk together the flour, baking powder, baking soda, and salt.

3. In a stand mixer with the paddle, combine the egg, oil, brown sugar, and vanilla. Mix on low speed until light and creamy, about 5 minutes. Add the flour mixture in three additions, alternating with the buttermilk, beginning and ending with the dry ingredients. Scrape down the sides and bottom of the bowl, mixing just until you no longer see streaks of flour. Fold in the fruit without breaking it up.

4. Evenly scoop the batter into the prepared muffin tins. Each cup should be about halfway full to make room for the crumb topping. Add a generous amount of crumb topping (about ¼ cup) to each muffin, squeezing the crumb together and then pressing gently on the muffins so it doesn't fall off.

5. Bake for 22 to 24 minutes, or until a cake tester inserted in the centers comes out clean.

6. Let the muffins cool in the pans for 5 to 10 minutes. Transfer to a rack to cool completely.

CAPPUCCINO CHIP MUFFINS

When we first introduced muffins to the bakery, we decided to rotate a daily selection of four different kinds. We wanted to be able to offer all our great flavors over the course of a week. But we soon learned from our customers that this muffin—and the Apple Walnut Muffin (page 191)—had to be a daily staple. Once you've tried these, you will understand why. Nothing goes better with that morning cup of joe.

MAKES 15 muffins

INGREDIENTS

2½ cups (337g/12oz) all-purpose flour

1 tablespoon baking powder

3 teaspoons instant espresso powder

½ teaspoon ground cinnamon

½ teaspoon salt

½ cup/1 stick (113g/4oz) unsalted butter, at room temperature

1 cup plus 2 tablespoons (225g/8oz) sugar

1 egg

1 egg yolk

2 teaspoons pure vanilla extract

1⅓ cups (320g/11.3oz) whole milk

1 cup (180g/6.3oz) semisweet chocolate chips

1. Preheat the oven to 325°F. Line 15 cups of two muffin tins with paper liners or coat with nonstick spray.

2. In a medium bowl, whisk together the flour, baking powder, espresso powder, cinnamon, and salt. Set aside.

3. In a stand mixer with the paddle, cream the butter and sugar on medium speed until light and fluffy, about 3 minutes. Scrape down the sides and bottom of the bowl. Add the whole egg and egg yolk, one at a time, and mix just until incorporated. Beat in the vanilla and scrape the bowl again.

4. Add the flour mixture in three additions, alternating with the milk, beginning and ending with the dry ingredients. Mix just until you see very few flour streaks. Remove the bowl from the mixer and scrape down the bottom and sides with a spatula, being sure all the ingredients are fully incorporated. Gently fold in the chocolate chips.

5. Evenly scoop the batter into the prepared muffin cups.

6. Bake for 23 to 25 minutes, or until a muffin top springs back when pressed and a cake tester inserted in the center comes out clean.

7. Let the muffins cool in the pans for 5 to 10 minutes. Transfer to a rack to cool completely.

CHOCOLATE CHIP CHERRY MUFFINS

This classic flavor duo is my mother's favorite, so I'm always developing special recipes with her in mind. Since chocolate and cherries are a combination beloved by many, it's no surprise these are a hit at the bakery. Be sure to use dried sour cherries or the muffins will be too sweet.

MAKES 15 muffins

INGREDIENTS

2¾ cups (372g/13.2oz) all-purpose flour

3 tablespoons (18g/0.67oz) unsweetened dark cocoa powder (22 to 24%), sifted

1 tablespoon baking powder

½ teaspoon baking soda

½ teaspoon salt

1 cup (150g/5.3oz) dried sour cherries

½ cup/1 stick (113g/12oz) unsalted butter, at room temperature

¾ cup (150g/5.3oz) granulated sugar

1 egg

1 teaspoon pure vanilla extract

½ teaspoon almond extract

1½ cups (360g/12.7oz) buttermilk

1 cup (180g/6.3oz) semisweet chocolate chips

1. Preheat the oven to 350°F. Line 15 cups of two muffin tins with paper liners or coat with nonstick spray.

2. In a medium bowl, whisk together the flour, cocoa, baking powder, baking soda, and salt. Set aside.

3. Place the dried cherries in a heatproof bowl, barely cover with boiling water, and let sit for 10 minutes. Drain. Chop into large chunks. Set aside.

4. In a stand mixer with the paddle, cream the butter and sugar on medium speed until light and fluffy, about 3 minutes. Scrape down the sides and bottom of the bowl.

5. In a liquid measuring cup, whisk together the egg, vanilla, and almond extract. Slowly pour into the mixer, mixing just until incorporated. Scrape down the sides and bottom of the bowl again.

6. Add the flour mixture in three additions, alternating with the buttermilk, beginning and ending with the dry ingredients. Remove the bowl from the mixer, and scrape down the bottom and sides, with a rubber spatula, being sure all ingredients are fully incorporated but being careful not to overmix. Gently fold in the cherries and chocolate chips.

7. Evenly scoop the batter into the prepared muffin cups.

8. Bake for 20 to 22 minutes, or until the muffin tops spring back when pressed and a cake tester inserted in the centers comes out clean.

9. Let the muffins cool in the pans for 5 to 10 minutes. Transfer to a rack to cool completely.

LEMON ZEST MUFFINS

These light and lemony pillows are made airy by the addition of whipped egg whites. To heighten the lemon flavor, I add a tart lemon glaze. If you love lemon sweets like I do, you'll be excited to pucker up!

MAKES 16 muffins

INGREDIENTS

2 cups (270g/9.6oz) all-purpose flour

2 teaspoons baking powder

½ teaspoon salt

1 cup/2 sticks (226g/8oz) unsalted butter, at room temperature

1 cup (200g/7.1oz) granulated sugar

4 eggs, separated

½ cup (112g/3.9oz) fresh lemon juice

2 teaspoons grated lemon zest

FOR THE LEMON GLAZE

1 cup (125g/4.4oz) powdered sugar, sifted

1 teaspoon grated lemon zest

2 tablespoons fresh lemon juice

1 tablespoon whole milk

1. Preheat the oven to 350°F. Line 16 cups of two muffin tins with paper liners or coat with nonstick spray.

2. In a small bowl, whisk together the flour, baking powder, and salt. Set aside.

3. In a stand mixer with the paddle, cream the butter and sugar until light and fluffy, about 3 minutes, occasionally scraping down the sides and bottom of the bowl. Add the egg yolks and mix well. Scrape down the sides and bottom of the bowl again.

4. Add the flour mixture in three additions, alternating with the lemon juice, beginning and ending with the flour. Mix until just incorporated, being careful not to overmix. Remove the bowl from the mixer and fold in the lemon zest. Mix until incorporated.

5. In a stand mixer with the whisk, beat the egg whites until stiff but not dry. Gently fold the whites into the lemon batter.

6. Evenly scoop the batter into the prepared muffin cups.

7. Bake for 20 to 23 minutes, or until a cake tester inserted in the center comes out clean.

8. Let the muffins cool in the pans for 5 to 10 minutes. Transfer to a rack to cool completely.

9. **MEANWHILE, MAKE THE LEMON GLAZE:** In a small bowl, whisk together the powdered sugar, lemon zest, lemon juice, and milk until smooth.

10. Before serving, drizzle the muffins with the lemon glaze.

APPLE WALNUT MUFFINS

This muffin is probably the most-requested breakfast item at Magnolia Bakery. We just can't seem to make enough of them. Each muffin is so laden with fruit, it's like biting into a whole apple. The batter barely coats all the ingredients, and that's just fine. The moisture from the apples brings it all together in the oven. These muffins are delicious when eaten while slightly warm. They won't last long in your house.

MAKES 20 muffins

INGREDIENTS

8 cups (1kg/36.5oz) unpeeled Granny Smith apple chunks (about 8 apples)

1½ cups (300g/10.6oz) granulated sugar

3 eggs, lightly beaten

¾ cup (155g/5.5oz) vegetable oil

2 teaspoons pure vanilla extract

3 cups (405g/14.3oz) all-purpose flour

1 tablespoon ground cinnamon

1 tablespoon baking soda

½ teaspoon salt

¾ cup (95g/3.4oz) fresh or frozen cranberries, chopped

¾ cup (90g/3.2oz) chopped toasted walnuts (see Tip, page 288)

1. Preheat the oven to 350°F. Line 20 cups of two muffin tins with paper liners or coat with nonstick spray.

2. In a very large bowl, toss the apples with the sugar until fully coated.

3. In a small bowl, whisk together the eggs, vegetable oil, and vanilla until creamy. Pour over the apples and toss until thoroughly combined.

4. In another bowl, whisk together the flour, cinnamon, baking soda, and salt. Add the flour mixture to the apple mixture and mix using a heavy spoon or spatula. The mixture will be heavy and thick. Fold in the cranberries and walnuts and mix until the flour is no longer visible. Be careful not to overmix.

5. Evenly scoop the mixture into the prepared muffin cups. It will seem like too much batter, but trust me, it's not.

6. Position the tins in the top third and bottom third of the oven. Bake for 24 to 26 minutes, rotating halfway through or until a cake tester inserted in the centers comes out clean.

7. Let the muffins cool in the pans for 5 to 10 minutes. Transfer to a cooling rack before serving.

CINNAMON SUGAR MUFFINS

I first tried these wonderful muffins at a charming bakery on Cape Cod. They were called "dirt bombs" (not the most enticing name), but I'll never forget how they tasted warm from the oven: like the freshly made cinnamon-sugar doughnuts from the bakery I went to as a child. The minute I got home from Cape Cod, I set about re-creating those flavors.

MAKES 16 muffins

INGREDIENTS

3 cups plus 3 tablespoons (429g/15.3oz) all-purpose flour

1 tablespoon baking powder

½ teaspoon salt

½ teaspoon grated nutmeg

¼ teaspoon ground cardamom

¾ cup/1½ sticks (170g/6oz) unsalted butter, at room temperature

1 cup (200g/7.1oz) granulated sugar

2 eggs

1 cup (240g/8.5oz) whole milk

FOR THE CINNAMON TOPPING

1 cup/2 sticks (226g/8oz) unsalted butter

¾ cup (150g/5.3oz) granulated sugar

1 tablespoon ground cinnamon

1. Preheat the oven to 325°F. Butter and flour 16 cups of two muffin tins or coat with nonstick spray. Do not use paper liners.

2. In a medium bowl, whisk together the flour, baking powder, salt, nutmeg, and cardamom. Set aside.

3. In a stand mixer with the paddle, cream the butter and sugar until light and fluffy, 3 to 4 minutes. Stop halfway through to scrape down the sides and bottom.

4. Add the eggs, one at a time, mixing well and scraping down the sides after each addition.

5. Add the flour mixture in three additions, alternating with the milk, beginning and ending with the flour. Scrape down the bottom and sides of the bowl.

6. Evenly scoop the batter into the prepared muffin cups.

7. Bake for 20 to 23 minutes, or until a cake tester inserted in the centers comes out clean.

8. Let the muffins sit in the pans while you are prepare the topping.

9. **PREPARE THE TOPPING:** Place the butter in a microwave-safe bowl and warm until melted, about 1 minute. In a separate bowl, whisk together the sugar and cinnamon.

10. Remove the muffins from the tins and place them on a cooling rack. Using a pair of tongs, dip the whole baked muffins into the butter until fully covered. Then, using a different set of tongs, dip in the cinnamon-sugar mixture to completely cover them. Place on a cooling rack. These are best eaten when warm!

COFFEE CAKE PECAN MUFFINS

These muffins taste just like good old-fashioned crumb coffee cake. Luckily, they come proportioned in conveniently individual sizes, making them perfect for an afternoon coffee or tea break. If you have the topping premade, it's a cinch to bake up a batch. They'll only keep, covered on the counter, for about 2 days, but can be wrapped and frozen for up to 3 months.

MAKES 16 muffins

INGREDIENTS

FOR THE STREUSEL TOPPING

½ cup (100g/3.5oz) granulated sugar

⅔ cup (133g/4.7oz) light brown sugar

⅔ cup (90g/3.2oz) all-purpose flour

2 tablespoons ground cinnamon

¼ cup/½ stick (56g/2oz) unsalted butter, cut into ½-inch cubes, at room temperature (but still firm)

½ cup (58g/2oz) coarsely chopped pecans

FOR THE MUFFIN BATTER

4 eggs

2 cups (460g/16oz) sour cream

1 tablespoon pure vanilla extract

2¾ cups (372g/13.2oz) all-purpose flour

1 cup (200g/7.1oz) granulated sugar

2 tablespoons baking powder

½ teaspoon salt

¼ cup/½ stick (56g/2oz) unsalted butter, cut into ½-inch cubes, at room temperature

1. **MAKE THE STREUSEL:** In a stand mixer with the paddle, combine both sugars, the flour, and cinnamon. Mix on low speed for 1 minute. Add the butter and mix on low speed until the mixture turns into moist, clumpy crumbs, about 2 minutes. Add the chopped pecans and mix until just combined.

2. Remove from the mixer bowl and set aside. This can be made ahead and stored in the refrigerator for up to 3 days.

3. **MAKE THE BATTER:** Preheat the oven to 350°F. Line 16 cups of two muffin tins with paper liners or coat with nonstick spray.

4. In a small bowl, whisk together the eggs, sour cream, and vanilla until no lumps remain. Set aside.

5. In a stand mixer with the paddle, mix the flour, sugar, baking powder, and salt on low speed for 1 minute. Add the butter and mix on low speed until the mixture resembles coarse sand. Remove from the mixer and scrape down the bottom and sides of the bowl.

6. Using a rubber spatula, gradually fold in the egg mixture until just combined. Scrape down the sides and bottom of the bowl again

7. Place one small scoop of batter in each muffin cup and top with 1 tablespoon of streusel topping. Add another scoop of batter and sprinkle with streusel topping. Gently pat the streusel topping with your fingers.

8. Bake for 25 to 27 minutes, or until light and golden.

9. Let the muffins cool in the pans for 5 to 10 minutes. Transfer to a rack to cool completely.

PUMPKIN PECAN MUFFINS

Pumpkin spice season seems to arrive earlier every year, though I'm not complaining. As soon as there's a chill in the night air, it's time to start making these moist, aromatic muffins. Pop them in the oven and your whole kitchen smells like fall.

MAKES 16 muffins

INGREDIENTS

1½ cups (202g/7.2oz) all-purpose flour

1½ teaspoons baking powder

1 teaspoon baking soda

2 teaspoons ground cinnamon

½ teaspoon ground allspice

¼ teaspoon grated nutmeg

¼ teaspoon salt

1¼ cups (250g/8.8oz) granulated sugar

3 eggs

¾ cup (155g/5.5oz) vegetable oil

1½ cups (360g/12.7oz) canned unsweetened pumpkin puree (preferably Libby's)

½ cup (58g/2oz) coarsely chopped pecans, lightly toasted (see Tip, page 288)

FOR THE MAPLE GLAZE (OPTIONAL)

2 tablespoons dark maple syrup

1½ teaspoons whole milk

½ cup (62g/2oz) powdered sugar, sifted

1. Preheat the oven to 325°F. Line 16 cups of two muffin tins with paper liners or coat with nonstick spray.

2. In a small bowl, whisk together the flour, baking powder, baking soda, cinnamon, allspice, nutmeg, and salt. Set aside.

3. In a stand mixer with the paddle, combine the granulated sugar, eggs, oil, and pumpkin puree on low until the ingredients are light in color, 3 to 4 minutes. Scrape the bottom and sides of the bowl.

4. Remove the bowl from the mixer and, using a large rubber spatula, fold in the flour mixture until no flour is visible, being careful not to overmix. Scrape down the sides and bottom of the bowl. Gently fold in the pecans.

5. Evenly scoop the mixture into the prepared muffin cups.

6. Bake for 23 to 25 minutes, or until a cake tester inserted in the center comes out clean.

7. Let the muffins cool in the pans for 10 to 15 minutes while you prepare the glaze, if using.

8. **MAKE THE GLAZE:** In a small bowl, whisk together the maple syrup, milk, and powdered sugar until smooth.

9. Remove the muffins from the pans and drizzle with the glaze.

SOUR CREAM COFFEE CAKE

Delicate, super moist, and delicious, this cake is perfect for breakfast, with afternoon tea, or as a hostess gift for any occasion. It's simple to make and easily adapted to any berry or soft fruit, such as peaches or plums. I found this recipe on an old recipe card from one of my grandmother's little recipe boxes. With a few adjustments I was able to update it for today's tastes.

SERVES 6 to 8

INGREDIENTS

1½ cups (203g/7.2oz) all-purpose flour

1½ teaspoons baking powder

¼ teaspoon baking soda

½ teaspoon salt

1 cup/2 sticks (226g/8oz) unsalted butter, at room temperature

¾ cup (150g/5.3oz) granulated sugar

¼ cup (50g/1.8oz) light brown sugar

1 egg

½ cup (115g/4oz) sour cream

⅓ cup (80g/2.8oz) whole milk

1 teaspoon pure vanilla extract

1. Preheat the oven to 375°F. Coat a 9-inch fluted tart pan with a removable bottom with nonstick spray.

2. In a small bowl, whisk together the flour, baking powder, baking soda, and salt. Set aside.

3. In a stand mixer with the paddle, cream the butter while slowly adding both sugars. Stop occasionally and scrape down the bottom and sides of the bowl. Mix until light and fluffy, 4 to 5 minutes. Add the egg and mix for 1 minute. Scrape down the bottom and sides of the bowl.

4. In a liquid measuring cup, whisk together the sour cream, milk, and vanilla until no lumps remain. Add to the butter mixture and mix until just incorporated. Scrape down the sides and bottom of the bowl.

5. With the mixer on low speed, carefully add the flour mixture until just incorporated. Be sure not to overmix. Stop the mixer and scrape down the paddle, bottom, and sides of the bowl.

6. Pour the batter into the prepared pan and smooth with an offset spatula.

7. **MAKE THE TOPPING:** Arrange the fruit in any design you want with the slices as close together as possible and with the cut sides down around the sides and center of the batter. Sprinkle with the granulated sugar.

8. Bake for 10 minutes. Reduce the oven temperature to 350°F and continue to bake for 40 to 45 minutes, or until light golden brown and a cake tester inserted in the center comes out clean.

9. Let cool for 30 minutes in the pan. Place on a decorative plate and dust with powdered sugar just before serving.

FOR THE TOPPING

Choice of fruit (see Toppings)

2 tablespoons granulated sugar

Powdered sugar, for serving

TOPPINGS

STRAWBERRY: about 3 cups (525g/18.5oz) halved strawberries (if really large, cut them into 3 or 4 slices)

PEACH: about 1½ cups (240g/9oz) peeled peaches, sliced into ¼-inch slices

BLUEBERRY: about 3 cups (480g/17oz) berries, rinsed and picked over for stems

PEACH-BERRY: about 2 peaches, peeled and cut into ¼-inch slices and about 1 cup (133g/4.7oz) raspberries or 1 cup (160g/5.7oz) fresh blueberries, rinsed and picked over for stems

LEMON VANILLA MINI-BUNDT CAKES

The Vanilla Bundt Cake has long been popular at Magnolia Bakery, with many devoted fans coming in to get their morning slice. I lightened the recipe a bit for these minis, which of course bake up in just 20 minutes and only need to cool for a bit before you pop them out of the pan. These are best eaten the same day you make them.

MAKES 16 mini-Bundt cakes

INGREDIENTS

¾ cup/1½ sticks (170g/6oz) unsalted butter, at room temperature (but still firm)

1½ cups (300g/10.6oz) granulated sugar

2 teaspoons grated lemon zest

3 eggs

2 teaspoons pure vanilla extract

1½ cups (202g/7.2oz) all-purpose flour

⅓ cup (80g/2.8oz) club soda

Powdered sugar, for dusting

1. Preheat the oven to 350°F. Butter and flour 16 cups of two mini-Bundt cake pans.

2. In a stand mixer with the paddle, cream the butter, sugar, and lemon zest on medium speed until light and fluffy, about 5 minutes. Scrape the bottom and sides of the bowl.

3. Add the eggs, one at a time, beating very well after each addition. Beat in the vanilla. Scrape down the bottom and sides of the bowl.

4. On low speed, add the flour in three additions, alternating with the club soda, beginning and ending with the flour. Mix just until combined. Scrape the bottom and sides of bowl and mix just until the flour has been fully incorporated; do not overmix.

5. Evenly scoop the batter into the prepared mini-Bundt pans.

6. Bake for 20 to 22 minutes, or until the cakes are golden and a cake tester inserted in the center comes out clean.

7. Let the cakes cool in the pan for 10 minutes, then pop them out of the pan while still slightly warm and dust with powdered sugar. Serve immediately.

VARIATION

LEMON VANILLA BUNDT CAKE: To make a full-size Bundt cake, double this recipe. Use a 10-inch Bundt pan with a 12-cup capacity and bake for at least 1 hour 20 minutes, or until a cake tester inserted halfway between the center tube and the edge of the cake comes out clean.

CHAPTER SEVEN

SCONES

Scones are a traditional British baked good, usually not too sweet and often eaten with butter, jam, and clotted cream. They are a versatile carrier for all kinds of flavors, both sweet and savory. Get creative with the fruits, spices, or other ingredients you add to come up with your own go-to scone. Seven recipes in this chapter are made with a freezer-friendly scone base. The base recipe makes 8 cups, and the individual recipes only require 2 cups. I always make the full quantity because I love having extra in my freezer, but if you'd prefer, you can make just the 2 cups required for any single recipe.

SCONE BASE

MAKES 8 cups (1.37kg/48oz)

INGREDIENTS

6 cups (810g/28.6oz) all-purpose
flour

3 tablespoons (36g/1.2oz) baking
powder

2 teaspoons salt

3 tablespoons (42g/1.5oz)
granulated sugar (optional)

1 cup/2 sticks (226g/8oz) unsalted
butter, frozen or very cold,
grated (see Tip on this page)

In a large bowl, whisk together the flour, baking powder, salt, and sugar. Gently stir in the frozen butter pieces, tossing them around to make sure they are all completely coated with the flour mixture. At this point you can refrigerate or freeze the base.

GRATING BUTTER

Cover a sheet pan with parchment paper. Place a large-hole box grater in the center of the pan. If your butter comes in 1-pound blocks, cut it into 4 pieces. Take one piece out of the freezer at a time. Roll one stick of butter in flour just to coat. Working quickly, grate the frozen or very cold butter, moving the grater across the pan as you go so that the butter does not clump into one pile. As soon as you are done with one piece, quickly continue grating the remaining pieces. Spread the shreds across the pan and place in the freezer.

MAKING AND SHAPING SCONES

Fold the dough over onto itself from back to front.

Determine the approximate size of the round using the width of your extended hand from pinky to thumb.

Cut the dough into 6 equal wedges.

The trick to flaky scones is to handle the dough as little as possible. The recipes in this chapter all use the same basic technique. Follow these simple steps and you will become a pro at making scones in no time.

1. Create a well in the flour mixture and add the wet ingredients. Stir only until the dough comes together.

2. Turn the dough out onto a lightly floured surface.

3. Using a bench scraper, fold the dough over onto itself from back to front. Give it a half turn and do it one more time.

4. Gently pat the dough into a 6- to 7-inch round about 1 inch thick. Use the width of your extended hand (pinky to thumb) to determine the approximate size of the round.

5. With a lightly floured chef's knife, cut the dough into 6 equal wedges.

6. Store the dough in a sealed plastic bag in the refrigerator for up to 5 days or in the freezer for up to 3 months.

APPLE CINNAMON SCONES

If you love apple pie, this is the scone for you. It has just the right touch of cinnamon to offset the sweet apple filling. If you're short on time, you can use canned apple pie filling, but be sure to drain it well so it doesn't add too much moisture.

MAKES 6 scones

INGREDIENTS

2 cups (342g/12 oz) Scone Base
(page 204)

¼ cup (50g/1.8oz) granulated sugar

½ teaspoon ground cinnamon

⅛ teaspoon grated nutmeg

1½ cups (300g/10.6oz) Apple Filling
(page 285) or store-bought apple
pie filling

½ cup (120g/4.2oz) heavy cream,
plus 1 to 2 tablespoons for brushing

1 egg

1 tablespoon coarse sanding sugar

1. Preheat the oven to 325°F. Line a baking sheet with parchment paper.

2. In a medium bowl, whisk together the scone base, granulated sugar, cinnamon, and nutmeg. Gently fold in the apple filling.

3. In a liquid measuring cup, whisk together the heavy cream and egg. Create a well in the flour mixture and gently stir in the cream and egg, stirring until it all comes together. Do not overmix. If you still have loose flour, you may need to add an additional tablespoon of cream.

4. Turn the dough out onto a lightly floured surface. Using a bench scraper, fold the dough over onto itself from back to front, give it half a turn, and repeat quickly until the dough is smooth and evenly incorporated. Do not overwork.

5. Gently pat the dough into a 6- to 7-inch round about 1 inch thick. With a lightly floured chef's knife, cut into 6 equal wedges.

6. Transfer to the prepared baking sheet, brush with the heavy cream, and sprinkle lightly with the sanding sugar.

7. Bake for 10 minutes. Rotate the pan front to back and continue baking for 8 to 10 minutes, or until golden brown.

8. Let the scones cool on a cooling rack for 10 to 15 minutes before serving.

BLUEBERRY-LEMON SCONES

Moist yet crumbly and loaded with blueberries, these scones are perfect for breakfast or afternoon tea. The lemon zest adds a welcome note of brightness. If you don't have fresh berries, you can use frozen ones straight from the freezer.

MAKES 6 scones

INGREDIENTS

2 cups (342g/12oz) Scone Base
  (page 204)

¼ cup (50g/1.8oz) granulated sugar

2 teaspoons grated lemon zest

1 cup (160g/5.7oz) fresh blueberries,
  rinsed and picked over for stems

2 teaspoons fresh lemon juice

½ cup (120g/4.2oz) heavy cream, plus
  2 tablespoons for brushing

1 egg, lightly beaten

2 tablespoons coarse sanding sugar

1. Preheat the oven to 325°F. Line a baking sheet with parchment paper.

2. In a medium bowl, whisk together the scone base, granulated sugar, and lemon zest. Gently fold in the blueberries.

3. In a liquid measuring cup, whisk together the lemon juice, heavy cream, and egg. Create a well in the flour mixture and gently stir in the cream and egg mixture until it all comes together. Do not overmix. If you still have loose flour, you may need to add an additional tablespoon of cream.

4. Turn the dough out onto a lightly floured surface. Using a bench scraper, fold the dough over onto itself from back to front, give it half a turn, and repeat quickly, until the dough is smooth and evenly incorporated. Do not overwork.

5. Gently pat the dough into a 6- to 7-inch round about 1 inch thick. With a lightly floured chef's knife, cut into 6 equal wedges.

6. Transfer to the prepared baking sheet, brush with the heavy cream, and sprinkle lightly with the sanding sugar.

7. Bake for 10 minutes. Rotate the pan front to back and continue baking for 8 to 10 minutes, or until golden brown.

8. Let the scones cool on a cooling rack for 10 to 15 minutes before serving.

FREEZING FRESH BERRIES

It's so wonderful to have access to local strawberries, raspberries, and blueberries, but they have a short shelf life and are very delicate. The good news is that they freeze so well. First, give them a quick rinse, then lay them out on paper towels to dry. Arrange them in a single layer on a baking sheet and freeze until firm. Once frozen, transfer to resealable freezer bags and freeze for up to 6 months. No need to thaw! Just add the frozen berries to any muffin, scone, pie, or crisp recipe.

CRANBERRY-PECAN SCONES

Cranberries add a pop of scarlet to these scones, which makes them ideal for a pretty holiday presentation. Use a food processor to quickly chop the cranberries—fresh or frozen cranberries both work well. If you can't find either, substitute dried cranberries that you reconstitute by soaking in boiling water for about 10 to 15 minutes, until they plump up.

MAKES 6 scones

INGREDIENTS

2 cups (342g/12 oz) Scone Base (page 204)

¼ cup (50g/1.8oz) granulated sugar

1 teaspoon grated orange zest

½ cup (50g/1.8oz) fresh cranberries, chopped

½ cup (58g/2oz) coarsely chopped pecans, lightly toasted (see Tip, page 288)

½ cup (120g/4.2oz) heavy cream, plus 2 tablespoons for brushing

1 egg

2 tablespoons coarse sanding sugar

1. Preheat the oven to 325°F. Line a baking sheet with parchment paper.

2. In a medium bowl, whisk together the scone base, granulated sugar, and orange zest. Gently fold in the chopped fresh cranberries and pecan pieces.

3. In a liquid measuring cup, whisk together the heavy cream and egg. Create a well in the flour mixture and gently stir in the cream and egg mixture until it all comes together. Do not overmix. If you still have loose flour, you may need to add an additional tablespoon of cream.

4. Turn the dough out onto a lightly floured surface. Using a bench scraper, fold the dough over onto itself from back to front, give it half a turn, and repeat quickly until the dough is smooth and evenly incorporated. Do not overwork.

5. Gently pat the dough into a 6- to 7-inch round about 1 inch thick. With a lightly floured chef's knife, cut into 6 equal wedges.

6. Transfer to the prepared baking sheet, brush with the heavy cream, and sprinkle lightly with the sanding sugar.

7. Bake for 10 minutes. Rotate the pan front to back and continue baking for 8 to 10 minutes, or until golden brown.

8. Let the scones cool on a cooling rack for 10 to 15 minutes before serving.

LEMON POPPY SCONES

There is something so wonderful about the combination of lemon and poppy seeds. The tart citrusy flavor is offset by the tiny, oily black seeds, which impart a subtle, nutty flavor and crunch. These are a crowd favorite at Magnolia Bakery and a personal favorite of mine, a lifelong lemon lover. They are delicious with or without the glaze, but I always prefer that extra hit of lemon.

MAKES 6 scones

INGREDIENTS

2 cups (342g/12 oz) Scone Base (page 204)

¼ cup (50g/1.8oz) granulated sugar

2 tablespoons (18g/0.7oz) poppy seeds

2 teaspoons grated lemon zest

1 egg, lightly beaten

2 teaspoons fresh lemon juice

½ cup (120g/4.2oz) heavy cream, plus 2 tablespoons for brushing

2 tablespoons coarse sanding sugar

FOR THE LEMON GLAZE

1 cup (125g/4.4oz) powdered sugar

1 teaspoon grated lemon zest

2 tablespoons fresh lemon juice

1 tablespoon whole milk

1. Preheat the oven to 350°F. Line a baking sheet with parchment paper.

2. In a medium bowl, whisk together the scone base, granulated sugar, poppy seeds, and lemon zest.

3. In a liquid measuring cup, whisk together the egg, lemon juice, and heavy cream. Create a well in the flour mixture and gently stir in the cream and egg mixture until it all comes together. Do not overmix. If you still have loose flour you may need to add an additional tablespoon of cream.

4. Turn the dough out onto a lightly floured surface. Using a bench scraper, fold the dough over onto itself from back to front, give it half a turn, and repeat quickly until the dough is smooth and evenly incorporated. Do not overwork.

5. Gently pat the dough into a 6- to 7-inch round about 1 inch thick. With a lightly floured chef's knife, cut the dough into 6 equal wedges.

6. Transfer to the prepared baking sheet and brush with the heavy cream and sprinkle with the sanding sugar.

7. Bake for 10 minutes. Rotate the pan front to back and continue baking for 8 to 10 minutes more, or until golden brown.

8. Let the scones cool on a cooling rack for 10 to 15 minutes before serving.

9. **MEANWHILE, MAKE THE GLAZE:** In a small bowl, whisk together the powdered sugar, lemon zest, lemon juice, and milk until smooth.

10. Before serving, drizzle the scones with the lemon glaze.

PEACH-RASPBERRY SCONES

When peaches are at their peak of ripeness, I look for every possible way to incorporate them into baked goods. Because they can go from ripe to overripe in a flash, don't wait to use them. While the pairing of peaches and raspberries seems like a natural combination, it's been attributed to French chef Auguste Escoffier, whose Peach Melba debuted in 1893.

MAKES 6 scones

INGREDIENTS

2 cups (342g/12 oz) Scone Base (page 204)

¼ cup (50g/1.8oz) granulated sugar

2 teaspoons grated lemon zest

½ cup (80g/2.8oz) sliced peeled peaches (cut ¼ inch thick)

¾ cup (100g/3.5oz) raspberries

1 egg, lightly beaten

2 teaspoons fresh lemon juice

½ cup (120g/4.2oz) heavy cream, plus 2 tablespoons for brushing

2 tablespoons coarse sanding sugar

1. Preheat the oven to 325°F. Line a baking sheet with parchment paper.

2. In a medium bowl, whisk together the scone base, granulated sugar, and lemon zest. Gently fold in the peach slices and raspberries.

3. In a liquid measuring cup, whisk together the egg, lemon juice, and heavy cream. Create a well in the flour mixture and gently stir in the cream and egg mixture until it all comes together. Do not overmix. If you still have loose flour, you may need to add an additional tablespoon of cream.

4. Turn the dough out onto a lightly floured surface. Using a bench scraper, fold the dough over onto itself from back to front, give it half a turn, and repeat quickly until the dough is smooth and evenly incorporated. Do not overwork.

5. Gently pat the dough into a 6- to 7-inch round about 1 inch thick. With a lightly floured chef's knife, cut the dough into 6 equal wedges.

6. Transfer to the prepared baking sheet, brush with the heavy cream, and sprinkle lightly with the sanding sugar.

7. Bake for 10 minutes. Rotate the pan front to back and continue baking for 8 to 10 minutes, or until golden brown.

8. Let the scones cool on a cooling rack for 10 to 15 minutes before serving.

PEAR-GINGER SCONES

Like peaches, pears can go soft quickly. If you have a couple of perfectly ripe pears and some scone base in your freezer, these come together in a snap. If you don't have any candied ginger, you can substitute ¼ teaspoon dried ginger, though it doesn't have the same sweet heat.

MAKES 6 scones

INGREDIENTS

2 cups (342g/12 oz) Scone Base (page 204)

¼ cup (50g/1.8oz) granulated sugar

1½ cups (283g/10oz) ½-inch cubes peeled pear (about 2 Bartlett pears)

½ cup (58g/2oz) candied ginger, diced

½ cup (120g/4.2oz) heavy cream, plus 2 tablespoons for brushing

1 egg

2 tablespoons coarse sanding sugar

1. Preheat the oven to 325°F. Line a baking sheet with parchment paper.

2. In a medium bowl, whisk together the scone base and granulated sugar. Gently fold in the cubed pears and candied ginger.

3. In a liquid measuring cup, whisk together the heavy cream and egg. Create a well in the flour mixture and gently stir in the cream and egg mixture until it all comes together. Do not overmix. If you still have loose flour, you may need to add an additional tablespoon of cream.

4. Turn the dough out onto a lightly floured surface. Using a bench scraper, fold the dough over onto itself from back to front, give it half a turn, and repeat quickly until the dough is smooth and evenly incorporated. Do not overwork.

5. Gently pat the dough into a 6- to 7-inch round about 1 inch thick. With a lightly floured chef's knife, cut the dough into 6 equal wedges.

6. Transfer to the prepared baking sheet, brush with the heavy cream, and sprinkle lightly with the sanding sugar.

7. Bake for 10 minutes. Rotate the pan front to back and continue baking for 8 to 10 minutes, or until golden brown.

8. Let the scones cool on a cooling rack for 10 to 15 minutes before serving.

PUMPKIN CHOCOLATE CHIP SCONES

Though pumpkin and chocolate may not jump out at you as a match made in heaven, they share a sweet, earthy richness that is quite delicious. Aromatic, warming spices add another dimension that brings these moist muffins to life.

MAKES 6 scones

INGREDIENTS

2¾ cups (371g/13.1oz) all-purpose flour

⅓ cup (66g/2.3oz) light brown sugar

1 tablespoon (12g) baking powder

¾ teaspoon salt

¾ teaspoon ground cinnamon

¼ teaspoon ground allspice

¼ teaspoon ground ginger

¼ teaspoon grated nutmeg

½ cup/1 stick (113g/4oz) unsalted butter, very cold or frozen, grated (see Tip, page 204)

1 cup (180g/6.3oz) semisweet chocolate chips

⅔ cup (150g/5.3oz) canned unsweetened pumpkin puree (preferably Libby's)

¼ cup (74g/2.6oz) dark maple syrup

1 egg

2 tablespoons heavy cream

2 tablespoons coarse sanding sugar

1. Preheat the oven to 350°F. Line a sheet pan with parchment paper.

2. In a large bowl, whisk together the flour, brown sugar, baking powder, salt, and spices.

3. Add the grated butter pieces, gently tossing them to make sure they are completely coated with the flour mixture. Stir in the chocolate chips and gently toss to coat.

4. In a liquid measuring cup, whisk together the pumpkin puree, maple syrup, and egg until smooth.

5. Create a well in the flour mixture and gently stir in the pumpkin mixture until it all comes together. Do not overmix. If you still have loose flour, you may need to add a tablespoon of cream.

6. Turn the dough out onto a lightly floured surface. Using a bench scraper, fold the dough over onto itself from back to front, give it half a turn, and repeat quickly until the dough is smooth and evenly incorporated. Do not overwork.

7. Gently pat the dough into a 6- to 7-inch round about 1 inch thick. With a lightly floured chef's knife, cut the dough into 6 equal wedges.

8. Transfer to the prepared baking sheet, brush with the heavy cream, and sprinkle lightly with the sanding sugar.

9. Bake for 10 to 12 minutes. Rotate the pan front to back and continue baking for 10 to 12 minutes, or until lightly golden brown. To test for doneness, stick a cake tester in the center; if it comes out clean, the scone is done.

10. Let the scones cool on a cooling rack for 10 to 15 minutes before serving.

VARIATION

MAPLE-GLAZED PUMPKIN CHOCOLATE CHIP SCONES: Omit the coarse sanding sugar on top. Make the maple glaze from Maple Pecan Scones (page 225). Once cool, drizzle the scones with the glaze.

STRAWBERRY SCONES

There is nothing better than sun-kissed strawberries picked fresh from the field. They tend to be smaller and sweeter than store-bought and will have a much shorter shelf life. Consider making several batches of these scones and freezing some for later. While you're at it, pick some extra berries and freeze those, too, to use in all the other wonderful strawberry desserts you can't wait to make.

MAKES 6 scones

INGREDIENTS

2 cups (342g/12 oz) Scone Base (page 204)

¼ cup (50g/1.8oz) granulated sugar

1 cup (175g/6.1oz) ½-inch chunks of strawberries, hulled

1 egg, lightly beaten

2 teaspoons fresh lemon juice

½ cup (120g/4.2oz) heavy cream, plus 2 tablespoons for brushing

2 tablespoons coarse sanding sugar

1. Preheat the oven to 325°F. Line a baking sheet with parchment paper.

2. In a medium bowl, whisk together the scone base and granulated sugar. Gently fold in the strawberries.

3. In a liquid measuring cup, whisk together the egg, lemon juice, and heavy cream. Create a well in the flour mixture and gently stir in the cream and egg mixture until it all comes together. Do not overmix. If you still have loose flour, you may need to add an additional tablespoon of cream.

4. Turn the dough out onto a lightly floured surface. Using a bench scraper, fold the dough over onto itself from back to front, give it half a turn, and repeat quickly until the dough is smooth and evenly incorporated. Do not overwork.

5. Gently pat the dough into a 6- to 7-inch round about 1 inch thick. With a lightly floured chef's knife, cut the dough into 6 equal wedges.

6. Transfer to the prepared baking sheet, brush with the heavy cream, and sprinkle lightly with the sanding sugar.

7. Bake for 10 minutes. Rotate the pan front to back and continue baking for 8 to 10 minutes, until golden brown.

8. Let the scones cool on a cooling rack for 10 to 15 minutes before serving.

CHERRY CHOCOLATE ALMOND SCONES

The classic combo of cherry and chocolate inspired me to make these scones (and my mother loves them). I added almonds here because they also pair beautifully with cherries. Turns out they're in the same family. You'll notice that a touch of almond extract really enhances the cherry flavor.

MAKES 6 scones

INGREDIENTS

2½ cups (337g/11.9oz) all-purpose flour

¼ cup (50g/1.8oz) granulated sugar

1 teaspoon baking powder

¼ teaspoon baking soda

½ teaspoon salt

⅔ cup (150g/5.3oz) very cold unsalted butter, cut into small pieces (or freeze the butter and grate it; see Tip, page 204)

½ cup (75g/2.6oz) dried cherries

½ cup (90 g/3.2oz) semisweet chocolate chunks

½ cup (60 g/2.1oz) slivered almonds

1 cup (240g/8.5oz) buttermilk

¼ teaspoon pure vanilla extract

¼ teaspoon almond extract

2 tablespoons heavy cream

2 tablespoons coarse sanding sugar

1. Preheat the oven to 325°F. Line a baking sheet with parchment paper.

2. In a medium bowl, whisk together the flour, sugar, baking powder, baking soda, and salt. Add the butter, gently tossing to make sure all the pieces are completely coated with the flour mixture.

3. In another bowl, combine the dried cherries, chocolate chunks, and almonds. Stir gently into the flour-butter mixture.

4. In a liquid measuring cup, whisk together the buttermilk, vanilla, and almond extract. Create a well in the flour mixture and gently stir in the buttermilk mixture, until it all comes together. Do not overmix. If you still have loose flour, you may need to add an additional tablespoon of cream.

5. Turn the dough out onto a lightly floured surface. Using a bench scraper, fold the dough over onto itself from back to front, give it half a turn, and repeat quickly until the dough is smooth and evenly incorporated. Do not overwork.

6. Gently pat the dough into a 6- to 7-inch round about 1 inch thick. With a lightly floured chef's knife, cut the dough into 6 equal wedges.

7. Transfer to the prepared baking sheet, brush with the heavy cream, and sprinkle lightly with the sanding sugar.

8. Bake for 10 minutes. Rotate the pan front to back and continue baking for 8 to 10 minutes, or until golden brown.

9. Let the scones cool on a cooling rack for 10 to 15 minutes before serving.

MAPLE PECAN SCONES

When I was pregnant with my first child, I craved the maple pecan scones at a certain well-known coffee shop. They were big, not too sweet, and loaded with nuts. I wound up developing my own recipe, so I could have them whenever I needed a fix. These are smothered with a maple glaze, which I recommend you apply liberally.

MAKES 6 scones

INGREDIENTS

2 cups (270g/9.6oz) all-purpose flour

¼ cup (50g/1.8oz) light brown sugar

1 tablespoon (12g) baking powder

1 teaspoon ground cinnamon

½ teaspoon salt

½ cup/1 stick (113g/4oz) very cold unsalted butter, cut into little pieces (or frozen and grated; see Tip, page 204)

1 cup (125g/4.4oz) toasted pecan pieces (see Tip, page 288)

1 egg

¼ cup (75g/2.6oz) dark maple syrup

¼ cup (60g/2.1oz) heavy cream, plus 1 tablespoon for brushing

1 tablespoon dark maple syrup

FOR THE MAPLE GLAZE

½ cup (62g/2oz) powdered sugar, sifted

¼ cup (75g/2.6oz) dark maple syrup

1. Preheat the oven to 350°F. Line a baking sheet with parchment paper.

2. In a medium bowl, whisk together the flour, brown sugar, baking powder, cinnamon, and salt. Add the butter, gently tossing the pieces to make sure they are completely coated with the flour mixture. Add the pecan pieces and toss to combine.

3. In a liquid measuring cup, whisk together the egg, maple syrup, and ¼ cup (60g/2.1oz) of the cream. Create a well in the flour mixture and gently stir in the egg mixture until it all comes together. Do not overmix. If you still have loose flour, you may need to add an additional tablespoon of cream.

4. Turn the dough out onto a lightly floured surface. Using a bench scraper, fold the dough over onto itself from back to front, give it half a turn, and repeat quickly until the dough is smooth and evenly incorporated. Do not overwork.

5. Gently pat the dough into a 6- to 7-inch round about 1 inch thick. With a lightly floured chef's knife, cut the dough into 6 equal wedges.

6. Transfer to the prepared baking sheet. Combine the remaining 1 tablespoon heavy cream and the maple syrup. Lightly brush the scones.

7. Bake for 10 minutes. Rotate the pan front to back and continue baking for 8 to 10 minutes, or until lightly golden brown.

8. Let the scones cool slightly on a cooling rack while you make the glaze.

9. **MAKE THE GLAZE:** In a small bowl, whisk together the powdered sugar and maple syrup to make a smooth, pourable glaze.

10. While the scones are still warm, slowly pour the glaze to completely cover them. Cool until the glaze hardens.

CHAPTER EIGHT

ICEBOX DESSERTS

Icebox desserts have been around since World War I, when new packaged ingredients gave housewives dessert options that needed little-to-no baking time. Many of these grocery store staples included a recipe on the back of the box. (Remember the "mock apple pie" on the box of Ritz crackers?) Among the most popular was the Chocolate Refrigerator Roll on the box of Nabisco Famous Chocolate Wafers. Layers of chocolate wafer cookies and whipped cream are assembled and then chilled, no baking required. This is a great summer dessert option, and you don't have to worry about how long you cream the butter or whether your cake will rise.

Icebox desserts have always been popular at Magnolia Bakery, from our signature (and trademarked) Icebox Cake to the peanut butter icebox pies and bars. Building on this theme, I added a few new ones to our repertoire, including tart Key Lime Bars with a whipped cream topping and Grasshopper Pie Icebox Bars that taste like thin chocolate mint candy.

TIPS FOR MAKING PERFECT ICEBOX DESSERTS

Many icebox desserts call for whipped cream, either in the main event or as a topping or garnish. I recommend using pasteurized (not ultra-pasteurized) heavy cream. Ultra-pasteurized heavy cream has been heated to 280°F and above to extend its shelf life and won't whip up as fluffy as just pasteurized. Make sure you purchase heavy cream, not whipping cream.

If it's hot in your kitchen, you'll never get fluffy whipped cream unless you chill all the elements involved. Before you begin, place your bowl and beaters in the freezer for 5 to 10 minutes. Start mixing on low speed so that you don't splash all over. As soon as the cream starts to thicken, increase the speed and whip until soft peaks form. Be careful not to overwhip or you will wind up with butter.

The cream cheese you purchase also makes a difference. Don't skimp on quality, as cheaper cream cheese can be wet. Low-fat cream cheese doesn't have the flavor and richness needed for these recipes, so always use full-fat cream cheese (preferably Philadelphia brand).

ICEBOX CAKE

A classic icebox cake has only two ingredients: rich chocolate wafers and whipped cream. To make the cake, carefully layer the cookies and cream (I tell you how!) and place in the fridge for a few hours to soften up the cookies and meld the flavors. The result is a remarkably delicious, delicately textured dessert. While you can use the Nabisco Famous Chocolate Wafers, this cake is much better if you make the wafers yourself. Your efforts will really pay off.

SERVES 6 to 12

INGREDIENTS

4 cups (903g/32oz) heavy cream

3 tablespoons (37.5g/1.3oz) granulated sugar

1 tablespoon pure vanilla extract

70 Chocolate Wafer Cookies (page 231)

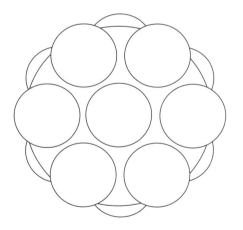

Use 7 wafers on each cake layer: Place 1 at center and 6 around the perimeter. Position each wafer on the perimeter directly between 2 wafers in the row below.

1. Place a 10-inch flat serving plate on a cake turner, if you have one, or the counter.

2. In a stand mixer with the whisk, start on low speed and whip the heavy cream. Slowly add the sugar and vanilla and continue mixing for 1 minute. Turn the mixer speed to medium and whip until medium peaks form, 4 to 8 minutes more.

3. To assemble, use an offset spatula to spread about 2 tablespoons of the whipped cream onto the center of the plate in a round about 7 inches in diameter. Place 7 wafer cookies on top of the round of cream, placing one in the middle and 6 around the edge, making sure the wafers stick out slightly from the edge of the whipped cream as shown in the diagram.

4. For the next layer, spread ¾ cup of the whipped cream on top of the wafers, leaving just the edges of the wafers visible. Use 7 more wafers, this time placing the wafers directly in between the previously placed wafers. It's like building a brick house. Follow the diagram.

5. Continue following these steps, alternating the wafers in the exact same pattern, until there are 10 layers of wafers and whipped cream. For the top layer of the icebox cake, use 1¾ cups of whipped cream and spread evenly over the top of the cake.

6. Place in a cake saver. If you don't have a cake saver, cover loosely with plastic wrap. Refrigerate for at least 5 hours before serving.

Use a scoop to portion the dough.

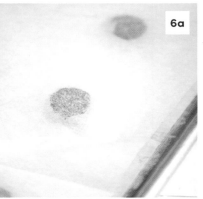

Cover the dough with parchment.

Gently press down the dough balls with a flat-bottomed measuring cup.

CHOCOLATE WAFER COOKIES

Why buy packaged wafer cookies when you can make your own? These flavorful cookies are essential for our beloved Icebox Cake (page 228). Though they require a bit of work, you can make a lot at once and store them in the fridge or freezer for the next icebox cake. Each cake uses 70 cookies and this recipe makes double that amount.

MAKES about 140 cookies

INGREDIENTS

4½ cups (607g/21.6) all-purpose flour

1 cup (120g/4.2oz) unsweetened dark cocoa powder (22 to 24%), sifted

4½ cups (900g/31.9oz) sugar

4½ teaspoons baking soda

1½ teaspoons baking powder

2 teaspoons salt

2¼ cups/4½ sticks (508g/18oz) unsalted butter, cut into 1-inch pieces, at room temperature

3 eggs

TIP

When you reuse a baking sheet for the next batch, be sure to let it cool before you place the cookies on them, and line it with a new piece of parchment.

1. Preheat the oven to 325°F. Line two to four (depending on how many you have) baking sheets with parchment paper.

2. In a stand mixer with the paddle, combine the flour, cocoa, sugar, baking soda, baking powder, and salt. Mix on low for 30 seconds, until the mixture looks like sand.

3. On low speed, add the butter pieces a little at a time. Beat until the mixture resembles damp soil, 3 to 4 minutes. Turn the mixer off until you are ready to add the eggs.

4. Whisk the eggs lightly, then add to the cocoa-butter mixture on low. Beat until the mixture comes together into a dough, about 15 seconds or until there are no streaks of flour.

5. Use a small (#70) ½-ounce scoop to portion the dough and place on the prepared baking sheets, 3 across and 4 down, for a total of 12 per baking sheet. You will ultimately need to bake 12 sheets of cookies.

6. Cover the dough balls with a piece of parchment paper and use a flat-bottomed measuring cup to gently press down (not smash) the dough balls to flatten them. Remove the top parchment.

7. Bake two sheets at a time for 14 minutes, rotating top to bottom, front to back halfway through baking time, until the cookies look crisp but are not overbaked. Repeat until all the cookies are baked.

8. Cool completely. Store in an airtight container for up to 2 weeks. These can be wrapped tightly and kept on the counter for several weeks, or they can be wrapped in foil and zipped into a resealable plastic bag before storing them in the freezer for up to 3 months.

BLUEBERRY JAMBOREE

This is among my favorite Magnolia Bakery desserts. The nutty crust, the sweet, smooth cream cheese, and the lemon-spiked blueberry filling all come together in the perfect bite. Make this recipe in July, when blueberry season is at its peak. You can bake the crust in a pie pan or in a square pan and serve it in squares. Either way, you might as well double the recipe—that's how much of a crowd-pleaser it's sure to be.

MAKES one 9-inch pie or one 8 × 8-inch pan; serves 6–8

INGREDIENTS

FOR THE PECAN SHORTBREAD CRUST

⅓ cup (75g/2.6oz) unsalted butter, melted

1 cup (135g/4.8oz) all-purpose flour

½ cup (58g/2oz) coarsely chopped pecans, lightly toasted (see Tip, page 288)

FOR THE CREAM CHEESE LAYER

1 cup (240g/8.5oz) heavy cream

1 cup (226g/8oz) full-fat cream cheese (preferably Philadelphia brand), at room temperature

1 cup (125g/4.4oz) powdered sugar, sifted

FOR THE TOPPING

About 3 cups Blueberry Filling (page 285)

1. Preheat the oven to 325°F. Lightly butter a 9-inch pie pan or an 8 × 8-inch baking pan.

2. **MAKE THE SHORTBREAD CRUST:** In a medium bowl, stir together the butter, flour, and pecans with a wooden spoon until it all just comes together. Be very careful not to overwork the dough.

3. Press the dough into the prepared pan. Bake for 12 to 15 minutes, or until fragrant and lightly golden brown. Cool on a rack. While the crust is cooling, make the filling. The crust can be made ahead and wrapped in plastic wrap for up to 3 days.

4. **MAKE THE CREAM CHEESE LAYER:** In a stand mixer with the whisk, whip the heavy cream on medium speed until stiff peaks form, 3 to 5 minutes. Transfer the cream to a bowl. Set aside.

5. In the same mixer bowl (you don't need to clean it) with the paddle, beat the cream cheese on medium-high speed until smooth and creamy. Scrape down the bottom and sides of the bowl. Add the powdered sugar and beat on medium until smooth and creamy, about 1 minute. Scrape down the bottom and sides of the bowl again.

6. Remove the bowl from the mixer. Use a rubber spatula to gently fold the whipped cream into the cream cheese mixture. Using an offset spatula, evenly spread the cream cheese filling over the cooled crust.

7. Top with the blueberry filling. Cover with plastic wrap and refrigerate for 2 to 4 hours or overnight until set.

GRASSHOPPER PIE ICEBOX BARS

This cool and refreshing dessert is a good choice for a hot summer day. The mint filling, so bright and fluffy, is anchored by the rich, dark chocolatey crust. The flavor is reminiscent of after-dinner mints, but the presentation is really quite elegant.

MAKES one 9 × 13-inch pan; serves 12

INGREDIENTS

FOR THE CRUST

2½ cups (320g/11.3oz) chocolate wafer crumbs, store-bought or homemade (page 283)

½ cup (100g/3.5oz) light brown sugar

½ cup/1 stick (133g/4oz) unsalted butter, melted

FOR THE FILLING

1 cup (240g/8.5oz) heavy cream

1 cup (240g 8.5oz) full-fat cream cheese (preferably Philadelphia brand), at room temperature

1 teaspoon peppermint extract

½ drop green gel food coloring (optional)

1 cup (125g/4.4oz) powdered sugar, sifted

¼ cup (49g/1.4oz) mini chocolate chips

FOR TOPPING

1 cup heavy cream, whipped to soft peaks

¼ cup (40g/1.4oz) mini chocolate chips, for garnish

1. **MAKE THE CRUST:** Preheat the oven to 325°F. Line a 9 × 13-inch pan with parchment paper leaving overhang on the sides (see Lining the Pan, page 141).

2. In a large bowl, stir together the chocolate wafer crumbs and brown sugar. Add the melted butter and stir until a wet crumb forms. Dump the crumbs into the prepared pan. Shape the crust by pressing it into the bottom of the pan.

3. Bake for 8 to 10 minutes, or until fragrant and lightly toasted. Let cool to room temperature.

4. **MEANWHILE, MAKE THE FILLING:** In a stand mixer with the whisk, whip the heavy cream on medium speed until stiff peaks form, 3 to 5 minutes. Transfer the cream to a bowl. Set aside.

5. In the same mixer bowl (you don't need to clean it) with the paddle, beat the cream cheese on medium-high speed until smooth and creamy. Add the peppermint extract and the green gel food coloring (if using—a tiny bit goes a long way). Mix until combined. Scrape down the bottom and sides of the bowl. Add the powdered sugar and beat on medium until smooth and creamy, about 1 minute. Scrape down the bottom and sides of the bowl.

6. Remove the bowl from the mixer and with a rubber spatula gently fold the whipped cream into the cream cheese mixture. Add the ¼ cup mini chips. and carefully fold into the filling. It is very important that the filling be light and fluffy.

7. Using an offset spatula, spread the cream cheese filling into the prepared crust. Refrigerate for 2 to 4 hours until completely set.

8. Cut into a 3 × 4 grid (for 12 bars). Top each bar with a large dollop of whipped cream and sprinkle with mini chips.

KEY LIME PIE BARS

Key lime pie is renowned as a Southern dessert, but Northerners also hold it very dear. There is an ongoing argument as to its origins, whether from the Florida Keys or from New York (though we know where the limes come from). Regardless, its sweet tartness is a unifying factor that shines in this popular bar. In Japan and Korea, where Magnolia Bakery has franchises, I swapped out the Key lime for yuzu, a local aromatic citrus. It's now an international favorite.

MAKES one 9 × 13-inch pan; 12 bars

INGREDIENTS

2 cups (220g/7.8oz) graham cracker crumbs

½ cup/1 stick (113g/4oz) unsalted butter, melted

3 (14-ounce) cans sweetened condensed milk

12 egg yolks

2 cups (500g/17.6oz) Nellie & Joe's Key lime juice

3 tablespoons grated lime zest (2 to 3 limes), plus more for garnish

2 cups (480g/17oz) heavy cream, whipped to soft peaks

1. Preheat the oven to 325°F.

2. In a medium bowl, combine the graham cracker crumbs and melted butter. Mix until thoroughly combined. Dump the crumbs into a 9 × 13-inch pan and press firmly to form a crust on the bottom of the pan.

3. Bake for 10 to 12 minutes, or until set and fragrant. Set aside to cool. Leave the oven on. The crust can be made ahead and wrapped in plastic wrap for up to 3 days.

4. In a large bowl, whisk together the sweetened condensed milk, egg yolks, and Key lime juice. Fold in the lime zest just to incorporate. Do not overmix. Carefully pour the filling into the prepared crust.

5. Return to the oven and bake for 30 to 35 minutes, or until the middle has set and is no longer jiggly.

6. Let cool on a cooling rack for 20 minutes. Refrigerate for at least 2 hours to completely set.

7. Using an offset spatula, spread the whipped cream over the bars. Cut into a 3 × 4 grid (for 12 bars) and garnish with lime zest.

PEANUT BUTTER ICEBOX BARS

When we were kids, my brother and I created a game with the jar of peanut butter that was always in the cupboard. Whoever opened a new jar first would carve a heart into the top layer of peanut butter. If the next user disturbed the heart, it meant you loved that person. Although it's almost impossible not to touch the heart, we always gave it our best. This recipe asks you to dig deep into your jar of peanut butter. It's been a Magnolia Bakery favorite for years and I find it absolutely irresistible. Making it into a bar allowed me to balance the ratio of crust to filling, because it really is all about the filling.

MAKES one 9 × 13-inch pan;
12 to 24 bars

INGREDIENTS

FOR THE CRUST

2½ cups (300g/10.6oz) Nilla wafer crumbs

½ cup (100g/3.5oz) light brown sugar

⅔ cup/1⅓ sticks (150g/5.3oz) unsalted butter, melted

FOR THE FILLING

1 cup (240g/8.5oz) heavy cream

1½ cups (340g/12oz) full-fat cream cheese (preferably Philadelphia brand), at room temperature

¾ cup (198g/7.7oz) Skippy creamy peanut butter

¼ cup (31g/1oz) powdered sugar, sifted

2 teaspoons pure vanilla extract

¼ cup (70g/2.4oz) caramel sauce, store-bought or homemade (page 287)

FOR THE TOPPING

1 cup (252g/9oz) chopped (¼-inch pieces) Reese's Peanut Butter Cups

¼ cup (30g/1oz) peanuts, finely chopped

1. Preheat the oven to 325°F.

2. **MAKE THE CRUST:** In a large bowl, stir together the cookie crumbs and brown sugar. Add the melted butter and mix with a wooden spoon until a wet crumb forms. Dump the crumbs into a 9 × 13-inch pan. Shape the crust by pressing a flat-bottomed cup into the bottom of the pan, being sure to get into the corners.

3. Bake for 10 to 12 minutes, or until fragrant and set. Let cool to room temperature. The crust can be made ahead and wrapped in plastic wrap for up to 3 days.

4. **MEANWHILE, MAKE THE FILLING:** In a stand mixer with the whisk, whip the heavy cream on medium speed until stiff peaks form, 3 to 5 minutes. Transfer the cream to a bowl. Set aside.

5. In the same mixer bowl (you don't need to clean it) with the paddle, beat the cream cheese on medium speed until smooth and creamy, about 3 minutes. Scrape down the bottom and sides of the bowl. Add the peanut butter, powdered sugar, and vanilla and beat until light and creamy, about 5 minutes. Remove the bowl from the mixer and gently fold in the whipped cream until completely combined and light and fluffy.

6. With a mini-offset spatula, spread the caramel in a thin layer on the top of the cooled crust. Using an offset spatula, spread the cream cheese filling over the caramel. To garnish, sprinkle the peanut butter cup pieces and the peanuts all over the top.

7. Refrigerate for 2 to 4 hours, or overnight, until thoroughly set. Cut in a 3 × 4 grid (for 12 bars) or a 4 × 6 grid (for 24 bars).

PUMPKIN ICEBOX PIE

Because fall takes our taste buds to a new place, I decided to add a pumpkin icebox pie to the Magnolia Bakery lineup. This creamy pie has a gingersnap crust and is beautifully decorated with sugared cranberries. It's the perfect no-bake pie for any holiday (especially when the oven is always filled with turkey and a million side dishes).

MAKES one 9-inch pie; serves 6 to 8

INGREDIENTS

1½ cups (340g/12oz) full-fat cream cheese (preferably Philadelphia brand), at room temperature

½ cup (100g/3.5oz) light brown sugar

½ cup (62g/2oz) powdered sugar, sifted

1 teaspoon pure vanilla extract

½ teaspoon ground cinnamon

½ teaspoon ground cloves

½ teaspoon ground ginger

⅛ teaspoon grated nutmeg

2 cups (450g/16oz) canned unsweetened pumpkin puree (preferably Libby's)

¼ cup (72g/2.5oz) sweetened condensed milk

Gingersnap Crust (page 282)

FOR SERVING

1 cup (240g/8.5oz) heavy cream

¼ cup (28.7g/1oz) coarsely chopped pecans, lightly toasted (see Tip, page 288) or Candied Pecans (page 288)

Sugared Cranberries (optional; page 288)

1. In a stand mixer with the paddle, beat the cream cheese on medium speed until smooth and creamy, about 3 minutes. Scrape down the bottom and sides of the bowl. Add the brown sugar, powdered sugar, vanilla, and spices and beat until light and creamy, about 5 minutes. Scrape down the bottom and sides of the bowl. Add the pumpkin and the sweetened condensed milk and mix about 1 minute more, until fully incorporated. Remove the bowl from the mixer and scrape down the paddle, bottom, and sides.

2. Spread the cream cheese filling in the cooled crust. Smooth the cream cheese a little, leaving the top slightly rounded.

3. Cover with plastic wrap and refrigerate for at least 5 hours or overnight to set.

4. Just before serving, in a stand mixer with the whisk, whip the heavy cream on medium speed until stiff peaks form, 3 to 5 minutes. Transfer the whipped cream to a piping bag and dollop whipped cream around the perimeter of the pie. To decorate as in the photo, top each dollop with a sugared cranberry. Sprinkle the center of the pie with chopped nuts or candied pecans.

CHOCOLATE PUDDING PIE

This classic pudding pie is rich and full-bodied—a no-bake dessert destined to conquer any chocolate-lover's heart. The luscious chocolate pudding is also wonderful on its own, maybe topped with whipped cream, and can also be layered with cake and whipped cream to create Chocolate Pudding Parfaits (see page 244).

MAKES one 9-inch pie; serves 6 to 8

INGREDIENTS

2 cups (400g/14oz) granulated sugar

1 cup (57g/2.5oz) unsweetened dark cocoa powder (22 to 24%), sifted

½ cup (68g/2.4oz) cornstarch, sifted

½ teaspoon salt

6¼ cups (1.5kg/52.9oz) whole milk

¾ cup (135g/4.8oz) semisweet chocolate chips or shaved dark chocolate

2 tablespoons pure vanilla extract

Chocolate Wafer Crumb Crust (page 283)

FOR SERVING

2 cups (480g/17oz) heavy cream

¼ cup (40g/1.4oz) chocolate shavings or mini chocolate chips

1. In a large pot, whisk together the sugar, cocoa, cornstarch, and salt until combined. Whisk in the milk. Set the pot over medium-high heat and cook, whisking constantly, until the mixture thickens and comes to a boil, 5 to 6 minutes. Once the mixture starts to boil, whisk 1 more minute and then remove from the heat. The mixture should be very thick.

2. Whisk in the chocolate chips and vanilla and continue whisking until smooth.

3. Pour the pudding into the cooled pie crust. Let cool slightly, then cover with plastic wrap, touching the surface of the pudding so that a skin doesn't form. Refrigerate for 4 hours, until completely set.

4. When ready to serve, in a stand mixer with the whisk, whip the heavy cream on low speed for 1 minute, then increase the speed to medium-high and continue until soft peaks form, about 2 to 3 minutes more.

5. Decorate the pie with the whipped cream and sprinkle with the chocolate shavings or mini chocolate chips.

CHOCOLATE PUDDING PARFAITS

Parfaits are so pretty and very easy to prepare ahead of time, which makes them convenient for parties and picnics. Use the cutest vintage glassware or jars that fit a single serving. Each one gets layered with slices of cake, pudding, and whipped cream, all sprinkled with mini chocolate chips.

MAKES 6 or 8 parfaits (depending on what size container you use)

INGREDIENTS

FOR THE CHOCOLATE PUDDING

1 cup (200g/7.1oz) granulated sugar

½ cup (60g/2.1oz) unsweetened dark cocoa powder (22 to 24%), sifted

¼ cup (30g/1oz) cornstarch, sifted

¼ teaspoon salt

3 cups (1.5kg/52.9oz) whole milk

½ cup (90g/3.2oz) semisweet chocolate chips

1 tablespoon pure vanilla extract

FOR ASSEMBLY

2 cups (480g/17oz) heavy cream

6 or 8 Super-Rich Chocolate Cupcakes (page 79), depending on how many servings

½ cup (80g/2.8oz) mini chocolate chips

1. **MAKE THE CHOCOLATE PUDDING:** In a large pot, whisk together the sugar, cocoa, cornstarch, and salt until combined. Whisk in the milk. Set the pot over medium-high heat and cook, whisking constantly, until the mixture thickens and comes to a boil, 5 to 6 minutes. Once the mixture starts to boil, whisk 1 more minute and then remove from the heat. The mixture should be very thick.

2. Whisk in the chocolate and vanilla and continue whisking until smooth.

3. Pour the pudding into a bowl. Let cool slightly, then cover with plastic wrap, touching the surface of the pudding so a skin doesn't form. Refrigerate for 1 hour, until the pudding is no longer warm but not completely set.

4. **TO ASSEMBLE:** In a stand mixer with the whisk, whip the heavy cream on low speed for 1 minute, then increase the speed to medium-high and continue until soft peaks form, 2 to 3 minutes.

5. Cut the cupcakes in half. Place the bottom of a cupcake into each of six or eight decorative glass cups or jars.

6. If making 8 servings, scoop in ¼ cup pudding, followed by ¼ cup whipped cream. If making 6 servings, increase to ⅓ cup for each layer. Sprinkle each with 1 teaspoon mini chips. Top with the other half of the cupcake and repeat with ¼ cup (or ⅓ cup) each pudding and whipped cream. Sprinkle with the remaining mini chocolate chips.

7. Refrigerate for at least 1 hour before serving.

CHAPTER NINE

BANANA PUDDING

True Magnolia Bakery insiders are deeply loyal to the banana pudding. Since opening our first shop in 1996, this pudding has been our not-so-well-kept secret. We actually sell more than a million containers of it every year! Our banana pudding is so beloved that we created a special food holiday in its honor. Since 2014, we've been celebrating National Banana Pudding Day on the last Thursday of August.

Until recently, we offered only the classic version—layers of vanilla pudding, vanilla wafers, and bananas. A couple of years ago, we began adding new flavors we love. The roster now includes more than a dozen versions that we rotate in our stores, including chocolate hazelnut, salted caramel, pumpkin-gingersnap, peanut butter, and java chip. We've even created special flavors for our stores around the world, such as choc-nut in the Philippines and lotus in the Middle East.

In this chapter, you'll find our recipe for the classic banana pudding along with some of our most popular specialty flavors. They all look beautiful in a large trifle bowl or you can create individual portions in small glass jars or mini trifle bowls. Individual portions are more time-consuming, but make a lovely presentation for a dinner party. Banana pudding is even presentable in a casserole dish to be scooped tableside. The number of servings depends on the size of your portions. If this is the only dessert offered, it may serve 8 people. If it's part of a dessert buffet, it could serve up to 16 people.

MAGNOLIA BAKERY'S FAMOUS BANANA PUDDING

Banana pudding has been around since the late 1800s, when faster steam ships meant bananas could make their way to US ports. It was first made with sponge cake but by the 1920s, cake was replaced with vanilla wafers. For this recipe, I use Nabisco Nilla wafers and strongly recommend you don't make any substitutions to ensure you get the crave-worthy texture of this iconic dessert.

MAKES 4 to 5 quarts; serves up to 16

INGREDIENTS

1 (14oz) can sweetened condensed milk

1½ cups (360g/12.7oz) ice-cold water

1 (3.4oz) package instant vanilla pudding mix (preferably Jell-O brand)

3 cups (720g/25.5oz) heavy cream

1 (11oz) box Nilla wafers

4 to 5 ripe bananas, sliced

1. In a stand mixer with the whisk, beat the condensed milk and water on medium speed until well combined, about 1 minute. Add the pudding mix and beat until there are no lumps and the mixture is smooth, about 2 minutes. Transfer the mixture to a medium bowl, cover, and refrigerate until firm, at least 1 hour or overnight.

2. In a stand mixer with the whisk, whip the heavy cream on medium speed for about 1 minute, until the cream starts to thicken, then increase the speed to medium-high and whip until stiff peaks form. Be careful not to overwhip.

3. With the mixer running on low speed, add the pudding mixture a spoonful at a time. Mix until well blended and no streaks of pudding remain.

4. To assemble, select a trifle bowl or a wide glass bowl with a 4- to 5-quart capacity, or individual serving bowls.

5. Saving 4 to 5 cookies for the garnish on top, begin assembly. Spread one-quarter of the pudding over the bottom and layer with one-third of the cookies and one-third of the sliced bananas (enough to cover the layer). Repeat the layering twice more. End with a final layer of pudding. Garnish the top with additional cookies or cookie crumbs.

6. Cover tightly with plastic wrap and refrigerate for 4 to 6 hours. Cookies should be tender when poked with a knife. This dessert is best served within 12 hours of assembling.

CHOCOLATE BANANA PUDDING

Our classic banana pudding was the sole flavor on the Magnolia Bakery menu from 1996 until 2014. Then we introduced chocolate. It was an instant hit and led to our developing a number of other specialty flavors.

MAKES 4 to 5 quarts; serves 8 to 16

INGREDIENTS

1 (14oz) can sweetened condensed milk

1½ cups (360g/12.7oz) ice-cold water

1 (3.9oz) package instant chocolate pudding mix (preferably Jell-O brand)

3 cups (720g/25.5oz) heavy cream

1 (9oz) box Nabisco Famous Chocolate Wafers or 1 (11oz) box Nilla wafers

4 to 5 ripe bananas, sliced

1 cup (240g/8.5oz) heavy cream whipped to soft peaks

1 cup (160g/5.6oz) mini chocolate chips

1. In a stand mixer with the whisk, beat the condensed milk and water on medium speed until well combined, about 1 minute. Add the pudding mix and beat until there are no lumps and the mixture is smooth, about 2 minutes. Transfer the mixture to a medium bowl, cover, and refrigerate until firm, at least 1 hour or overnight.

2. In a stand mixer with the whisk, whip the heavy cream on medium speed for about 1 minute, until the cream starts to thicken, then increase the speed to medium-high and whip until stiff peaks form. Be careful not to overwhip.

3. With the mixer running on low speed, add the pudding mixture a spoonful at a time. Mix until well blended and no streaks of pudding remain.

4. To assemble, select a trifle bowl or a wide glass bowl with a 4- to 5-quart capacity, or individual serving bowls.

5. Spread one-quarter of the pudding on the bottom and layer with one-third of the cookies, one-third of the sliced bananas (enough to cover the layer), and ¼ cup of the mini chips. Repeat the layering twice more. End with a final layer of pudding.

6. Cover tightly with plastic wrap and refrigerate for 4 to 6 hours. Cookies should be tender when poked with a knife. Before serving, garnish with dollops of whipped cream and sprinkle with the remaining ¼ cup of mini chips.

7. This dessert is best served within 12 hours of assembling.

JAVA CHIP BANANA PUDDING

This banana pudding has a delectable mocha flavor that appeals to coffee connoisseurs. Each bite delivers a nice crunch thanks to the mini chocolate chips. It's definitely one way to enjoy your daily caffeine fix!

MAKES 4 to 5 quarts; serves up to 16

INGREDIENTS

1 teaspoon instant espresso powder

1½ cups (360g/12.7oz) brewed coffee, at room temperature

1 (14oz) can sweetened condensed milk

1 (3.4oz) package instant vanilla pudding mix (preferably Jell-O brand)

3 cups (720g/25.5oz) heavy cream

1 (11oz) box Nilla wafers (no substitutions!)

4 to 5 ripe bananas, sliced

1 cup (180g/6.3oz) mini chocolate chips

1. Add the espresso powder to the coffee and stir until dissolved.

2. In a stand mixer with the whisk on medium speed, beat the condensed milk and coffee mixture until well combined, about 1 minute. Add the pudding mix and beat until there are no lumps and the mixture is smooth, about 2 minutes. Transfer the mixture to a medium bowl, cover, and refrigerate until firm, at least 1 hour or overnight.

3. In a stand mixer with the whisk, whip the heavy cream on medium speed for about 1 minute, until the cream starts to thicken, then increase the speed to medium-high and whip until stiff peaks form. Be careful not to overwhip.

4. With the mixer running on low speed, add the pudding mixture a spoonful at a time. Mix until well blended and no streaks of pudding remain.

5. To assemble, select a trifle bowl or a wide glass bowl with a 4- to 5-quart capacity, or individual serving bowls.

6. Spread one-quarter of the pudding on the bottom and layer with one-third of the cookies, one-third of the sliced bananas (enough to cover the layer), and ¼ cup of the mini chips. Repeat the layering twice more. Top with a final layer of pudding. Sprinkle with the remaining ¼ cup mini chips.

7. Cover tightly with plastic wrap and refrigerate for 4 to 6 hours. Cookies should be tender when poked with a knife. This dessert is best served within 12 hours of assembling.

PEANUT BUTTER BANANA PUDDING

This peanut butter version of our classic banana pudding was introduced for Magnolia Bakery's twentieth anniversary. The fans went wild. I took it a step further by adding Reese's pieces, which boosts the chocolate quotient. I think you'll love this as much as I do.

MAKES 4 to 5 quarts; serves up to 16

INGREDIENTS

1 (14oz) can sweetened condensed milk

1½ cups (360g/12.7oz) ice-cold water

1 (3.4oz) package instant vanilla pudding mix (preferably Jell-O brand)

1 cup (266g/9.4oz) Skippy creamy peanut butter

3 cups (720g/25.5oz) heavy cream

1 (11oz) box Nilla wafers

4 to 5 ripe bananas, sliced

½ cup (70g/2.4oz) chopped peanuts

½ cup (110g/3.9oz) Reese's pieces, chopped

1. In a stand mixer with the whisk, beat the sweetened condensed milk and water on medium speed until well combined, about 1 minute. Add the pudding mix and beat until there are no lumps and the mixture is smooth, about 2 minutes. Transfer the mixture to a medium bowl, cover, and refrigerate until firm, at least 1 hour or overnight.

2. Remove the pudding mixture from the refrigerator and place it in the bowl of the stand mixer with the whisk. Add the peanut butter and whisk until thoroughly combined. Set aside.

3. In a clean bowl of the stand mixer with the whisk, whip the heavy cream on medium speed for about 1 minute, until the cream starts to thicken, then increase the speed to medium-high and whip until stiff peaks form. Be careful not to overwhip.

4. With the mixer running on low speed, add the pudding mixture a spoonful at a time. Mix until well blended and no streaks of pudding remain.

5. To assemble, select a trifle bowl or a wide glass bowl with a 4- to 5-quart capacity, or individual serving bowls.

6. Spread one-quarter of the pudding on the bottom and layer with one-third of the cookies, one-third of the sliced bananas (enough to cover the layer), and one-quarter of the chopped peanuts and Reese's pieces. Repeat the layering twice more. End with a final layer of pudding. Sprinkle the top with the remaining chopped peanuts and Reese's Pieces.

7. Cover tightly with plastic wrap and refrigerate for 4 to 6 hours. Cookies should be tender when poked with a knife. This dessert is best served within 12 hours of assembling.

CHOCOLATE HAZELNUT BANANA PUDDING

If you like to indulge in Nutella by the spoonful, you're already sold on this chocolate hazelnut banana pudding. It's an even more satisfying way to enjoy copious amounts of your favorite hazelnut spread. Magnolia Bakery originally launched this flavor right before Valentine's Day in 2019, and fans and staff alike fell in love. It's now a featured monthly flavor, but this recipe invites you to make it for yourself any time you're in the mood.

MAKES 4 to 5 quarts; serves up to 16

INGREDIENTS

1 (14oz) can sweetened condensed milk

1½ cups (360g/12.7oz) ice-cold water

1 (3.4oz) package instant vanilla pudding mix (preferably Jell-O brand)

3 cups (720g/25.5oz) heavy cream

1 (11oz) box Nilla wafers (no substitutions!)

4 to 5 ripe bananas, sliced

2 cups (600g/21.2oz) Nutella

1. In a stand mixer with the whisk, beat the condensed milk and water on medium speed until well combined, about 1 minute. Add the pudding mix and beat until there are no lumps and the mixture is smooth, about 2 minutes. Transfer the mixture to a medium bowl, cover, and refrigerate until firm, at least 1 hour or overnight.

2. In a stand mixer with the whisk, whip the heavy cream on medium speed for about 1 minute, until the cream starts to thicken, then increase the speed to medium-high and whip until stiff peaks form. Be careful not to overwhip.

3. With the mixer running on low speed, add the pudding mixture a spoonful at a time. Mix until well blended and no streaks of pudding remain.

4. To assemble the pudding, select either a trifle bowl or a wide glass bowl with a 4- to 5-quart capacity, or individual serving bowls.

5. Spread one-quarter of the pudding on the bottom and layer with one-third of the cookies, then one-third of the bananas (enough to cover the layer). Place the Nutella in a piping bag and drizzle one-quarter over the banana slices. Repeat the layering twice more. Top the pudding with a final layer of pudding and drizzle with the remaining Nutella.

6. Cover tightly with plastic wrap and refrigerate for 4 to 6 hours. Cookies should be tender when poked with a knife. This dessert is best served within 12 hours of assembling, if you can wait that long!

SALTED CARAMEL BANANA PUDDING

Who can resist rich, buttery caramel? (It's a rhetorical question.) This inspired iteration of our banana pudding—yet another fan favorite—reminds me of the bananas Foster made tableside at premium steak houses in the 1970s. That pinch of sea salt brings all the flavors together so beautifully.

MAKES 4 to 5 quarts; serves up to 16

INGREDIENTS

1 (13.4oz) can Nestle's La Lechera dulce de leche sweetened condensed milk

1½ cups (360g/12.7oz) ice-cold water

1 (3.4oz) package instant vanilla pudding mix (preferably Jell-O brand)

3 cups (720g/24oz) heavy cream

1 (11oz) box Nilla wafers

4 to 5 ripe bananas, sliced

1 cup Salted Caramel Sauce (page 287)

1. In a stand mixer with the whisk, beat the dulce de leche and water on medium speed until well combined, about 1 minute. Add the pudding mix and beat until there are no lumps and the mixture is smooth, about 2 minutes. Transfer the mixture to a bowl, cover, and refrigerate for 1 to 2 hours or overnight.

2. In a stand mixer with the whisk, whip the heavy cream on medium speed for about 1 minute, until the cream starts to thicken, then increase the speed to medium-high and whip until stiff peaks form. Be careful not to overwhip.

3. With the mixer running on low speed, add the pudding mixture a spoonful at a time. Mix until well blended and no streaks of pudding remain. To assemble the pudding, select a trifle bowl or large, wide glass bowl with a 4- to 5-quart capacity, or individual serving bowls.

4. Spread one-quarter of the pudding on the bottom and layer with one-third of the cookies and one-third of the bananas (enough to cover the layer). Drizzle with ¼ cup of the salted caramel. Repeat the layering twice more. End with a final layer of pudding. Drizzle with the remaining ¼ cup salted caramel.

5. Cover tightly with plastic wrap and refrigerate for 4 to 6 hours. Cookies should be tender when poked with a knife. This dessert is best served within 12 hours after assembly, if you can wait that long!

PUMPKIN-GINGERSNAP BANANA PUDDING

Pumpkin desserts—from cupcakes to pies to bars—are an important part of the repertoire at Magnolia Bakery, but at first I wasn't sure about a pumpkin banana pudding. I used gingersnaps instead of the typical vanilla wafers and incorporated the classic fall spices. From the very first bite, I knew it was a winner.

MAKES 4 to 5 quarts; serves up to 16

INGREDIENTS

1 (14oz) can sweetened condensed milk

1½ cups (360g/12.7oz) ice-cold water

1 (3.4oz) package instant vanilla pudding mix (preferably Jell-O brand)

1½ cups (360g/12.7oz) canned unsweetened pumpkin puree (preferably Libby's), drained if wet

1 teaspoon pumpkin pie spice

3 cups (720g/25.5oz) heavy cream

1 (16oz) box Nabisco Ginger Snaps

4 to 5 ripe bananas, sliced

1. In a stand mixer with the whisk, beat the condensed milk and water on medium speed until well combined, about 1 minute. Add the pudding mix and beat until there are no lumps and the mixture is smooth, about 2 minutes. Transfer the mixture to a medium bowl, cover, and refrigerate until firm, at least 1 hour or overnight.

2. Remove the pudding mixture from the refrigerator and place it in the bowl of the stand mixer with the whisk. Add the pumpkin puree and pie spice and whisk until thoroughly combined. Set aside.

3. In a clean bowl of the stand mixer with the whisk, whip the heavy cream on medium speed for about 1 minute, until the cream starts to thicken, then increase the speed to medium-high and whip until stiff peaks form. Be careful not to overwhip.

4. With the mixer running on low speed, add the pudding mixture a spoonful at a time. Mix until well blended and no streaks of pudding remain.

5. To assemble, select either a trifle bowl or a wide glass bowl with a 4- to 5-quart capacity, or individual serving bowls.

6. Saving 4 to 5 cookies for garnish, begin assembly. Spread one-quarter of the pudding on the bottom and layer with one-third of the cookies and one-third of the sliced bananas (enough to cover the layer). Repeat the layering twice more. End with a final layer of pudding. Garnish with additional cookies or cookie crumbs.

7. Cover tightly with plastic wrap and refrigerate for 4 to 6 hours. Cookies should be tender when poked with a knife. This dessert is best served within 12 hours of assembling.

> **NOTE**
> Because gingersnaps are a harder cookie than Nilla wafers, they may take additional time to soften.

RED VELVET BANANA PUDDING

Coming up with new banana pudding flavors is not as easy as you might think. Our staff and fans make suggestions all the time, but not all of them resonate. When someone asked for red velvet banana pudding, we all got excited. I tested multiple recipes over many weeks and, after eating more banana pudding than I thought humanly possible, I came up with my ultimate version. It has the perfect cake-to-pudding ratio and a wonderful tang, thanks to the addition of cream cheese. You're welcome.

MAKES 4 to 5 quarts; serves up to 16

INGREDIENTS

Batter for Red Velvet Cake (page 52)

1 (14oz) can sweetened condensed milk

1½ cups (360g/12.7oz) ice-cold water

1 (3.4oz) package instant vanilla pudding mix (preferably Jell-O brand)

1 (8oz) package full-fat cream cheese (preferably Philadelphia brand), cut into 8 pieces, at room temperature

3 cups (720g/25.5oz) heavy cream

4 to 5 ripe bananas, sliced

1 cup plus 1 tablespoon (160g/5.6oz) mini chocolate chips or chocolate shavings

1. Preheat the oven to 325°F. Butter and flour a 9 × 13-inch pan.

2. Scrape the batter for the red velvet cake into the prepared pan. Bake for 40 to 45 minutes, or until the top springs back when touched and a cake tester inserted in the center of the cake comes out clean.

3. Let the cake cool in the pan for at least 30 minutes. Transfer the cake to a cooling rack to cool completely. Note: The cake can be made ahead, and wrapped in plastic wrap for up to 3 days.

4. In a stand mixer with the whisk, beat the condensed milk and water on medium speed until well combined, about 1 minute. Add the pudding mix and beat until there are no lumps and the mixture is smooth, about 2 minutes. Transfer the mixture to a medium bowl, cover, and refrigerate until firm, at least 1 hour or overnight.

5. Transfer the pudding mixture to a stand mixer with the whisk, add the softened cream cheese, and mix until thoroughly combined and smooth. Refrigerate while you prepare the whipped cream.

6. In a clean bowl in a stand mixer with the whisk, whip the heavy cream on medium speed for about 1 minute, until the cream starts to thicken, then increase the speed to medium-high and whip until stiff peaks form. Be careful not to overwhip.

7. With the mixer running on low speed, add the pudding mixture a spoonful at a time. Mix until well blended and no streaks of pudding remain.

8. Remove the red velvet cake from the pan and cut into a 4 × 2-inch grid for 8 rectangular pieces. Cut each rectangle in half for 16 ½-inch-thick pieces. Set aside.

9. To assemble the pudding, select either a trifle bowl or wide glass bowl with a 4- to 5-quart capacity, or individual serving bowls.

10. Spread one-quarter of the pudding on the bottom and layer with enough slices of the red velvet cake to cover the layer. Add one-third of the sliced bananas (enough to cover the cake) and 1/3 cup of the mini chips. Repeat the layering twice more. End with a final layer of pudding. Sprinkle the top layer with crumbled red velvet cake and a tablespoon of mini chips. Cover with plastic wrap and refrigerate for 4 hours or overnight before serving. Note: You may have a couple of pieces of cake left over for snacking.

BASE RECIPES

Buttercreams and Icings

American-style buttercream, meringue butter cream (a meringue base with added butter), and meringue icing (made with cooked sugar)—how do you choose? It's all about personal preference, though American buttercream is sweeter and faster to make than meringue. All of my buttercreams and icings work with a number of different cakes and cupcakes. When I feel strongly about a particular combination, I let you know. I prefer quite a bit of buttercream on my cakes, up to 5 cups, depending on the cake and the design. If that's too much for you, simply cut the recipe in half.

Store buttercream at room temperature in an airtight container for 2 to 3 days. Check the consistency before using and re-whip if it has stiffened. If you have extra, you can refrigerate it for up to 1 week or freeze it for up to 2 months. Just bring it to room temperature before using. You will have to re-whip it for a few minutes until it's smooth and fluffy. Store icings made with cream cheese in the refrigerator if you're not using them the same day; bring them to room temperature before using.

TIPS ON TINTING BUTTERCREAM

- You can use food coloring in the form of drops, but I prefer gel paste for its concentrated color and that it adds minimal liquid to a recipe. Also see Food Coloring, page 17.
- Add color in tiny increments with a clean toothpick, then mix with a spoon until blended.
- Wait 1 to 2 hours before decorating. As it sets, color deepens in buttercream.
- Keep extra buttercream on hand in case you don't like how a color sets.
- Store the decorated cake in a cool place, out of direct light.

MAGNOLIA BAKERY VANILLA BUTTERCREAM

Magnolia Bakery's classic vanilla and chocolate cupcakes are iced with an American-style vanilla buttercream in our trademark swirl. All bakers need a reliable recipe in their arsenal when it comes to decorating cakes and cupcakes. This one is sweet, but not so sweet it hurts your teeth. If you make it correctly, it shouldn't be gritty or heavy. You must mix this on low speed—if you get impatient and go too fast you will create air bubbles, which makes it difficult to get a smooth finish on your cakes. Adjusting the amount of milk or cream changes the consistency. This buttercream is great for icing cakes with more complex designs, as it holds a shape really well.

MAKES about 4 cups
(enough for one 9-inch cake or 24 cupcakes)

INGREDIENTS
1 cup/2 sticks (226g/8oz) unsalted butter,
    at room temperature
1 teaspoon pure vanilla extract
4 cups (500g/17.6oz) powdered sugar, sifted
3 to 4 tablespoons whole milk
Food coloring (optional)

1. In a stand mixer with the paddle, cream the butter on medium speed until light and fluffy, 3 to 4 minutes. Add the vanilla and mix for 1 minute. Scrape down the bottom and sides of the bowl.

2. With the mixer running on low speed, gradually add the powdered sugar, 1 cup (125g/4.4oz) at a time. Scrape down the bottom and sides of the bowl again. When you have added the third cup of sugar, the mixture will start to thicken and appear dry. Add 3 tablespoons

of the milk, then add the rest of the sugar and add more milk if the buttercream is too stiff. The desired consistency is creamy and smooth. Scrape down the bottom and sides of the bowl. The great thing about this buttercream is that you can adjust the quantities of sugar and milk to achieve the consistency you desire.

3. Continue to beat the icing on low speed for 1 to 2 minutes longer, until smooth and creamy. Do not mix on medium or high, as it will add too much air and be too fluffy. If desired, add a few drops of food coloring, one drop at a time, and mix thoroughly to get the right color.

4. Store the icing at room temperature in an airtight container for up to 3 days.

CHOCOLATE BUTTERCREAM

This chocolate buttercream (and its mocha variation) is incredibly smooth and luscious. It has the perfect amount of chocolate flavor without being overpowering on a vanilla or chocolate cake. It's also a decadent choice to go with the peanut butter or banana cakes. Using the best quality chocolate will make a significant difference.

MAKES about 5 cups
(enough for one 9-inch cake or 24 cupcakes)

INGREDIENTS

2 cups/4 sticks (452g/16oz) unsalted butter,
    at room temperature

2 teaspoons pure vanilla extract

3 cups (375g/13.2oz) powdered sugar, sifted

2 cups (360g/12.7oz) semisweet chocolate chips,
    melted but not hot

1 tablespoon heavy cream or milk,
    if needed to thin the buttercream

1. In a stand mixer with the paddle, beat the butter until smooth and creamy, starting on low speed to break up the clumps, then on medium for about 4 minutes. Stop and scrape down the paddle, bottom, and sides of the bowl. Add the vanilla and beat for another minute

2. On low speed, add the sugar, mixing until combined. Stop and scrape down the paddle, bottom, and sides of the bowl.

3. Carefully pour the melted chocolate into the mixer bowl, being careful not to let it touch the sides of the bowl or the paddle. If the butter is colder than the chocolate, the chocolate will seize up when it touches the cold bowl or paddle. Mix on low speed until all the chocolate has been added. Scrape down the bottom and sides of the bowl.

4. Once fully combined, turn the mixer to medium speed and mix for about 4 minutes. Scrape down the bottom and sides of the bowl. Mix again on low speed until you no longer see streaks of butter, 1 to 2 minutes.

5. Remove the bowl from the mixer and scrape the paddle, bottom, and sides of the bowl with a spatula. Return to the mixer on medium speed for about 10 seconds, just to incorporate any of the butter bits from the bottom. If you mix too much, the icing will be too light. Add the tablespoon of cream or milk if you need to adjust the consistency of the buttercream for it to spread easier.

6. Store the icing at room temperature in an airtight container for up to 3 days.

VARIATION

CHOCOLATE MOCHA BUTTERCREAM: Add 2 teaspoons instant espresso powder and mix on low speed for 10 to 15 seconds just until incorporated.

PEANUT BUTTER BUTTERCREAM

Since I'm so passionate about peanut butter, this buttercream is one of my favorites. It's essentially just a sweeter, lighter version of peanut butter. I recommend Skippy, which has a rich, peanutty flavor and the ideal smooth texture. Using this buttercream to ice the PB&J Cupcakes (page 96) is a no-brainer, but it's equally good on our chocolate and banana cupcakes.

MAKES about 5 cups
(enough for one 9-inch two-layer cake
or 24 cupcakes)

INGREDIENTS

1½ cups/3 sticks (340g/12oz) unsalted butter,
   at room temperature

1½ cups (396g/14oz) Skippy creamy peanut butter

1½ teaspoons pure vanilla extract

3¾ cups (469g/16.5oz) powdered sugar, sifted

In a stand mixer with the paddle, cream the butter on medium speed for about 1 minute, just until smooth. Add the peanut butter and vanilla and mix until combined. With the mixer running on low, add the sugar one cup at a time. Stop the mixer and scrape down the bottom and sides. Mix for another 30 seconds until fully blended. Store the icing at room temperature in an airtight container for up to 3 days.

NUTELLA BUTTERCREAM

This buttercream is extremely rich, so use a light hand when icing your cakes.

MAKES 3 cups
(enough for 24 cupcakes; double the recipe
for a 9-inch two-layer cake)

INGREDIENTS

1 cup/2 sticks (226g/8oz) unsalted butter,
   at room temperature

1 cup (300g/10.6oz) Nutella

1 teaspoon pure vanilla extract

2½ cups (312g/11oz) powdered sugar, sifted

1 tablespoon heavy cream or milk,
   if needed

In a stand mixer with the paddle, cream the butter on medium speed for about 1 minute, just until smooth. Add the Nutella and vanilla and mix until combined. With the mixer running on low speed, slowly add the sugar. Stop the mixer and scrape down the bottom and sides. Mix for another 30 seconds, until fully blended. Add cream or milk if your icing is not smooth enough. Store the icing at room temperature in an airtight container for up to 3 days.

CHOCOLATE GANACHE

There are so many uses for chocolate ganache, beginning with eating it with a spoon from morning to night. It's just what you want to fill a cake or to create those decorative drizzles down the sides. If you chill ganache, it firms up and you can use it to make truffles—and you can use *those* to fill your chocolate cupcakes! Because who ever heard of too much chocolate?

MAKES 2 cups

INGREDIENTS
2 cups (360g/12.7oz) semisweet chocolate chips
1 cup (240g/8.5oz) heavy cream

1. Place the chocolate chips in a heatproof glass or stainless steel bowl.

2. In a small saucepan, bring the cream to a gentle simmer over medium heat, stirring occasionally so that the bottom does not scorch. Pour the warm cream over the chocolate. Let it set for a few minutes to soften the chocolate. Using a rubber spatula, stir the chocolate-cream mixture until completely smooth.

3. Ganache can be made ahead and stored in the refrigerator for up to 3 weeks. Bring it to room temperature before using (either as whipped ganache or as a glaze).

4. **FOR CHOCOLATE GLAZE:** To use this for cake drizzles and to coat cupcakes, the ganache should be pourable but not hot. You can warm it up in the microwave in 30-second increments until just pourable.

5. **FOR WHIPPED GANACHE:** Beat stiff but not cold ganache on medium speed for 3 to 5 minutes until creamy and mousse-like in texture.

CREAM CHEESE ICING

I am not a fan of super-sweet cream cheese icing, mostly because I feel the sweetness can overpower the tangy flavor. For recipes like our Ultimate Carrot Cake (page 58) and Red Velvet Cake (page 52), this icing really lets the cream cheese shine through.

MAKES about 4 cups
(enough for one 9-inch two-layer cake or 24 cupcakes)

INGREDIENTS
4 (8oz) packages full-fat cream cheese (preferably Philadelphia brand), broken into large chunks, at room temperature (but not too soft)
1 tablespoon pure vanilla extract
1½ cups (118g/6.6oz) powdered sugar, sifted

1. In a stand mixer with the paddle, beat the cream cheese on low speed until smooth, about 2 minutes. Scrape down the sides and bottom of the bowl. Add the vanilla and beat just until incorporated. With the mixer running on low, gradually add the sugar, ½ cup (62g/2oz) at a time, beating until smooth but not creamy. Scrape the bottom and sides of the bowl. Be careful not to overbeat or the icing will become gummy.

2. Use immediately. If the icing looks a little gummy (you overmixed), you can cover and refrigerate it for 2 to 3 hours to thicken. It's best to use this the same day. If you want to make it ahead of time, refrigerate covered for up to 3 days. Bring to room temperature before use. You may need to beat it again to soften.

Scrape down the sides and bottom of the bowl. Add the vanilla and mix just until incorporated. With the mixer running on low speed, add the cream cheese about 2 ounces at a time. (I grab big blobs of it with my fingers and throw it into the bowl.) Beat until smooth but not creamy. You want to just get the lumps out. Scrape the bottom and sides of the bowl. Best if used immediately.

VARIATION

LEMON CREAM CHEESE ICING: In place of the vanilla, add 2 teaspoons each grated lemon zest and lemon juice. Let sit for 30 minutes before using so the flavors blend.

MAPLE CREAM CHEESE ICING

Irresistibly tangy with a subtle maple flavor, this icing goes so well with our Pumpkin Spice Cupcakes (page 100). You have the option of boosting the maple flavor with a few drops of maple extract.

MAKES about 4 cups
(enough for one 9-inch two-layer cake or 24 cupcakes)

INGREDIENTS
2½ cups (312g/11oz) powdered sugar, sifted
¼ cup (80g/2.8oz) dark maple syrup
½ teaspoon pure vanilla extract
½ teaspoon maple extract (optional)
⅛ teaspoon salt
3 (8oz) packages full-fat cream cheese
    (preferably Philadelphia brand),
    cut into big chunks, at room temperature
    (but not too soft)

In a stand mixer with the paddle, mix the sugar, maple syrup, vanilla (and maple extract if using), and salt on low speed until sandy. With the mixer on low speed, add the cream cheese in chunks. Continue mixing on medium until combined and smooth, being careful not to overmix. Scrape down the bottom and sides of the bowl. Mix until smooth and combined. Best if used immediately.

SWEET CREAM CHEESE ICING

This recipe is typical of a Southern-style cream cheese icing. It's sweeter than our Cream Cheese Icing (opposite) and pairs beautifully with the Hummingbird Cake (page 60).

MAKES about 4 cups
(enough for one 9-inch two-layer cake or 24 cupcakes)

INGREDIENTS
6 tablespoons/¾ stick (85g/3oz) unsalted butter,
    cut into small pieces, at room temperature
    (but still firm)
5 cups (625g/22oz) powdered sugar, sifted
1½ teaspoons pure vanilla extract
2 (8oz) packages full-fat cream cheese
    (preferably Philadelphia brand),
    at room temperature (but not too soft)

In a stand mixer with the paddle, beat the butter on medium speed until smooth and creamy, about 2 minutes. Add the sugar and mix until it looks like crumbly sand.

CARAMEL CREAM CHEESE ICING

Caramel adds a voluptuous sweetness with delicious burnt sugar notes that make this the right choice for icing our Pumpkin Spice Cake (page 71). It requires an extra step, but it's well worth the effort.

MAKES about 6 cups
(enough for one 9-inch cake or 24 cupcakes)

INGREDIENTS

1 cup (227g/8oz) water

2 cups (400g/14.2oz) granulated sugar

1 tablespoon pure vanilla extract

1½ cups/3 sticks (340g/12oz) unsalted butter, cut into 1-inch pieces, at room temperature (but still firm)

¼ cup (60g/2.1oz) heavy cream

4 (8oz) packages full-fat cream cheese (preferably Philadelphia brand), at room temperature (but not too soft)

1. In a saucepan, combine the water, sugar, and vanilla. Set over medium heat and cook, stirring occasionally, until the sugar is completely dissolved. Use a wet pastry brush to wash down any sugar crystals on the sides of the pan.

2. Attach a candy thermometer to the side of the pan and bring the mixture to a rolling boil over medium heat, until the thermometer reads 360°F. Be very careful not to burn the caramel.

3. Immediately remove from the heat and place the saucepan on a towel. Working rapidly, whisk the butter and heavy cream into the caramel.

4. Once the butter is completely incorporated, transfer the caramel to a large measuring cup and place in the refrigerator for about 45 minutes. The caramel must be set before continuing. (The caramel can be made ahead and stored in the refrigerator for up to 1 week. Bring back to room temperature before using.)

5. In a stand mixer with the paddle, beat the cream cheese on medium speed until light and creamy, about 3 minutes, making sure there are no lumps. Scrape down the bottom and sides of the bowl.

6. With the mixer running, slowly pour the caramel into the cream cheese. Mix until the caramel is completely incorporated, scraping down the sides and bottom of the bowl. Transfer the icing to a container and refrigerate for at least 5 hours before using.

WHIPPED VANILLA ICING

This unusual icing is what makes our Red Velvet Cake (page 52) so different from all the rest. It's an old-fashioned boiled milk icing, also known as "ermine frosting," made with a roux starter of milk and flour. Its light, whipped texture is a great alternative to a classic powdered sugar frosting and also provides an eggless option to meringue buttercream. I consider a stand mixer essential for making this icing.

If you are going to decorate a cake with rosettes, you will need to double or even triple this recipe. The more decorative the cake or cupcakes, the more buttercream you will need.

MAKES about 5½ cups
(enough for one 9-inch two-layer cake decorated with rosettes or 24 cupcakes)

INGREDIENTS

6 tablespoons (48g/1.7oz) all-purpose flour

2 cups (480g/17oz) whole milk

2 cups/4 sticks (452g/16oz) unsalted butter, at room temperature

2 cups (400g/14.2oz) granulated sugar

2 teaspoons pure vanilla extract

1. In a medium saucepan, whisk the flour into the milk until smooth. Set over medium-high heat and cook, *stirring constantly,* being sure to get into the corners, until very thick and bubbling, about 3 minutes. Remove from the heat and strain through a fine-mesh sieve into a heatproof glass or metal bowl. Place a piece of plastic wrap directly on the surface. Refrigerate for at least 1 hour to chill. (This can be made up to 2 days ahead.)

2. To make the icing, remove the roux from the refrigerator and let sit at room temperature for at least 30 minutes.

3. In the stand mixer with the paddle, beat the butter on medium speed for 3 minutes, until smooth and creamy. Gradually add the sugar, scraping down the sides and bottom of the bowl occasionally, until all the sugar has been incorporated. Beat for a full 10 minutes, until creamy and very pale. Add the vanilla and beat well.

4. Add the room temperature roux to the bowl and beat with the paddle on medium speed until very smooth and white in color, 10 to 15 minutes. Scrape down the sides and bottom of the bowl occasionally. Switch to the whisk and whip on medium speed until light and fluffy, 2 to 3 minutes. Rub the icing between your thumb and forefinger. If it's at all grainy, continue to mix for another 5 to 10 minutes, or until creamy with no graininess.

5. I recommend using the icing right away. The texture remains creamy and it's easier to decorate with it at this time. If making the icing ahead, store at room temperature. Before using, place in a stand mixer with the paddle and beat for 5 to 10 minutes, until fluffy and creamy.

MARSHMALLOW MERINGUE ICING (AKA 7-MINUTE ICING)

This meringue-based icing, with its fluffy high peaks and glossy sheen, has been popular since the early 1900s. It's often referred to as having a marshmallow consistency and its light, airy texture makes for an impressive presentation. I slather our mile-high Coconut Cake (page 50) with it and cover our Chocolate White-Out Cake (page 46) and Coconut Cupcakes (page 82) with peaks of this glossy icing.

MAKES enough for one 9-inch cake or 24 cupcakes

INGREDIENTS
2¼ cups (450g/16oz) granulated sugar
½ cup (120g/4.2oz) water
¾ teaspoon cream of tartar
5 egg whites
1 teaspoon pure vanilla extract

1. In a medium saucepan, combine the sugar, water, and cream of tartar. Stir to moisten all the sugar. Bring to a boil over medium-high heat without stirring. If necessary, use a moistened pastry brush to wash down any sugar that remains on the sides of the pan.

2. Meanwhile, in a stand mixer with the whisk, combine the egg whites and vanilla and beat on medium speed.

3. When the sugar mixture comes to a boil, clip a candy thermometer to the side of the pan. Do not stir the mixture at all. Bring the sugar syrup to 223°F.

4. As soon as the sugar syrup reaches 223°F, increase the mixer speed to high.

5. Watch the syrup carefully. When it comes to 230°F, remove from the heat. By this point the egg whites should be fluffy and about one-third of the way up the bowl and almost white.

6. Carefully and gradually pour the hot syrup in a thin stream into the egg whites as they are beating on high speed. Be sure to pour the syrup onto the side of the bowl (and not onto the whisk) and let it drizzle down into the beating whites.

7. On high speed, continue to whip the meringue mixture for about 5 minutes. The icing is finished when it pulls away from the sides of the mixer bowl and puffs up in the center. You should have firm, shiny peaks that curl slightly at the ends when the whisk is removed. This icing must be used immediately.

MERINGUE BUTTERCREAM BASE

Buttercream usually calls to mind the American-style icing that's made with powdered sugar and butter. This meringue-based buttercream, however, also contains egg whites, which give it a beautiful, creamy texture and glossy sheen. It's a blank canvas for flavors: See the list of options below.

MAKES 5 cups
(enough for one 9-inch cake or 24 cupcakes)

INGREDIENTS

1½ cups (300g/10.6oz) granulated sugar

½ cup (120g/4.2oz) water

¼ teaspoon cream of tartar

6 egg whites

¼ teaspoon salt

2 cups/4 sticks (452g/16oz) unsalted butter, cut into 1-inch pieces, at room temperature (but still firm)

Flavoring of choice (options follow)

TROUBLESHOOTING

If your buttercream is soupy, stop mixing it and place the bowl in the refrigerator or freezer for a few minutes, then beat again. It should thicken up.

---

1. In a medium saucepan, combine 1 cup (200g/7.1oz) of the sugar, the water, and cream of tartar. Stir to moisten all the sugar. Bring to a boil over medium-high heat without stirring.

2. Meanwhile, in a stand mixer with the whisk, beat the egg whites on low speed.

3. When the sugar mixture comes to a boil, increase the mixer speed to medium. Clip a candy thermometer to the side of the saucepan. Do not stir the mixture at all.

4. When the egg whites are frothy, stream in the remaining ½ cup (100g/3.5oz) sugar and continue to beat on medium speed. When the sugar syrup reaches 235°F, increase the mixer speed to high. The egg whites are ready when they reach a soft peak.

5. Watch the syrup carefully. When it comes to 240°F, remove the syrup from the heat and slowly pour it in a thin stream into the egg whites as they are beating on high speed. Be sure to pour the syrup onto the sides of the bowl (and not onto the whisk) and let it drizzle down into the beating whites. If the syrup is poured directly onto the whisk, it will end up on the sides of the bowl and never reach the egg whites.

FLAVOR OPTIONS

RASPBERRY MERINGUE BUTTERCREAM
Add ½ cup (170g/6oz) raspberry jam

STRAWBERRY MERINGUE BUTTERCREAM
Add ½ cup (170g/6oz) strawberry jam

PEPPERMINT MERINGUE BUTTERCREAM
Add 1½ teaspoons peppermint extract

LEMON MERINGUE BUTTERCREAM
Add 2 tablespoons fresh lemon juice and 2 teaspoons grated lemon zest

VANILLA BEAN MERINGUE BUTTERCREAM
Scrape in the seeds from ½ vanilla bean

MAPLE MERINGUE BUTTERCREAM
Add ½ cup pure maple syrup

WHITE CHOCOLATE RASPBERRY MERINGUE BUTTERCREAM
Add 2 cups (340g/12oz) white chocolate, melted but not hot, and ½ cup (170g/6oz) raspberry jam

CARAMEL MERINGUE BUTTERCREAM
Add 1 cup (300g/10.6oz) caramel sauce (page 287)

1

Making sugar syrup.

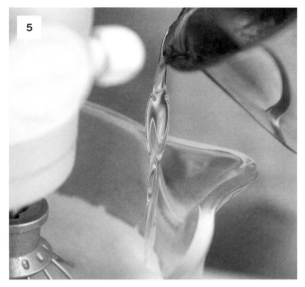

5

Pouring sugar syrup into the egg whites.

6

Adding the butter.

8

Light and fluffy buttercream.

6. Reduce the mixer speed to medium and continue to whip the meringue mixture until it cools to room temperature. As it whips, add the salt. When the egg white mixture has cooled to room temperature, start adding butter on high speed as it whips. Add about a tablespoon at a time, watching carefully until mixed before adding more. When all the butter is added the buttercream should be light and fluffy.

7. After all of the butter has been added, add the flavoring of choice and mix on medium-high speed for another minute. You can make the base ahead (without adding the flavoring). Store in an airtight container for up to 2 days. To add flavor, place the buttercream in a stand mixer with the paddle and whip for a minute just to smooth the buttercream. Then add the flavoring and mix on medium-high speed for another minute.

PIPING A BUTTERCREAM ROSE

Flowers are things of beauty, and at Magnolia Bakery we like to create piped flowers that are as delightful to look at as they are to eat. To make the rose shown below, you'll need a Wilton #104 decorating tip. For instructions on filling a piping bag, see page 18.

Pipe a dollop of buttercream in the center of the cupcake to start the bud of the rose.

Wrap 3 petals around the center bud; stagger them as you go.

For the second round, pipe 4 petals, staggering them between the previous 3 petals.

Continue as shown in images #2 and #3, creating staggered petals, dragging the piping bag longer with each round to create a fan effect.

Crumbs and Crusts

Without crust, a pie is just a bowl of fruit. As the foundation of all pies, crusts deserve consideration and careful preparation. Whether you're perfecting pie dough—and I take you through the entire process, step by step—or discovering the delightful simplicity of our nut and cookie crusts, you'll come to appreciate the flavor and structure of these essential components.

PERFECT PIE DOUGH EVERY TIME: A PRIMER

Pie dough can be so intimidating. But practice makes perfect. And really understanding the technique goes a long way toward helping you build confidence. Once you acquire some skill, making pie becomes so fast and easy that cleaning up will take more time than making the dough. Read through this step-by-step process before you attempt your first dough. Then get all your tools and ingredients set up and dive in!

1. In a large bowl, whisk together the flour and salt. If your room is hot, place the bowl in the refrigerator or freezer while prepping the butter.

2. Be sure the butter is cold and use fresh butter. It really does make a difference. Cut the butter into ½-inch pieces. If your kitchen is hot, place the bowl in the freezer for a few minutes.

3. When the recipe says ice water, it really means ice water. Fill a 2-cup measuring cup with ice and then add water. Measure the amount you need from this cup, keeping it very cold. Be careful not to add the ice cubes.

4. Cut your butter into the flour and salt mixture. A food processor is the fastest and easiest way to do this, but then you must wash it. I prefer to do this step by hand, using a similar procedure as when I make scones. (If you have warm hands, place them in cold water, then dry them.) It's the pinch of the thumb and fingers, then push technique, like snapping your fingers. Pinch the flour-coated butter between your thumb and fingers then "snap" your fingers together, pushing the dough at the same time. If your butter, flour, and hands are cold, you will have a very flaky dough. Do this until you have a shaggy dough with some cranberry-sized chunks of flour-coated butter. You can also cut the butter in using a pastry blender.

Add butter.

Add water.

Place the dough on a lightly floured surface.

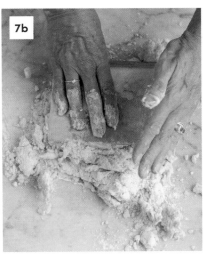

Fold the dough.

Divide the dough in half.

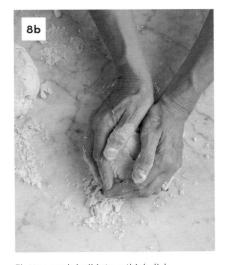

Flatten each ball into a thick disk.

5. Gently sprinkle the cold water 1 tablespoon at a time around the outside of the mixture. You may not need all the water, or you may need more. Using your fingers or a large wooden spoon, gently toss the mixture until the water is somewhat incorporated.

6. Continue to add water a bit at a time until the dough just holds together when you squeeze it, being very careful not to overwork the dough.

7. Once the dough comes together, remove it from the bowl and lay it on a lightly floured surface. Press the dough with the palm of your hand and push the dough away, using a bench scraper and folding as you go. Make a quarter-turn and do this step two more times, being careful not to knead the dough.

8. Divide the dough in half. Flatten each into a thick disc, wrap in plastic wrap, and refrigerate for at least 30 minutes or up to 3 days. You can also freeze the dough for up to 3 months.

HOW TO ROLL OUT PIE DOUGH

To make a perfect pie crust, you will need the following tools: a rolling pin, bench scraper, pastry brush, scissors, and 9-inch pie pan. Have all these tools at hand and follow these simple steps.

1. Take one disc of dough out of the refrigerator at a time. Let the dough sit at room temperature for about 10 minutes, then place it on a lightly floured surface.

2. Dust a rolling pin and your hands with flour to prevent sticking. I like to keep a dry pastry brush handy to brush excess flour from the dough.

3. Hit the dough a few times with the rolling pin just to confirm it's soft enough to roll. If it's too firm, give it a few more minutes before you start rolling or you will tear the dough.

4. Press the rolling pin in the center of the dough and, using light pressure, roll away from you.

5. Give the dough a quarter-turn and repeat these steps a few times, occasionally flipping the dough over. Roll out to an even 11-inch round. Brush off the excess flour.

6. If the dough starts to stick to the counter, lift it gently with a bench scraper, turn it over, and lightly dust the counter with more flour.

7. Place a 9-inch pie pan upside down over the crust to confirm that it will be large enough to fit your pan. Fold the dough in half, brush off the excess flour again, then fold it in half again, creating a triangle.

8. Press the dough into the pan, but do not stretch the dough. With scissors, trim the edges to leave about a ½-inch border.

9. If you are making a single crust pie, fold the dough under. Crimp the edges by pinching the dough with the thumb and pointer finger of your nondominant hand, pushing the dough with your pointer finger of your other hand. Rotate the pie pan as you go around the dough.

10. If you're making a double-crust pie, leave the ½-inch overhang while you roll out the top crust.

11. Keep the crust chilled while preparing fillings. I even put my pie crust in the freezer for 15 minutes before baking. The colder the crust the better.

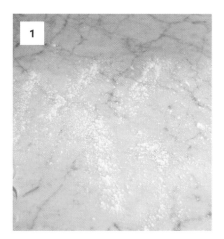

Flour the surface.

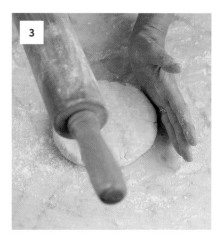

Test the dough for texture before rolling.

Brush off any excess flour.

Confirm the dough will fit in the pan.

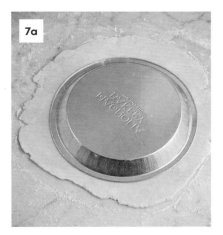

Fold the pie dough in half.

Brush off the excess flour again.

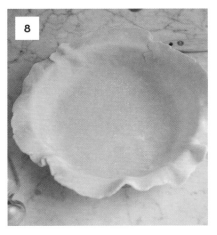

Create a triangle.

Allow a ½-inch overhang.

Crimp the dough.

BAKING A PIE SHELL

Baking a pie crust without any filling is referred to as blind baking. First you bake the crust with pie weights to help the dough keep its shape. Then you remove the weights and bake the crust again, either partially (parbaked) or fully, depending on the type of pie filling. Here's how to do it.

1. Roll out pie dough following the instructions on pages 278-279.

2. Cover the bottom of the pan with parchment paper or foil. Fill with ceramic pie weights or dried beans to keep the sides of the dough from drooping. (I like to fill mine with about 2 cups of beans, which is about two-thirds full.) Place in the refrigerator to chill for about 30 minutes.

3. Preheat the oven to 375°F.

4. Remove the pie shell from the refrigerator and bake for 15 minutes.

5. Remove the pie crust from the oven and then the parchment paper and pie weights or beans.

6. **TO PARBAKE:** If you are making a pie with a filling that needs to be cooked, like pecan or pumpkin pie, return the pie crust to the oven for only 5 to 8 minutes, just to cook the bottom a little longer; you don't want a fully cooked crust.

7. **TO FULLY BAKE:** If you are making a pie with a filling that does not need to be baked, such as a cream pie, the pie crust needs to be baked completely. Prick the bottom of the crust with a fork to keep the crust from bubbling up and return the pie to the oven for 15 minutes, or until the crust is lightly golden.

A beautifully shaped crust.

Cover the crust with parchment paper or foil.

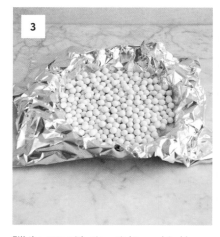

Fill the pan with pie weights or dried beans to keep the sides of the dough upright.

MAGNOLIA BAKERY'S CLASSIC PIE DOUGH

This makes the ideal flaky pie crust. And an all-butter crust has the most delicious flavor. I like to double this recipe and freeze a disc so that I always have pie dough on hand. The dough can be frozen, wrapped well, for up to 3 months. To thaw, place in the refrigerator for 24 hours before using.

MAKES two 9-inch crusts

INGREDIENTS

2¼ cups (303g/10.7oz) all-purpose flour

1 teaspoon salt

1 cup/2 sticks (226g/8oz) cold unsalted butter,
   cut into ½-inch chunks

6 to 8 tablespoons ice water

1. In a food processor, combine the flour and salt. Pulse for 10 seconds to blend.

2. Add the butter chunks and toss together to coat the butter with flour. Pulse several times, until the butter pieces are the size of small peas. (Note: If you don't have a food processor, you can use your hands or a pastry cutter to cut in the butter.)

3. Remove from the food processor and place the flour-butter mixture in a large bowl. Slowly add the water, starting with 4 tablespoons. Toss the mixture using your fingertips. Add more water as you go, until the mixture holds together when pinched. You should not see any loose flour.

4. Dump the mixture onto the counter.

5. Fold the dough in half, gently pushing across the table away from you. Give the dough a third turn.

6. Using a bench scraper, fold the dough over again and push out. Do this one more time using the bench scraper. Fold and turn a total of 3 times, pressing the dough away from you each time until you have a cohesive dough. DO NOT KNEAD the dough.

7. Form into a large flat disc, then cut in half.

8. Place each half on a piece of plastic wrap, shape into a ball, and flatten into a thick disc.

9. Wrap well in the plastic and refrigerate for at least 1 hour and up to 3 days. You can also freeze the dough at this point for up to 3 months. Remove from the freezer and place in the refrigerator for 24 hours before rolling out.

PECAN SHORTBREAD CRUST

This crust creates the perfect nutty foundation for our Blueberry Jamboree (page 233). I also like to use it with any no-bake pie fillings.

MAKES enough for one 9-inch round pie or one 9 × 13-inch pan

INGREDIENTS

¾ cup/1½ sticks (169.5g/6oz) unsalted butter, melted

2 cups (270g/9.6oz) all-purpose flour

1 cup (115g/4oz) coarsely chopped pecans,
   lightly toasted (see Tip, page 288)

1. Position a rack in the center of the oven and preheat the oven to 325°F. Lightly butter a 9-inch round pie pan or a 9 × 13-inch glass baking dish.

2. In a stand mixer with the paddle, mix together the butter, flour, and pecans just until it all comes together and is crumbly. Be very careful not to overwork the dough.

3. Press the dough into the prepared pan and chill for 15 minutes.

4. Bake for 12 to 15 minutes, or until fragrant and lightly golden brown. Cool on a rack. The crust can be made ahead and wrapped in plastic wrap for up to 3 days.

SHORTBREAD COOKIE CRUST

This shortbread cookie crust is so buttery, flaky, and delicious, you'll be tempted to eat it on its own. The crust balances the bright lemon curd of our popular Lemon Bars (page 156) beautifully.

MAKES enough for one 9 x 13-inch pan cut into 12 bars

INGREDIENTS

2 cups (270g/9.6oz) all-purpose flour

1 cup/2 sticks (226g/8oz) cold unsalted butter, cut into ½-inch pieces

½ cup (62g/2oz) powdered sugar, sifted

¼ teaspoon salt

1. Position and oven rack in the center of the oven and preheat the oven to 325°F. Butter a 9 × 13-inch pan, then line it with parchment paper or foil, leaving overhand on the sides (see Lining a Pan, page 141).

2. In a food processor, combine the flour, butter, powdered sugar, and salt and mix until a coarse meal is formed and just holds together when you pinch your fingers together. You want the dough to be crumbly. Evenly sprinkle the dough into the prepared pan, then gently press the dough, making sure it is level and the pan is fully covered in the corners (Also see page 141).

3. Bake for 25 to 30 minutes, or until golden brown and firm and just dry to the touch. Cool on a rack. The crust can be made ahead and wrapped in plastic wrap for up to 3 days.

BROWN SUGAR SHORTBREAD CRUST

I love this crust for its toasty, buttery flavor—I sometimes make it as cookies just to satisfy my craving. But I also like that it's sturdy enough to provide a solid handhold when topped with something creamy.

MAKES enough for one 9 × 13-inch pan
(divide in half if using an 8 × 8-inch square pan)

INGREDIENTS

1 cup/2 sticks (226g/8oz) unsalted butter, at room temperature

¾ cup (150g/5.3oz) light brown sugar

3 cups (405g/14.3oz) all-purpose flour

½ teaspoon salt

1. Position a rack in the center of the oven and preheat the oven to 375°F. Butter a 9 × 13-inch pan, then line it with foil leaving overhang on the sides (see Lining the Pan, page 141).

2. In a stand mixer with the paddle, cream the butter and brown sugar on medium speed until light and fluffy, about 5 minutes.

3. Add the flour and salt, mixing just until combined but crumbly. Dump all the dough into the pan. Evenly press the dough into the bottom of the prepared pan.

4. Bake for 15 minutes, then reduce the oven temperature to 325°F and continue to bake for another 10 to 12 minutes, or until lightly golden brown.

5. Cool on a rack. The crust can be made ahead and wrapped in plastic wrap for up to 3 days.

GINGERSNAP CRUST

The fragrance of a baking gingersnap crust is so evocative of fall. We use this crust for our Pumpkin Icebox Pie (page 282). I suggest you use store-bought gingersnaps, but you can also make your own.

MAKES enough for one 9-inch pie

INGREDIENTS

1½ cups plus 3 tablespoons (230g/8.1oz) gingersnap crumbs

½ cup/1 stick (113g/4oz) unsalted butter, melted but cooled

1. Position a rack in the center of the oven and preheat the oven to 350°F.

2. In a medium bowl, combine the crumbs and melted butter and stir with a spatula until the mixture comes together and the crumbs are thoroughly moistened. The mixture will look like wet sand.

A 16-ounce box of Nabisco gingersnaps will make about 3 cups plus 6 tablespoons of crumbs. I usually just grind the entire box at one time; if I'm only making one pie, I save the other half for later.

The gingersnaps are large and hard, so you will need to break them into pieces before adding to your food processor. Grind until you have fine crumbs. If you don't have a food processor, place the crackers in a sturdy resealable plastic bag. Smash them with a rolling pin and roll back and forth until you have fine crumbs.

3. Dump the crumb mixture directly into a 9-inch pie pan. Using the bottom of a cup, press the crumbs into the bottom of the pan until set and use your fingers to press the crumbs up the sides of the pan, not quite making a full border but close.

4. Bake for 12 to 15 minutes to set. Cool on a rack. The crust can be made ahead and wrapped in plastic wrap for up to 3 days.

GRAHAM CRACKER CRUST

This crust is the base for several of our recipes, including our Key Lime Pie Bars (page 236) and Grasshopper Pie Icebox Bars (page 235). It acts as a strong foundation to support the filling, while still being delicate enough to cut through easily, so you can lift the entire creamy slice out in one piece.

MAKES enough for one 9-inch pie

INGREDIENTS
1¼ cups (140g/5oz) graham cracker crumbs

1 tablespoon brown sugar

6 tablespoons/¾ stick (85g/3oz) unsalted butter, melted and slightly cooled

1. Position a rack in the center of the oven and preheat the oven to 350°F.

2. In a medium bowl, combine the crumbs and brown sugar. Stir until combined. Add the melted butter and stir with a spatula until the mixture comes together

and the crumbs are thoroughly moistened. The mixture will look like wet sand.

3. Dump the crumb mixture directly into a 9-inch pie pan. Using the bottom of a cup, press the crumbs into the bottom until set and use your fingers to press the crumbs up the sides of the pan, not quite making a full border but close.

4. Bake for 15 minutes to set. Cool on a rack. The crust can be made ahead and wrapped in plastic wrap for up to 3 days.

Inside a box of Nabisco Graham Crackers there are three sealed packages ("sleeves"). Each one weighs about 140g/5oz. One of these sleeves will produce about 1¼ cups crumbs, enough for one 9-inch pie pan.

Hand-crumble the graham crackers into a food processor and grind the crumbs until fine. If you don't have a food processor (I never had one growing up), you can also go old school and place the crackers in a sturdy resealable plastic bag. Smash them with a rolling pin and roll the pin back and forth until you have fine crumbs. This method is fun for the kids to get involved in, too, or for you to let off a little steam.

CHOCOLATE WAFER CRUMB CRUST

This dark, flavorful crust is essential for the bakery's chocolate cream pie. You can always make the homemade chocolate wafers (page 231) or purchase chocolate crumbs in the grocery store or online.

MAKES enough for one 9-inch pie

INGREDIENTS
1¼ cups (137g/4.9oz) chocolate wafer crumbs

¼ cup (50g/1.8oz) light brown sugar

¼ cup/½ stick (56g/2oz) unsalted butter, melted

1. Position a rack in the center of the oven and preheat the oven to 325°F.

2. In a medium bowl, combine the crumbs and brown sugar. Stir until combined. Add the melted butter and

stir with a spatula until the mixture comes together and the crumbs are thoroughly moistened. The mixture will look like wet sand.

3. Dump the crumb mixture directly into a 9-inch pie pan. Using the bottom of a cup, press the crumbs into the bottom until set and use your fingers to press the crumbs up the sides of the pan, not quite making a full border but close.

4. Bake for 15 minutes to set. Cool on a rack. The crust can be made ahead and wrapped in plastic wrap for up to 3 days.

CINNAMON CRUMB TOPPING

This versatile crumb topping is great on our Apple Crumb Pie (page 168), Blueberry Crumb Pie (page 169), Berry-Buttermilk Crumb Muffins (page 183), or any baked good that needs a topping of big, crunchy crumbs. You can make this ahead of time in a large batch, so it's always ready when you need it. It keeps for 1 week in the fridge and can be frozen for up to 3 months. Bring it to room temperature before using.

MAKES about 5 cups

INGREDIENTS
2 cups (270g/9.6oz) all-purpose flour
1 cup (200g/7.1oz) light brown sugar
½ cup (100g/3.5oz) granulated sugar
1 teaspoon ground cinnamon
¼ teaspoon salt
¾ cup/1½ sticks (170g/6oz) cold unsalted butter,
   cut into small pieces

In a stand mixer with the paddle, mix together the flour, both sugars, the cinnamon, and salt just until combined. Add the butter and mix on medium speed until crumbly and it holds together when pinched with your fingers, about 3 minutes.

STREUSEL CRUMB TOPPING FOR CRISPS

This streusel cooks up quickly and soaks up some of the juices in fruit crisps. If you love oats and pecans in your crumb topping, this is the one for you. Bonus: It's quick and easy to throw together.

MAKES about 3½ cups

INGREDIENTS
1 cup (135g/4.8oz) all-purpose flour
1 cup (80g/2.8oz) old-fashioned rolled oats
1 cup (200g/7.1oz) light brown sugar
½ cup/1 stick (113g/4oz) unsalted butter, melted
⅓ cup (38g/1.4oz) coarsely chopped pecans,
   lightly toasted (see Tip, page 288) (optional)

In a medium bowl, toss together the flour, oats, and brown sugar. Add the melted butter, mixing with a rubber spatula until distributed evenly. Stir in the pecans, if using.

STREUSEL TOPPING FOR MUFFINS

A simple streusel that lets the toasty flavor of the nuts shine through.

MAKES about 3½ cups

INGREDIENTS
1⅓ cups (153g/5.4oz) coarsely chopped pecans
⅔ cup (133g/4.7g) light brown sugar
¾ cup (102g/3.6oz) all-purpose flour
6 tablespoons/¾ stick (85g/3oz) cold unsalted butter,
   cold, cut into 1-inch pieces

1. In a stand mixer with the paddle, combine the pecans, brown sugar, and flour. Mix on low speed for 1 minute.

2. Add the cold butter and mix on low speed until the mixture turns into moist, clumpy crumbs, about 2 minutes.

3. This can be made ahead and stored in the refrigerator for up to 3 days.

Fillings and Sauces

It's very handy to have some delicious fillings and sauces in your kitchen arsenal. Fruit fillings keep well and can be used for pies, to create crisps and bars, and even to spoon over yogurt or ice cream. Our caramel sauce, with or without salt, is wonderful drizzled over baked apples and essential for a banana split.

APPLE FILLING

Make a big batch of this with your fall apples and use it as the filling for our Apple Crumb Bars (page 160) and our Apple Crisp (page 170). Because the filling is precooked, the bake time for hand pies and crisps is just to brown the crust.

MAKES about 8 cups

INGREDIENTS
¾ cup plus 1 tablespoon (162g/5.6oz) granulated sugar

1⅓ cups (266g/9.4oz) light brown sugar

1 teaspoon grated nutmeg

2 teaspoons ground cinnamon

¼ teaspoon ground ginger

½ teaspoon salt

16 Golden Delicious apples, peeled, cored, and cut into 1½-inch pieces

1 tablespoon fresh lemon juice

1½ teaspoons pure vanilla extract

½ cup/1 stick (113g/4oz) unsalted butter, cut into pieces

3 tablespoons cornstarch

1 tablespoon water

1. In a medium bowl, whisk together both sugars, the spices, and salt.

2. In a large, heavy pot, toss the apples with the lemon juice and vanilla. Set over medium heat, add the butter, and stir until it melts. Add the sugar mixture, stirring to combine. Increase the heat to medium-high and cook, stirring occasionally, until the mixture comes to a simmer, 4 to 5 minutes. The apples will exude their juices and begin to soften.

3. In a small bowl, stir together the cornstarch and water. Add to the apples and stir well. Bring the mixture to a boil, then reduce the heat to a simmer and cook, stirring occasionally, until the mixture thickens and the apples are tender but not mushy, about 4 minutes. Don't stir too much, as it breaks up the apples. Check the apples for tenderness by sticking a knife into one. If it gives slightly, immediately remove the pot from the heat.

4. Spread the apple filling on a baking sheet in a single layer. Let cool to room temperature. Use the filling at room temperature or store in the refrigerator for up to 3 days. This filling also freezes beautifully.

> Be sure you cook the filling enough after adding the cornstarch. It needs 3 to 5 minutes to thicken and cook off the starch flavor. This filling holds well in the refrigerator for up to 3 days.

BLUEBERRY FILLING

When blueberries are in season, we use this filling as the basis for our Blueberry Jamboree (page 233). It's also especially good as a topping for vanilla ice cream. The lemon zest really brightens up the flavor of the blueberries.

MAKES about 3 cups

INGREDIENTS
2 tablespoons cornstarch

2 tablespoons water

5 cups (800g/28.5oz) fresh blueberries, rinsed and picked over for stems

⅔ cup (132g/4.8oz) granulated sugar

⅓ cup (67g/2.4oz) light brown sugar

1. In a small bowl, whisk together the cornstarch and water. Set aside.

2. In a heavy medium pot, combine 2 cups (300g/11.4oz) of the blueberries and both sugars. Cook over medium-high heat, stirring constantly, until the sugar has dissolved and the mixture starts to boil, about 5 minutes. You want to see that the blueberries have released their juices and started to pop.

3. Once the mixture has come to a boil, add the cornstarch-water mixture. Stir until the mixture is dark and thick, 3 to 5 minutes.

4. Remove the pot from the heat and pour the mixture into a heatproof bowl. Add the remaining 3 cups (500g/17.1oz) blueberries, gently stirring until fully combined. Be careful not to burst or smash the blueberries.

5. Cover and refrigerate until completely chilled. The filling keeps well in the refrigerator for up to 3 days.

> Be sure you cook the filling enough after adding the cornstarch. It needs at least 3 to 5 minutes to thicken and cook off the starch flavor.

COCONUT FILLING

Sweet and thick, this makes a delectably chewy addition to our impressive three-layer Coconut Cake (page 50). It's also wonderful sandwiched between cookies.

MAKES about 3 cups
(enough for a 9-inch three-layer cake)

INGREDIENTS
1½ cups (357g/12oz) whole milk
¾ cup (150g/5.3oz) granulated sugar
¼ cup (34g/1.2oz) all-purpose flour
4 cups (448g/15.8oz) sweetened shredded coconut
2 teaspoons pure vanilla extract

1. In a medium pot, whisk together the milk, sugar, and flour. Set over medium heat and cook, stirring constantly with a wooden spoon, until it comes to a slow boil, 10 to 12 minutes.

2. Remove the pan from the heat and add the coconut and vanilla. Stir until combined. Pour the mixture into a shallow bowl to cool quickly. Cover with plastic wrap and refrigerate until completely chilled before using.

VARIATION

COCONUT-LEMON FILLING: Stir together 2 cups of the coconut filling with 1 cup Lemon Cream Filling (recipe below).

LEMON CREAM FILLING

This is my guilty pleasure. I love it so much that I often double the recipe just so I can eat it straight from the jar when no one is looking. Use this filling between cake layers, folded into whipped cream as a pie filling, combined with our coconut filling to make Coconut-Lemon Filling (variation above) or to fill a tart shell.

MAKES about 2 cups
(enough for a 9-inch two-layer cake or 24 cupcakes)

INGREDIENTS
¾ cup (150g/5.30oz) sugar
1 tablespoon plus 1 teaspoon grated lemon zest
3 eggs
½ cup plus 1 tablespoon (135g/4.5oz) fresh lemon juice
1 cup/2 sticks (226g/8oz) cold unsalted butter, cut into ½-inch pieces

1. In a medium saucepan, bring a few inches of water to a medium simmer over medium-low heat.

2. In a heatproof bowl, combine the sugar and zest. Rub them together using your hands until moist and fragrant.

3. In a small bowl, whisk the eggs together lightly, then whisk them into the lemon sugar until completely combined. Whisk in the lemon juice. Set the heatproof bowl over the pot of simmering water. As the mixture cooks, stir with a heatproof spatula—frequently, but not constantly—until the mixture reaches 180°F on a candy thermometer. It should be thick and have a mayonnaise-like consistency.

4. Remove the bowl from the heat and strain through a fine-mesh sieve into a food processor. Let cool for about 8 minutes. With the food processor running, add the cold butter about 5 pieces at a time. Stop occasionally and scrape down the sides. Once all the butter has been added, continue to process until light and airy, about 3 minutes.

5. Store refrigerated in an airtight container. Can be stored for up to 3 days.

CARAMEL SAUCE

One of the best things about this buttery amber sauce is that it keeps in the refrigerator for weeks. Use it as a topping for ice cream, drizzled on cakes, and in the base for our decadent Billionaire Brownies (page 144). Once you get the hang of making it, you'll never buy caramel again. Be mindful when making caramel, as you're working with very high temperatures. Use a candy thermometer and the right size pot to prevent the caramel from boiling over. Wear burn gloves when stirring the caramel or adding cream to avoid hot splatters. Keep kids and pets at a good distance from the stove when making caramel. It's a process that needs your undivided attention.

MAKES about 3 cups

INGREDIENTS
3 cups (600g/21.2oz) granulated sugar

1 cup (227g/8oz) water

½ teaspoon fresh lemon juice

2 cups (480g/17oz) heavy cream

1½ teaspoons pure vanilla extract

½ teaspoon salt

1. Place a folded towel on the counter. In a large heavy-bottom pot, combine the sugar, water, and lemon juice and gently stir with a wooden spoon or spatula, making sure all the sugar is moistened with the water.

2. Set the pot over high heat. Clip a candy thermometer to the side of the pot and bring the mixture to a rolling boil. Do not stir. Allow the mixture to boil while watching the thermometer closely. The syrup must come to 330°F. As it cooks, be careful not to stir. If the syrup starts to color unevenly, you can swirl the pan to even it out. At 330°F, immediately remove the pot from the heat and carefully place on the folded towel. Be very cautious, as the mixture is extremely hot and can cause bad burns.

3. Pour the cream into the pot while standing back a little. The mixture will bubble vigorously. When it subsides, stir with a whisk. Whisk in the vanilla and salt.

4. Return the pot to medium heat and allow to come to a simmer again, stirring with the whisk until the mixture all comes together with a beautiful caramel color.

5. Remove the pot from the heat and pour into a heatproof bowl.

6. When the mixture is completely cool, store in a sealed container in the refrigerator for up to 1 month.

VARIATION

SALTED CARAMEL SAUCE: Stir in 2 tablespoons Maldon sea salt flakes after you pour the caramel into the heatproof bowl.

Adornments

These are the final touches, the little additions that make your desserts really stand out. While making them yourself is optional, the result is special and sure to impress—not to mention they taste fantastic!

SUGARED CRANBERRIES

These bright cranberries offer the perfect sweet-tart flavor to complement our Pumpkin Spice Cake (page 71) and Pumpkin Icebox Pie (page 240).

MAKES 1 cup cranberries

INGREDIENTS
1 cup (227g/8oz) water
1 cup (200g/7.1oz) sugar
1 cup (100g/3.5oz) fresh or frozen cranberries
½ cup (100g/3.5oz) superfine sugar

1. In a small saucepan, combine the water and sugar and cook over low heat until the sugar dissolves. Bring to a simmer and remove from the heat. Do not boil, or the cranberries will burst when added.

2. Add the cranberries and stir gently to coat all the berries. Pour the mixture into a heatproof container, cover, and refrigerate until completely cool, at least 1 hour.

3. Drain the cranberries in a colander set over a bowl. (Note: The cranberry syrup can be stored for up to 1 week and used as a beverage sweetener.)

4. Line a baking sheet with parchment paper. Place the superfine sugar in a shallow dish, add the cranberries, and roll them around until they are fully coated with the sugar. Spread the sugared cranberries in a single layer on the lined baking sheet. Let stand at room temperature for at least 1 hour to dry.

5. Store in a single layer in a cool, dry place. It's best to use these within a day, as the sugar will start to dissolve.

> **HOW TO TOAST NUTS**
> Preheat the oven to 350°F. Place the nuts on a baking sheet and roast for 12 to 15 minutes, or until lightly browned and fragrant. Immediately remove from the pan to cool.

CANDIED PECANS

These spiced pecans are useful for decorating pies and bars, but also delicious just for snacking.

MAKES about 3 cups

INGREDIENTS
2 cups (200g/7oz) pecan halves
1¼ cups (250g/8.8oz) light brown sugar
1½ teaspoons ground cinnamon
¼ teaspoon grated nutmeg
½ teaspoon ground ginger
1 egg white, lightly beaten

1. Position an oven rack in the center of the oven and preheat the oven to 325°F. Line a baking sheet with parchment paper or foil and coat lightly with nonstick spray. You can also use a silicone baking mat.

2. In a large bowl, combine the pecans, brown sugar, cinnamon, nutmeg, and ginger. Add the egg white to the mixture and toss to ensure the pecans are thoroughly coated.

3. Spread the pecans on the lined baking sheet so that they lie flat, taking care not to cluster the pecans.

4. Bake for 10 to 15 minutes, or until the pecans appear dry. Keep a watchful eye on them—they can go from perfectly cooked to overcooked in a minute. Start checking at 10 minutes.

5. Let the pecans cool completely on the pan on a cooling rack, then place in an airtight container. These can be made ahead and stored for up to 1 month.

HOW TO DYE COCONUT

For each color you choose, place the sweetened shredded coconut in a bowl, add a drop at a time of gel coloring, using any color you like. I prefer pastels like pink, green, blue, and lavender. Stir with a spoon until you get the desired color. Gel coloring goes a long way, so a tiny bit is all you need.

Add a drop at a time of gel coloring.

Stir with a spoon until you get the desired color.

ACKNOWLEDGMENTS

When I signed the contract to write this book, I was told I had almost two years from that time to the actual publication date. I thought, No big deal, how hard could this be. I already had a lot of the recipes and had been making them for years. Well, I discovered that writing a cookbook is not a small undertaking. It takes an army of very patient people to make it come together.

First, my deepest thanks to my loving husband, Mark, and our two kids, Luca and Mina, for putting up with my working late nights and long weekends, for understanding why I had to make ten recipes a day while on a vacation in Cape Cod, and for suffering through years of recipe tasting. Thank you, too, to my grandmothers and mother, who flamed the baking fire in my soul, and my friends, for their belief in my ability to write a book and their unfailing encouragement along the way.

I'd like to thank my work family for making every day feel like a party. To Steve Abrams—my business partner, dear friend, and brother in crime for more than twenty-five years—and his wife, Tyra Abrams: We've celebrated a lot of successes together and suffered through a few losses with humor and dignity. Thank you both for your support and for letting me run with some of my crazy ideas. Together we built this little company into an international brand and got to see the world while we were at it.

To Cheryl Saenz, I'm grateful for your loving support over the many years we have worked together. You have an amazing eye, which is clearly reflected in the photographs here. You matched the props to each recipe perfectly and effortlessly. We laughed and danced through an insane few weeks of attempting to shoot more than 150 recipes—and we did it. You keep me sane. To Ned Semoff, Magnolia Bakery's creative director and photographer extraordinaire, who shot the gorgeous images in this book, I am thankful that I work with you. You are insanely talented and a blast to be with. Your music choices keep me dancing and singing every day. Thank you to Sara Gramling and Lexi Portrait, for not only building the Magnolia Bakery brand, but also your editorial contributions to the book. Your suggestions always make me sound smarter.

My thanks to the many talented bakers and cake icers at Magnolia Bakery. Thank you, Joely Anderson, for working morning, noon, and night during the photo shoots to "get it right" just one more time. Thank you to Amy Tamulonis, Sarah Wallace, Sarah Kirkwood, and Jennifer Edwards for the last round of tweaking, and to America Salazar, for all the buttercream recipes she tested and the beautiful cakes she decorated. Thank you to my friend Cara Tannenbaum and to Olivia Mack McCool for jumping on board at the last minute to test entire chapters.

I would also like to thank everyone who has worked at Magnolia Bakery over the years; each of you has contributed to what we do and helped us grow. Thank you to Sina, Abby, Christa, Jaimie, Angel, Sam Z., and so many more dedicated bakers who tested, tested, and tested recipes over the years. Without your love for Magnolia Bakery, creative input, testing, tasting, feedback, and support, this book would not exist.

To my editor, Elizabeth Viscott Sullivan, I knew the minute I met you that you were the editor I wanted to work with. Thank you for believing in me, holding my hand through this tireless process— and for our late-night chats and emails that encouraged me when I thought I could never get the book done. You promised me the hardest work would be over soon and that you would deliver a beautiful book, and you did. To Laura Silverman, thank you for your help and writing support. When I told you I was struggling with the recipe headers because I'm not a writer, your reply—"You just wrote a cookbook, you *are* a writer."—made me more confident. You helped me find my voice and made my stories come to life.

To Tricia Levi, who spent hour upon hour reviewing the recipes to make sure the instructions made sense and that every gram and ounce was correct, my deep thanks. Your attention to detail is unsurpassed.

To the team at Harper Design—art director Lynne Yeamans, production director Susan Kosko, and book designer Michelle Cohen—thank you for your stunning work on the book design and printing.

Finally, I'd like to thank all the loyal Magnolia Bakery customers, fans, families, and partners from around the world. You are why we're here.

SOURCES

HOUSEWARES

Bed Bath and Beyond

bedbathandbeyond.com

From cookware and bakeware to kitchen knives and bread pans, you can't go wrong at Bed Bath and Beyond. They carry most of the basic supplies I suggest at a great price—and you can always get one of their 20-percent-off coupons if you sign up for their emails.

Sur la Table

surlatable.com

If you are looking for any specialty pans or premium cookware, this is the place to go. They carry all the top brands and have a very knowledgeable staff that can help lead you in the right direction. They also have locations all over the country.

New York Cake

nycake.com

118 West 22nd Street, New York, NY 10011

New York Cake is a wonderful source for specialty baking supplies and ingredients. They carry most of what the home or professional baker needs to make anything in this book and beyond. From gel food colorings, piping bags, tips, and cake and cupcake pans to all the paper supplies you need, like parchment paper and cake boards.

Michaels Craft Stores

www.michaels.com

Michaels is a national retailer that carries all the Wilton brand cake-decorating supplies, from pastry bags and tips to specialty sprinkles and decorations. They have a large selection of specialty baking pans and liners. You can also find gel dye sets and icing wands.

JB Prince

www.jbprince.com

36 East 31st Street, New York NY 10016

This iconic New York City culinary restaurant supply store is one of the best shops ever for anything you need as a professional chef or baker. Even if you don't need to purchase anything, go just for the experience of walking the aisles to see all the interesting equipment and supplies.

SPECIALTY BAKING INGREDIENTS

For specialty decorating ingredients—like colored sugars, sugar pearls, nonpareils, edible glitter, disco dust, quins, seasonal and holiday decorations, and food coloring—these are some of my favorite sources.

Fancy Flours

www.fancyflours.com

Fancy Flours offers everything from bakeware to fun holiday decorations and packaging ideas.

Pfeil & Holing, Inc.

www.thebakerynetwork.com

www.cakedeco.com

P & H is a good source for sprinkles, De-cons, decorating supplies, specialty boxes, and cake boards.

INDEX

HarperCollins books may be purchased for educational, business, or sales promotional use.
For information, please email the Special Markets Department at SPsales@harpercollins.com.

First published in 2020 by
Harper Design
An Imprint of HarperCollins*Publishers*
195 Broadway
New York, NY 10007
Tel: (212) 207-7000
Fax: (855) 746-6023
harperdesign@harpercollins.com
www.hc.com

Distributed throughout the world by
HarperCollins*Publishers*
195 Broadway
New York, NY 10007

ISBN 978-0-06-288721-4
Library of Congress Control Number: 2018965711

Book design by HYPHENATE DESIGN/Michelle Cohen and Laura Klynstra
Front and back cover photographs by Ned Semoff

Printed in Thailand
First Printing, 2020

ABOUT THE AUTHOR

Bobbie Lloyd is chief baking officer at Magnolia Bakery, where she has played an integral role in expanding the bakery from its original location in New York City's West Village to its multiple locations across thirteen cities around the world. She brings the homemade essence of Magnolia Bakery to customers through the creation and development of new recipes and the perfection of old favorites. Born and raised in the Chicago area, Lloyd began her epicurean journey at eight with her first cooking class. She cultivated this interest through her formal education at Chef's and Company in Boston and working in restaurants. Throughout her career she has been involved in all aspects of the restaurant and bakery business. She lives in New York City.

Instagram @bobbielloyd

Twitter @bobbielloyd

Website: http://www.magnoliabakery.com

Official Magnolia Bakery Instagram @magnoliabakery

Official Magnolia Bakery Facebook: facebook.com/MagnoliaBakery

Official Magnolia Bakery Twitter @magnoliabakery

Official Magnolia Bakery Pinterest: pinterest.com/magnoliabakery/